CANADA
SOUTHERN
COUNTRY

Robert D. Tennant, Jr.

THE BOSTON MILLS PRESS

Canadian Cataloguing in Publication Data

Tennant, Robert D., 1942-
  Canada Southern country

Includes bibliographical references and index.
ISBN 1-55046-007-2

1. Canada Southern Railway Company – History.
2. Railroads – Ontario – History. I. Title.

HE2810.C35T4 1991   385'.06'57133   C91-094057-6

Published in Canada by:
THE BOSTON MILLS PRESS
132 Main Street
Erin, Ontario N0B 1T0
(519) 833-2407
Fax: (519) 833-2195

Designed by John Denison, Erin
Cover Design by Gill Stead, Guelph
Typography by Justified Type Inc., Guelph
Printed by Ampersand, Guelph

The Publisher gratefully acknowledges the assistance of
the Canada Council and the Ontario Arts Council.

American Association
for State and Local History
Award of Merit

Winners of the
Heritage Canada
Communications Award

OVERLEAF:
Number 7943, with a clean face, was photographed near the CASO
roundhouse in St. Thomas, Ontario.

Larry Broadbent

TABLE OF CONTENTS

*To my Father and late Mother,
who kindled in me an abiding
interest in and respect for
the labours of our foreparents
in building this great land.*

FOREWORD

When I visited Ontario Northland's yard at Englehart, Ontario, on 10 September 1965, little did I suspect that I would become captivated by the discovery of some hopper cars labelled CANADA SOUTHERN. I took some photographs and began wondering about this railway, but at the time I was a student en route back to university following work in the "clay belt," and I had other, more pressing concerns.

Over a period of several years I searched out bits of information, but bits they remained. Later I began to search in earnest; I became like a detective on a challenging case. I was soon hooked. The trail would take me over virtually every mile of the Canada Southern Railway (CSR) line in Ontario. I would visit or contact archives, libraries and museums in Canada and the United States, both along the CSR route and well removed from it. Hours and miles passed. I met many people who shared generously of their time and treasures. Without such people this book would not only have been significantly different, it would never have been finished.

The scope of this work ranges from the railway's humble beginnings in post-Confederation Ontario in 1868 to the bitter, protracted battles about the line's future before the Canadian Transport Commission in the 1980s. The railway was born at a time when railway fever convinced ill-prepared backers that money could be made out of nerve and dreams. The railway almost died at more recent time, a victim of the struggle of mega-railways whose well-prepared backers were equally convinced that they could make money out of nerve alone.

The purpose of this book is to provide a general history of the Canada Southern Railway Company, its subsidiary and related companies, and to contribute to our understanding of railway history in Ontario and Michigan.

I happily acknowledge the contributions of others to the making of the book's strengths; its remaining weaknesses are my own.

R.D.T.
Halifax, N.S.
26 July 1989

In 1873 Thomas Henry, an enterprising resident of Waterford, built this commodious three-storey brick hotel at a cost of more than $2,800. For many years he operated it under an agreement with the Canada Southern, whose railway line was nearby. The hotel was strictly a temperance establishment. The CSR hotel and its barns were among the many buildings destroyed by the great Waterford fire of 1903.

— *Historical Atlas of Norfolk County,*
Offset Edition, 1972, by permission Mika Publishing Company

ACKNOWLEDGEMENTS

The preparation of this book has been made possible because of the ready assistance of many individuals and organizations.

For the provisions of contacts, research, information, photocopying, photographs and typing, I express my appreciation to the following people: John E. Abercrombie, Christopher A. Andreae, C. Peter Anthony, Byron C. Babbish, Edward D. Bradt, Larry Broadbent, Cyril A. Butcher, Carlos Cacola, L. Bruce Chapman, Mrs. Margaret Crawford, Mrs. W.R. Crawford, James M. Courtright, Gary S. Daniels, Percy Dean, Thomas J. Dworman, C. Dorval Fox, Harold L. Elder, L.F. Gillam, Ross D. Gray, J. David Harding, G. Bruce Hollett, Kirk F. Hise, Miss Bev Hubley, Lorne J. Hymers, John D. Knowles, Ms. Betty Liebrock, William R. Linley, Lewis M. Ludlow, Allister W.D. MacBean, Herb MacDonald, Orin P. Maus, Greg McDonnell, J. Douglas Murray, Kenneth W. Noble, Al Paterson, Everette J. Payette, John A. Riddell, Ron Roels, Robert J. Sandusky, George Seibel, Mrs. H. Sinclair, Mareea Steedman, Julian O. Strong, John D. Thompson, George E. Thorman, Harold Usher, Mrs. Evelyn Couch Walker, Nemo Warr, Jay White, and three persons who wish to remain anonymous.

I acknowledge my deep indebtedness to Kenneth A.W. Gansel, C. Gerald Elder, (the late) John R. Lee and Michael P. McIlwaine for granting such ready access to their photographic collections.

I am grateful for the assistance of the Archives of Ontario, the Michigan State Archives, the Public Archives of Canada, (PAC, NAC) the Public Archives of Nova Scotia (particularly Allan C. Dunlop), and the United States National Archives.

The assistance of numerous public and university libraries is gratefully noted. In particular I thank Bowling Green State University, the Earl W. Bridges Public Library in Niagara Falls, N.Y., Detroit Public Library (particularly the Burton Historical Collection), Dalhousie University, Lambton County Public Library, London Public Library, Monroe County Library System, St. Thomas Public Library and Welland Public Library for permission to use illustrations from their holdings.

I acknowledge, too, the assistance of several societies and museums. In particular I wish to cite the Dossin Great Lakes Museum, Elgin County Pioneer Museum, Grosse Ile Historical Society, Hiram Walker Historical Museum, Lundy's Lane Historical Museum and Society, Munroe County Historical Commission, the Moore Museum, New York Central System Historical Society, Niagara Falls Historical Society, Niagara Historical Museum and Society, the Railway Museum of Pennsylvania, and the Spruce Row Museum (Waterford and Townsend Historical Society) for permission to include photographs from their collections.

Various other organizations granted permission to use their photographs. I thank Alco Historic Photos (Mohawk & Hudson Chapter of the National Railway Historical Society), Canadian Pacific Limited, Canapress, Consolidated Rail Corporation, the Diesel Division of General Motors of Canada Limited, the *Leamington Shopper*, the *London Free Press*, Mika Publishing Company, National Steel Car Corporation, Ontario Hydro, the *St. Thomas Times-Journal*, the *Sarnia Observer*, Union Pacific Railroad Company, and the *Windsor Star* for permission to use their photographs in this work.

In addition, I acknowledge permission from the National Gallery of Canada and Woodside National Historical Park to reproduce paintings by Robert Whale showing a Canada Southern passenger train at Niagara Falls. I am grateful also to the Metropolitan Toronto Library Board, who granted me permission to reproduce pen-and-ink sketches from the J. Ross Robertson Collection. I thank Mr. Michael Graston for his permission to include his cartoon.

A most important source of assistance has been the reading of my original and rather lengthy manuscript from differing viewpoints. To Mrs. Ruth Bedwell, Mr. C. Gerald Elder, Mr. Ian T. Pyatt, and Dr. Donald P. Cunningham, I express my heartfelt appreciation for the many helpful suggestions and constructive criticisms. I am grateful, too, for the advice of my publisher. The present work is a significantly shortened and hopefully more readable version of my original manuscript, "Canada Southern Railway."

One of the most prominent backers of the Canada Southern Railway was Isaac Buchanan (1810-1883). He was a merchant, economic theorist, politician and indefatigable railway promoter. Isaac, in partnership with his brother Peter, carried on an international wholesale and retail business in such centres as Hamilton, London, Montreal, Glasgow and New York City. Their trading firm carried on business under the name Buchanan & Company and several others. He was an advocate of currency reform in Canada. From 1841 to 1867 Isaac Buchanan was a member of the Legislative Assembly of the Province of Canada. He lost no opportunity to advance the cause of railways in what became southwestern Ontario. This was not entirely an altruistic view, for he was a financial backer to numerous enterprises himself. His pet project was the Great South Western Railway, an idea which was later embodied as the Canada Southern.
— NAC C100595

I

IN SEARCH OF A RAILWAY

Before the "Southern" Railway

The absence of significant railway construction was a characteristic of southwestern Ontario during the 1860s. This was due to the overbuilding which had occurred in the previous decade. The investment communities held differing views, but the results were the same. Domestic private capital was too preoccupied with the rate of return on any potential investment to advance funds for what could only be classed as developmental railway construction. British investors were already smarting under the lessons learned from the Great Western and Grand Trunk railways, and for its part the government of the Province of Canada was as a matter of policy not interested in subsidizing railways.

A second factor affecting this part of the province was the profound effect which the American Civil War had had on the regional economy. At first, the Great Western Railway had profited under an upsurge of traffic with its U.S. connections, but now inter-railway competition caused such traffic to collapse. The subsequent great discount on American currency combined with this declining traffic to cause the Great Western considerable suffering in its dealings with the United States' railways. The Grand Trunk was severely affected by this foreign war, too. Because of their declining purchasing power, Canadians reduced their purchases of British goods, and the GTR found itself with both lower tonnages and lower profits.

The rivers of Niagara and Detroit set limits to the peninsula; linking these rivers without descending the great Niagara escarpment was the quintessence of the "southern"[1] railway. As a concept and a hope, the "southern" railway would wax and wane for 40 years before finally being brought to fruition. Even with the construction of the Great Western Railway, which was partially intended to serve American through traffic, the concept of a southern rail line would not be laid to rest. Despite its potential to the Americans, they could not be enticed into supporting it in any of its forms, ever since the failure to re-charter the Niagara & Detroit Rivers Railway in 1846. The initials for railways covering all or a portion of the distance between these rivers read like alphabet soup, and they were just as easily rearranged. Among them was the Woodstock & Lake Erie Railway, which was partially controlled by Hamilton merchant, railway promoter and politician Isaac Buchanan. Buchanan was deeply involved with various projects, which he hoped to consolidate into a single railway linking the two great rivers of the peninsula. This was his Great Southern Railway. Samuel Zimmerman, a notorious railway contractor, became interested in the scheme, but just when Buchanan thought that he had found someone to build his line, Zimmerman was killed in the Desjardins Canal railway accident, one of the worst in Canadian history. It was ironic. After much wheeling and dealing, bribery and personal financial sacrifice, Buchanan had gained control of the much-dreamed-of project; now Zimmerman, his principal source of finance and construction expertise, was dead. Would the Great Southern project shortly follow suit? Buchanan's prized project might have foundered there and then if it had not been for James Morton of Kingston. Morton was a brewer, believed to be rich, and he had contracting experience. Buchanan had found Zimmerman's replacement, or so he thought. Morton "saw the contract as a golden opportunity to make money, he knew the background of the road and was fully aware of the kind of person with whom he was dealing and, since his own ethical principles were not particularly high, he was quite capable of looking after his own interests."[2]

In assembling the various charters which he owned or controlled, Buchanan had borrowed extensively, much of it from the Bank of Upper Canada. Morton seemed willing to buy out Buchanan and to finance the construction of the Great Southern Railway. Whenever Buchanan and Morton found agreement for a contract, however, Morton's lawyer, John A. Macdonald, would find some fault in the proposal. Having become suspicious with the interminable delays, and realizing that Morton was intending to back out, Buchanan sued him. Although he won a judgment of 50,000 pounds sterling, Buchanan was unable to collect, for Morton was broke. The suit was the latest in a long line of misunderstandings, suits, and countersuits which had come to be the hallmark of any dealings concerning the Great Southern Railway. So convoluted and corrupted were the dealings surrounding much of the railway's history, that a Select Legislative Committee of the Assembly of the Province of Canada had to investigate the whole tangled, sordid affair in 1857.

Buchanan, who was now too heavily in debt to abandon the project, began to look for financial help, this time below the border. This is curious, since during the aforementioned hearings before the Assembly, Buchanan had charged that the backers of the New York Central and Michigan Central railways had sought control of a southern railway through Ontario. He continued, in tones at times defensive and righteous, to say that by his controlling the Great Southern, the Americans would be thwarted in their designs and the Great Western spared financial ruin.[3] The intentions of American capitalists and Buchanan's own apparent nationalistic concerns proved to be more illusory than his own scheming and bribing, to which the committee had addressed considerable attention. This had not deterred Buchanan in the least, and in February 1860 he left to visit the United States money markets and likely financiers. He soon found that the attitudes towards such an enterprise were unchanged. John W. Brooks, president of the Michigan Central Railroad, was "no advocate of another line through Canada."[4] He said this despite the shabby service his road received from the Great Western. Buchanan turned to the New York Central & Hudson River Railroad, but its president, Erastus Corning, was equally cold to the invitation. There was little point in looking abroad. With the U.S. Civil War under way, British investors had one more reason to be cautious about investing in a turbulent continent.

After the Civil War ended, the prospects for the southern railway remained dim despite the tantalizing statistics. Although the volume of freight traffic carried between Michigan and New York via Canada was 50 percent higher in 1867 than in 1864 — and fully three times higher than that of only a decade earlier[5] — it was no cause for optimism with regard to actually getting the Niagara–Detroit railway built. Canadians were generally hesitant about seeking U.S. financial support for their railways, yet they could advance little risk capital themselves. The Fenian Raids of 1866-70 rekindled the fears which had been etched deeply on the young national psyche by the War of 1812. Canadians were somewhat jittery about the proximity of a large, victorious, disengaged American army. The Americans were irritated by the sympathies which some Canadians had extended to the Confederates. For its part, the entrepreneurial class in the United States was preoccupied with railways in its own country. British investors were reluctant to invest in a colony where war might erupt; they also had a considerable number of railway projects at home. Thus the time was not ripe for the construction of a southern railway across Ontario's southwestern peninsula.

Late in the 1860s, hopes for the incorporation of a southern railway dramatically improved when William A. Thomson, an energetic backer of depression-era railways, conceived of extending his portage railway as a bridge line between Canada and the United States. He was the principal backer behind the Fort Erie Railway Company, which had been incorporated in 1857. The FER purchased the feeble Erie & Ontario Railroad after it had defaulted on its mortgage and was foreclosed by the town of Niagara. To reflect this change, the FER renamed itself the Erie & Niagara Railway that same year, 1863. Within two years Thomson completed the E&N from Lake Erie to Lake Ontario following, where possible, the route of the Niagara River. This success behind them, Thomson and his associates turned to the concept of a Niagara-to-Detroit railway. Before Thomson could do anything, however, some of his friends formulated a proposal for a southern railway, and although it was endorsed by an experienced E&N contractor, James Beachell, and by George MacBeth, it failed in the Legislature in 1865. A second, different attempt a year later met the same fate. On both occasions Buchanan and John A. Macdonald (then representing Morton's widow) led the opposition, Thomson himself being involved in neither venture.

Thomson, who was also a member of the Legislature, used the occasions to assess his adversaries' strengths, and having satisfied himself of his eventual success, he waited quietly, confident that he would get his opportunity to extend the Erie & Niagara Railway westward. It was soon to come.

Inception at Last

While Buchanan was out of the country looking for financial backing for the Great Southern, Thomson saw his opportunity to enter the southern railway debate in a personal way by introducing to the House in January 1868 his own concept for such a railway. Inside the Legislature, Macdonald and Marcus Smith, an engineer who was deeply in debt as a result of Buchanan's scheme, led the opposition until Buchanan could join the political fray himself. Outside the Legislature, the rhetoric was equally acrimonious. Here, Great Western's general manager, Thomas Swinyard, spearheaded the opposition forces with charges that Thomson's bill was unnecessary, unprofitable and undesirable. Then he accused its backers of being a group of bankrupt speculators who were seeking a charter for the purpose of extorting money.[6] Thomson argued persuasively and when the voting was finished he had won. Thus, on 28 February 1868 his proposal for a southern railway was incorporated under the name Erie & Niagara Extension Railway Company.[7] It was empowered to build from Fort Erie via St. Thomas to either Sandwich or Windsor on the Detroit River.

The initial board of directors consisted of ten men. The only notables were Thomson and a Toronto lawyer, Adam Crooke.[8] The other eight men were involved in civic politics and, outside their own immediate townships, they were little known. Most did have some, albeit limited, experience of sitting on railway boards. Thomson shortly left for the United States to discuss funding for his railway with business contacts he had cultivated for five or more years. He came home empty-handed and discouraged that such groundwork had proven fruitless. For the first time Thomson and his associates began to realize that without adequate financial backing they were in danger of losing their charter. This prompted the development of friendly relations with Buchanan, to their mutual benefit. Although he was now retired from politics and still had large debts, he was able to bring to the Erie & Niagara Extension Railway the very things Thomson could not, money and influence. To begin with, in December 1868 Isaac Buchanan agreed to sell his maps, plans and profiles of earlier southern railway schemes to Thomson with the price to be determined at a later date. Thomson was then able to explain to prospective investors and contractors the prospects and feasibility of the E&NE. In addition, Buchanan was to advance Thomson $5,000 to cover his promotional travel, to foster public goodwill, to appease the provisional directors and to gain further financial backing. For his part Thomson would turn over $80,000 in cash, bonds or shares by the time of the railway's completion.

During the balance of 1868 and 1869 William Thomson travelled extensively in the United States in search of financial support for the E&NE. He visited the Boston, New York, Buffalo, Detroit and Chicago markets. Although these trips stirred up some interest in the southwestern Ontario railway in American financial circles, the sought-after funds proved to be as elusive as ever. Once again Thomson tried the direct approach to specific railways. Michigan Central's James Joy was aloof to the whole idea. Commodore Vanderbilt of the NYC&HR, smug with his recent takeover of the Lake Shore road, greeted Thomson with a grim smile. Vanderbilt stated tersely that he was not interested in a new Canadian railway; the Great Western was quite enough. Neither Thomson nor Buchanan accepted the rebuffs. The promoters were convinced that their bridge railway through Canada would be attractive to American railways, eventually. And so they kept searching.

The protracted search for substantial financial backing took its toll on the board. There were squabbles, heated arguments and rebellions to the point of near collapse of both the board and the railway. Buchanan, Thomson and their associates finally prevailed with the board, and they took their proposals for improvements to the Legislature, where they were successful in having their charter amended. This bill, which received Royal Assent on 24 December 1869, empowered the company to take a new name, The Canada Southern Railway. The bill also authorized a new slate of directors, 50 percent of whom could now be drawn from American contractors or promoters. The time to secure the $200,000 deposit was extended eight months, to November 1870. The

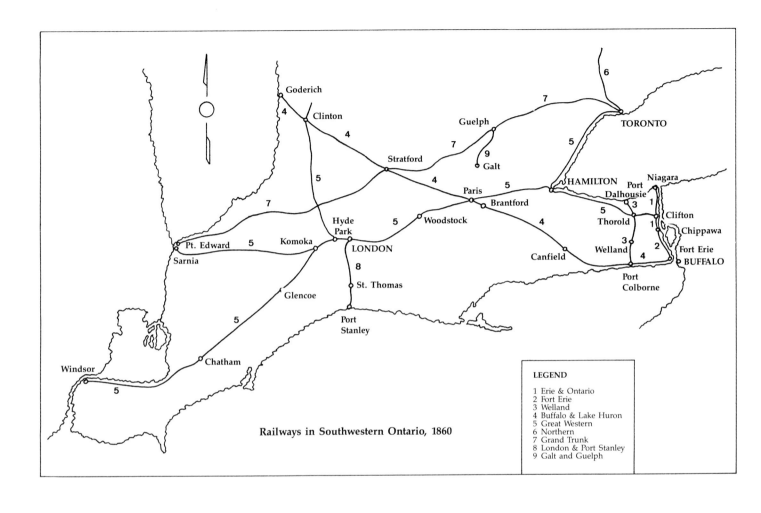

Railways in Southwestern Ontario, 1860

Goderich
Clinton
Stratford
Guelph
Galt
TORONTO
HAMILTON
Port Dalhousie
Niagara
Paris
Brantford
Woodstock
Thorold
Clifton
Chippawa
Hyde Park
Komoka
LONDON
Canfield
Welland
Fort Erie
BUFFALO
Pt. Edward
Sarnia
St. Thomas
Port Colborne
Glencoe
Port Stanley
Windsor
Chatham

LEGEND

1 Erie & Ontario
2 Fort Erie
3 Welland
4 Buffalo & Lake Huron
5 Great Western
6 Northern
7 Grand Trunk
8 London & Port Stanley
9 Galt and Guelph

company won the right to select its gauge and the CSR chose the Stephenson gauge, something Thomson considered essential to the viability of the entire project.

It is thought that the railway's new name was American in origin, since it was used to identify various nebulous schemes to link the western U.S. railways with the American northeast via a route through southern Canada. The idea for such a route was envisioned at least as early as 22 February 1852, when Richard P. Morgan, the chief engineer of the Peoria & Oquawka Railroad, wrote to Erastus Corning of the NYC&HRR concerning the extension of the Aurora Branch to Peoria and Burlington (for which line Morgan was the builder), thence from Burlington to Galesburg, Aurora, Chicago, Detroit and through Canada to Albany.[9] Nine months later to the day, MCRR's John W. Brooks wrote to Erastus Corning (a director of MCRR, GWR and CB&Q among others) of virtually the same projection.[10] Consequently, both Brooks and Corning knew of such a Canadian route prior to Buchanan's pitch for financial backing, and because they likely saw Canada Southern as a potential rival, it seemed best not to encourage it. That its early promotion had been so financially trying to Buchanan provided a convenient excuse to show disinterest. Their disinterest was feigned, for they could ill afford to be uninterested. The mere fact that a number of western American railroads had conceived of a possible line through Canada was cause enough for the Michigan Central and the NYC&HR lines to be alert.

Over time it became apparent to Buchanan and Thomson that they had done a better job promoting the Canada Southern project in the United States than they had thought. These efforts came home to roost. In the autumn 1869 sitting of the Ontario Legislature, three groups began to push, on behalf of their respective American and Canadian backers, two schemes similar to the CSR and one quite different plan. One group claimed its backers were in New York State, but they remained quite secretive as to who these backers were. They may well have represented the Buffalo Detroit Railway, whose notice seeking parliamentary legislation had been announced a few years earlier.[11] Rumours abounded that Vanderbilt sought an Ontario charter for a railway which would cover the same territory. The Michigan Air Line Railway openly sponsored a proposal to build a railway between the Niagara River and the St. Clair River. Both the Canada Southern and the Great Western railways opposed these proposed railways, but for different reasons. The former did so because it saw these schemes as threats to its own existence, which was precarious enough. The latter opposed them because it was determined to savour its prospective triumph over this upstart competitor.

Towards this end, in 1862 the GWR formed the Canada Air Line Railway and strengthened this with federal incorporation in 1871. The CAL would link the Niagara River with the GWR at a point west of London (Glencoe was selected), whereby the Great Western would gain a more direct line between Buffalo and Detroit while also traversing Canada Southern territory from St. Thomas to Fort Erie. The CAL idea had been proposed in 1854, but the general economic depression and insufficient capital kept postponing the project. As well, the GWR's Detroit and Milwaukee Railway Company syphoned off considerable capital and operating funds. When Great Western foreclosed on D&M's two mortgages in 1860, the latter's banker, the Commercial Bank of Canada, was toppled into sensational ruin.[12] If the Canada Southern were to succeed, the Great Western might well be reduced to a branch line. A.T. Dakin, GWR's president, cautioned his shareholders that despite the financial hardships the company could ill afford to ignore the issue a second time.

The chartering of both the Canada Southern and the Canada Air Line railways fostered confusion and mixed reactions in the financial community and the general public. To some it demonstrated how sound an idea the southern railway was and that its early construction should proceed. To others, there could be only unnecessary rivalry which would delay construction by pressing existing contractors beyond reasonable limits and escalate the costs of what construction could be achieved.

Meanwhile, Buchanan went to England to seek funding, but he returned empty-handed in November 1869. The following spring he repeated his efforts, but to no avail. Similar attempts at fund-raising in the United States proved just as fruitless.

As has been mentioned, Thomson, too, sought funding for the CSR, and whenever the opportunity presented itself, he drew attention to an ominous threat against competition in the area. Vanderbilt held controlling interest or other influence in the New York Central & Hudson

River, the Michigan Central, the Chicago, Rock Island & Pacific, and now the Great Western. Thomson (and later his successor, Milton Courtright) played up the prospect of a monopoly developing in southwestern Ontario.

The CSR's long-term viability lay in its being an integral part of an eastern extension for one of the big western American railways. Thomson's promotions of the CSR included bridging the Niagara River and tunnelling beneath the Detroit River. Such grandiose ideas, however, needed connections, very good connections. The Chicago & North Western, the Rock Island, and the Union Pacific were ambitious enterprises longing to forge a new line from Chicago to New York.[13] Thomson's ideas fitted into theirs. If Canada Southern itself could build to Chicago, the possibilities were tantalizing.

Large railways were not the only ones interested in such ideas. Major J.E. Kitton, later a director of CSR, said that his road, the Michigan Midland Railway, was indeed interested in such a grand scheme. This was not purely an altruistic suggestion, since his own road was facing bitter opposition both in and outside the Michigan Legislature. A Canadian ally could do no harm. Indeed, it might actually help. His offer to assist the Canada Southern was promptly accepted.

Through Kitton and his associates the arrangement for a $2 million subscription in Canada Southern stock was made during May 1870.[14] The principal backers subscribed as follows:[15]

Milton Courtright	$500,000
John F. Tracy	$250,000
Daniel Drew	$250,000
Sidney Dillon	$375,000
William L. Scott	$250,000
William A. Thomson	$250,000
John Ross	$125,000

Of this amount, ten percent was counted out in gold scrip and received by the London, Ontario, branch of the Merchant's Bank of Canada.[16] It was then deposited to the joint credit of the Canada Southern Railway and the Treasurer of Ontario in equal portions, to be held by branches of each of the Merchant's Bank of Canada and the Ontario Bank. This money was to be paid out for bona fide work on the railway or to the stockholders upon dissolution of the company. In those days such a deposit represented a commitment to build a railway.

The successful placement of the stock subscription was but one of a number of steps the Canada Southern undertook to improve its financial outlook. Another was the hiring of a new president. The provisional board sought someone who had both financial and contracting contacts in the United States. The promoters settled upon Milton Courtright of Erie, Pennsylvania. He was a graduate of Gambier College, Ohio, and had started his career as an engineer on the Erie Canal, later becoming superintendent.[17] In 1850 he had formed a partnership with J. Avery Tracy to conduct a contracting business, and they had taken as their first job a 28-mile section of the Erie Railroad's western division. An astute investment in the Michigan Southern had made Courtright a large amount of money. He was also a director of both the Rock Island and the Lake Shore. Courtright had the advantage of being knowledgeable about Canadian railway affairs in southwestern Ontario through his acquaintanceship with both Samuel Zimmerman and Isaac Buchanan. Also, he knew Sidney Dillon, a major railway contractor.

At its annual meeting in June 1870, the following men constituted the first elected board of directors of the Canada Southern Railway:[18]

Milton Courtright	Erie, Penn.
John F. Tracy	Chicago, Ill.
Daniel C. Drew	New York, N.Y.
Sidney Dillon	New York, N.Y.
William L. Scott	Erie, Penn.
William A. Thomson	Queenston, Ontario
John Ross	New York, N.Y.
O.S. Chapman	Boston, Mass.
Benjamin F. Ham	New York, N.Y.

William Alexander Thomson (1816-1878), a native of Wigtonshire, Scotland, had immigrated to the United States at an early age. He lived in Buffalo, N.Y., for a number of years before immigrating again, this time to Canada. He settled near Queenston in 1843. Chief among his interests were economics, politics and railway — though not always in that order, nor were they completely separable. Kind-hearted, socially sensitive and enterprising in spirit, William Thomson was a staunch advocate of radical agrarian economic doctrine about the time of Confederation. He had published in 1863 a lengthy pamphlet, "An Essay on Production, Money and Government," in which he went to great length to set forth his views for the improvement of society. His socioeconomic theories, predating the Canadian Social Credit Movement, caused him to enter politics in the federal general election of 1867. The voters of Niagara riding, however, rejected him. Defeat was no deterrence, for he heartily chose to try again, in the 1872 by-election for Welland riding. He was elected then and again in the 1874 general election. He promoted railways as economic tools with which to develop the country. He believed in hands-on experience and was deeply involved with the Fort Erie, Erie & Ontario and Canada Southern railways as a director or officer. Thomson was the first president of the Canada Southern. Deteriorating health caused him to withdraw from politics prior to the 1878 general election, but he was still promoting railways, this time in Manitoba. He died on 1 October 1878 at Glencairn near Queenston, Ontario. — PAC PA25398

Sidney Dillon was born in Northampton, Montgomery County, New York, on 7 May 1812. At age seven he became a waterboy on the Mohawk & Hudson Railroad. Although he had a meager education, he was willing to learn, persistent and resourceful. By his twenties he had become established in contracting, and he had a lengthy career in railway construction. He was instrumental in building many railways, until the 1870s. He was involved with the Rutland & Burlington, the Central of New Jersey, the Pennsy, the Canada Southern and the Union Pacific. After 1870 he became more known as a financier, and was closely associated with Jay Gould. Dillon was a major stockholder of the Canada Southern and served on its board of directors for a number of years, beginning in June 1870. He was a long-serving member of the board of directors of UPRR and twice served as president (1873-83 and 1890-92). Sidney Dillon was a good speaker and negotiator, qualities which contributed to his capable management of UPRR's affairs. He died on 9 June 1892. — Union Pacific Museum

During the reorganization process, Thomson stepped down and Buchanan stepped out. Not only had Canadian representation declined to one-ninth of the board, but the significant American representation far exceeded that authorized under the company's amended charter. The directors' participation, however, brought to the Canada Southern line the financial maturity it so desperately needed. John F. Tracy was the president of the Chicago, Rock Island & Pacific Railroad. Daniel Drew, a strange individualist, was a Wall Street financier of railways and steamships.[19] He recognized few obligations to stockholders, conventional business practices or competitors. Drew would later hold fully one-half of Canada Southern's common stock.[20] Sidney Dillon, a native of Northampton, Long Island, N.Y., started his lengthy railway career as an errand boy on the Mohawk & Hudson, and at the age of 28 he picked up part of a contract for the construction of the Western Railroad between Boston and Albany.[21] From here he entered the contracting business as Dillon, Clyde & Company and built many important lines in New Jersey, New England and Iowa, as well as the Canada Southern.[22] A tall, well-built man with finely chiselled features, Dillon conducted his extensive business dealings in a brisk yet courteous manner, ever mindful of the value of a dollar. He boasted before a Congressional hearing in 1873 that he would not take any contract on which he could not make 20 percent.[23] He was involved with Credit Mobilier, and for nearly three decades he was a director, and later president, of the Union Pacific Railroad. In 1851 William Scott, a native of Washington, D.C., became involved in a coal business in Erie, Pennsylvania. The business (later under the name of W.L. Scott & Company) prospered, and through it Scott owned upwards of 70,000 acres of coal lands, giving employment to 12,000 people in four states.[24] Although he was not physically strong, he had a prodigious memory with the ability to tabulate copious figures. His penetrating glance, soft voice and rapid speech drew attention if not agreement.[25] With his brother-in-law, John F. Tracy, he extended the Rock Island line to the Missouri River. As a contractor, director, or officer he was involved with many railways: the Erie & Pittsburgh, the Philadelphia & Norfolk, the Lake Shore, the C&NW, the Michigan Central and the CPR, among others. Scott, along with Courtright, was behind the Albermarle & Chesapeake Canal Company.[26] Benjamin F. Ham of New York City was the treasurer of Credit Mobilier,[27] an organization which financed the Union Pacific's construction contracts. These then were the members of the inaugural elected board of directors of the Canada Southern Railway.

Buchanan and Thomson had endeavoured to raise $500,000 in the form of municipal bonds from the towns and townships through which the railway was to be built. This was the second source of funds, and they were not easily obtained. The following municipalities provided bonuses for about 80 percent of the goal:[28]

County of Elgin	$200,000
County of Kent	80,000
Township of Townsend	30,000
Town of St. Thomas	25,000
Township of Amherstburg	15,000
Township of Anderson	15,000
Township of Dereham	15,000
Township of Malden	15,000
Township of South Norwich	15,000
Total bonuses	$410,000

The third source of funding was the provincial government. On 20 April 1871 the Lieutenant-Governor of Ontario approved an order-in-council which authorized the payment of $200,000 to the Canada Southern Railway and the Provincial Treasurer as co-payees. One-half was to be paid through each of the Merchant's Bank of Canada and the Ontario Bank. The railway was to benefit under the provisions of Ontario statute 33 Victoria, Chapter 32, Section 9, and conditional upon the report of William H. Boulton, who was the government's appointee to examine the Canada Southern. On 25 July 1871 Boulton submitted his progress report, which indicated that the railway was in satisfactory condition.[29] During September of that year the Canada Southern Railway received moneys from the Railway Subsidy Fund.

The long and complicated formation of the CSR and its board of directors was finally over. Financing had been secured and now construction was about to begin.

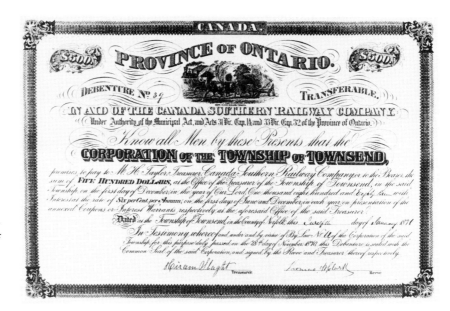

A debenture of $500 from the township of Townsend in aid of the Canada Southern for 1871.

This view from the early 1870s shows a Canada Southern construction train which has just arrived with fresh navvies at the work site near St. Thomas. The men have finished shovelling a load of fill from flat cars on to the embankment. Note the rather diminutive 4-4-0 steam locomotive with a large steam dome, balloon stack and four-wheel tender.

— Elgin County Pioneer Museum

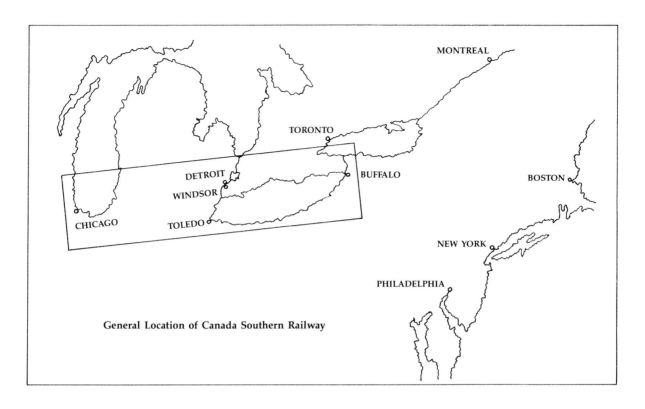

General Location of Canada Southern Railway

This representative view shows a surveyor at work in the field. Surveyors and their helpers walked hundreds of miles across southwestern Ontario, preparing the reconnaissance or preliminary survey along with the more detailed location surveys, often with optional routes around natural obstacles. Days and months were spent in all kinds of weather, amid clouds of black-flies or mosquitoes, as the arduous, painstaking work was carried out. The field notes and physical descriptions would be forwarded to the office of the chief engineer, under whose direction the various routes would be plotted on large rolls of paper. These would then be discussed with the company, and the railway's final route would be determined.
— PAC PA45699

Under the Stake, Under the Maul

The opening sentence of the company's *Prospectus* stated it clearly: "The object of the promoters of the Canada Southern Railway is to form with other roads a cheap line of traffic between Chicago and New York, so located and constructed as to reduce the cost of transporting the products of the interior to the lowest limit."[30] This document extolled the virtues of a railway that was to be 96 percent tangent track in Ontario, with nearly as favourable an alignment on the U.S. portion to Chicago. And it was to be level. Both the Canadian and American sections were to have grades no greater than 15 feet per mile facing the direction of the greater volume of revenue traffic.

Surveys commenced on 1 June 1870, with the line being located by 1 January 1871.[31] The surveying was conducted in an atmosphere of increasing rivalry, as the managements of the Great Western and the Canada Southern remained confident in their respective enterprises, each sure that the other was bluffing about building to Buffalo.

On 8 August 1870 the Canada Southern announced that specifications for grading and bridging would be released on September 17, with tenders to be called but three days later. In January 1871 the railway let its first contract, which covered the first 50 miles west from Fort Erie. By November of that year construction had progressed sufficiently for Courtright to announce that the whole of the line was expected to be graded by 1 April 1872. His chief engineer, F.N. Finney, reported in the trade press that approximately 200 miles of road had been graded and that main-line bridging was nearly completed.[32] So smoothly had work been progressing that late in 1871 management confirmed that the scheduled completion date was that prescribed in the railway's charter, 28 February 1873.[33] The construction pace, which had slackened for a few months, now resumed a brisk schedule. By 1 February 1872 fully 207 miles of road had been graded and the requisite number of ties had been delivered. The railway's impressive 1,365-foot wooden trestle across Kettle Creek was completed. Canada Southern had purchased a supply of 60-pound steel rails, the first quantity of which was scheduled for delivery by 1 May 1872.[34]

Late the previous autumn Canada Southern had taken delivery of two Baldwin 4-4-0 steam locomotives weighing 20 tons each. In February 1872 the CSR placed another order with Baldwin for two additional locomotives of the same type. These were to be delivered in May, in time for the railway to accelerate its construction schedule.

Construction was progressing well and the company decided to sell its first mortgage bonds. In July 1872 the railway's financial agents reported that the entire issue had been placed at 90 percent of the face value.[35] The fact that so much of the railway construction had either been finished or was well in hand prior to the offering of the bonds facilitated their quick sale.

On 1 August 1872 the first CSR locomotive was driven through St. Thomas on the company's own track.[36] Even though these tracks were isolated, the occasion raised the spirits of employees. During the same month the railway ordered sufficient numbers of locomotives, coaches, express cars and freight cars so that it might engage business by the end of October using two mixed trains.[37] In addition, 26 locomotives and 600 freight cars were under construction for delivery by 1 December 1872.[38] The Canada Southern awarded the Wason Manufacturing Company of Springfield, Illinois, the contract to build 50 passenger cars and 12 mail-and-baggage cars at a total cost of $330,000.[39]

Track gangs, meanwhile, continued their sweaty work. After reaching Wallacetown from the east on 24 October 1872, they proceeded to lay track westward at the rate of one-half mile per day.[40] By the end of that month the eastward-working track crew had laid track to within one-half mile of Comber, 40 miles east of Amherstburg.[41] By 9 November 1872, 154 miles of track had been laid between Amherstburg and Fort Erie. About 74 miles of trackwork remained.[42] By now, the construction crews were laying track at the rate of three miles a day.

Construction work on the two divisions of the Canada Southern continued in earnest. The Western Division (linking Amherstburg and St. Thomas) was completed first. Crews had been working from both ends, and they met on Friday, 13 December 1872, at approximately 11:30 a.m.[43] The first through train over this division arrived in St. Thomas at approximately 8 p.m. A small work crew was left behind to clean up the right-of-way during the winter in order that the work could resume once the weather permitted in the spring. The remaining work force of approximately 200 men was discharged. On the Eastern Division, as of 21 December 1872, there

This inspection walkway snaked its way through the upper portion of the wooden Kettle Creek Bridge. Taken about 1875, this view affords a look at the type of construction.

— George Thorman Collection

To the west of St. Thomas, the CSR's main line was to span the deep Kettle Creek valley on an impressive, single-track structure. The contractors laboured on the massive wooden trestle during 1871-72. Taken on 13 October 1871, this view shows the raising of bent No. 26 under somewhat festive circumstances and lax safety practices. When it was completed on 15 February 1872, the trestle stood 92 feet high and 1,365 feet long.

remained 60 miles of track to lay. The railway expected to accomplish this by 10 January 1873 using two track crews of 90 men each, with each crew laying from 1.5 to 3 miles per day. The last spike on the Canada Southern Railway was driven on Thursday, 20 February 1873, at Townsend, Ontario, a point 64 miles west of Fort Erie. The Western Division was opened for local traffic on 20 May 1873 with one train per day each way.[44] The first timetable was published two days later. The first timetable for the Eastern Division was published on 26 June 1873, although it was effective the previous day.[45]

Both the Great Western and the Canada Southern railways were finished. Despite its earlier completion, however, the GWR had not been able to marshal a through train. The first such train over the Canada Southern reached Fort Erie on 15 November 1873.[46] One month to the day would pass before the GWR could boast of its first through train from the Detroit River.[47]

The two railways, now physically complete, entered a great struggle for survival. Both expected to derive most of their earnings from the bridge traffic between Michigan and upper New York State. Both wished to supplement this with freight service generated within the peninsula itself. The companies, however, placed different emphasis on these objectives. With the Michigan Central–Great Western traffic agreement in effect, the Canada Southern was obliged to build through Michigan, a decision which entailed grave financial risks.[48] Locally, the CSR would limit itself to three branches. The Great Western, feeling somewhat secure with its Michigan connection — the Detroit & Milwaukee notwithstanding — believed its traffic weakness to lie in there being too few branch lines. Management consequently set out to acquire or lease several uneconomic branch lines, thereby adding some $2 million in debt. The more cautious shareholders began to object and the intra-company battle would eventually contribute to the Great Western's demise. As if these financial problems were not sufficiently taxing, both railways threw prudence and reserve to the winds by enthusiastically engaging in excursion fever. Railway excursions joined barn-raising bees as occasions of great fellowship and public benevolence, while the companies' treasuries hemorrhaged.

The Canada Southern Railway now linked Toledo in the west with Fort Erie in the east, with its own railway car ferry on the Detroit River between Stony Island, Michigan, and Amherstburg, Ontario. Complete as it was, the company's well-being would depend upon financial solvency in Ontario and the development of a direct connection with Chicago. To succeed, the Canada Southern needed the forebearance of its competitors and plain good luck. It was destined to have neither.

Sixty-four miles west of Fort Erie was the village of Townsend Centre. It was here, on 20 February 1873 at 11:30, that the last spike was driven to complete the Canada Southern Railway. The picture shows the diminutive station sometime after the installation of a signalling system, circa 1920.

— Spruce Row Museum

23

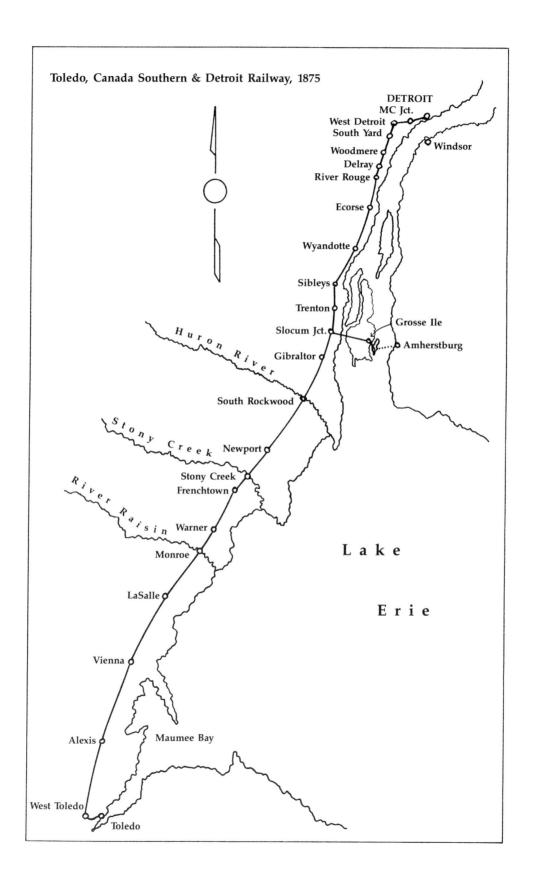

Toledo, Canada Southern & Detroit Railway, 1875

DETROIT
MC Jct.
West Detroit
South Yard
Windsor
Woodmere
Delray
River Rouge
Ecorse
Wyandotte
Sibleys
Trenton
Grosse Ile
Slocum Jct.
Amherstburg
Gibraltor
Huron River
South Rockwood
Stony Creek
Newport
Stony Creek
Frenchtown
River Raisin
Warner
Monroe
L a k e
LaSalle
E r i e
Vienna
Alexis
Maumee Bay
West Toledo
Toledo

II

CROSSING THE PLEASANT PENINSULA

Although its ultimate goal was Chicago, the Canada Southern first had to establish a revenue base on the American side of the Detroit River. In order to minimize the overall distance between Buffalo and Chicago, the proposed route would lie between Detroit and Toledo. There were already charters for railways linking these cities, and so the CSR moved swiftly to acquire and consolidate these charters in southeastern Michigan. Once this had been accomplished, work could begin on the crucial extension to Chicago.

Monroe County's Symbol of Worth

The earlier of the two acquired charters was that for the Detroit & State Line Railroad, which had been organized on 21 February 1872.[1] This railway was conceived as a 60-mile road to connect Detroit and the state's boundary with Ohio, whence the line would be projected to Toledo. Although the Detroit & State Line Railroad was capitalized at $800,000, only $3,000 worth was sold.[2] The later charter was that for the Junction Railway of Ohio, whose certificate was filed with the State of Ohio on 8 March 1872.[3] Capitalized at $2 million, the Junction Railway was empowered to construct a line wholly within Lucas County, from the northern boundary of Ohio, in the township of Manhattan, southward to Toledo.

Under articles of agreement the two railways agreed to merge on 29 May 1872, with the resulting corporation to be known as the Toledo, Canada Southern & Detroit Railway Company.[4-5] Its authorized capital was set at $2 million. The railway's documents indicated a rail line to be built from Springwells, Michigan, to Toledo. Once the new road had obtained assurances of adequate financial backing, it was speedily organized and set out at once to make arrangements for construction. From its inception the TCS&D aroused no antagonism. It secured its right of way, materials and labour promptly, and proceeded to construct its road as quickly as the crossing of the many rivers and ravines would permit. With the exception of about ten miles, the rail line was completed by October 1872.[6] Within two months the grading for the remaining stretch was virtually finished and track crews had laid eight miles of rail.

With the advent of the TCS&D the citizens of Monroe County had found a corporate hero in the making, and they supported it energetically. To understand this, it is necessary to know that Monroe saw itself as the commercial rival of Toledo. The earliest tool to carry out this objective had been the Erie & Kalamazoo Railroad, the county's first. In 1849 this enterprise was taken over by the Michigan Southern under a perpetual lease. This company gradually transferred its terminal business to Toledo. By the early 1870s growth in Monroe had peaked, declined and stagnated. Tracks had been torn up and what few were left were overgrown with grass and shrubs. Empty warehouses rotted on Monroe's wharves. This decline had engendered such bitterness against the Michigan Southern that being a representative of that railway had become a most unenviable position.[7] Meanwhile, the county's second railway, the Detroit, Monroe & Toledo, although seemingly independent, had been built by shareholders of the Lake Shore & Michigan Southern in the interests of that company.[8] When local people turned to the Flint & Pere Marquette, they found much to their chagrin that that railway's path had been rerouted away from Monroe because an important bridge had not been built for the F&PM by the Lake Shore & Michigan Southern. The thwarting of a third competing line raised to new heights the fury of the community.

Consequently, they championed the cause of the Canada Southern, since in it they saw their hopes rekindled for a competing railway which would advance their long-sought commercial prosperity.

By early January 1873 track on the Toledo, Canada Southern & Detroit had been laid northwestward from Toledo for a distance of 20 miles.[9] From there to Trenton, Michigan, grading of the rail line had been finished. Within months construction crews had graded the route from Detroit to Trenton. The bridge across the River Rouge had been started while that over the Ecorse River was being completed.[10] In fact, work had progressed so well by May that some expected the line to be opened during the summer. By the end of June track had been laid from Toledo to Trenton, where a connection was made with the small but important railway of the Canada Southern Bridge Company. Construction crews had laid rails as far as River Rouge by September. This was just below a junction with the Grand Trunk some three miles from Detroit. Trains were soon expected to be running into Detroit, using the MCRR depot initially.

The Toledo, Canada Southern & Detroit Railway opened for business on 13 November 1873, with the occasion suitably celebrated by an excursion train.[11] The opening of the railway brought a marked improvement in the business of Monroe County, so much so that the railway was indeed regarded as the county's symbol of prosperity.

During the construction and initial operation of the CSR's line along the Detroit River, the Canada Southern and the Lake Shore clashed repeatedly. Working conditions on the TCS&D were more attractive, and numerous LS&MS employees went to work for the Canadian-backed road. The battle between the two companies was bitter and cutting. Each railway had its official tariffs, but the freight agents would quote such figures as would be likely to draw business away from the rival.[12] Shipping rates were likened to a fire sale. The Lake Shore dropped its rates below cost and the Canada Southern, in matching or bettering these, would for three years fail to earn revenues sufficient to cover costs. This cutthroat competition did not augur well for Canada Southern's own viability, let alone its planned extension to Chicago, when the CSR had to cover, out of its own pocket, the financial drain of its TCS&D subsidiary.

Before commencing the line to Chicago, however, the TCS&D had to be connected to the Canada Southern's main line in Ontario to improve its financial well-being.

Of Bridges and Ferries

As previously mentioned, there were three projects which were key to the accomplishment of Canada Southern's grand scheme as a bridge line between western U.S. railways and upper New York State.

One of these was the crossing of the Detroit River, eventually by a tunnel, but for now a ferry service was crucial. The first corporate entity was the incorporation in 1872, of the Detroit River Railway Bridge Company under Canadian federal authority on petition of the CSR.[13] This company was empowered to build a bridge across the Detroit River from Amherstburg, Ontario, to Grosse Ile, Michigan. Subsequent legislation a year later further empowered the company to tunnel beneath the river, and altered the firm's name to the Detroit River Railway Bridge & Tunnel Company.[14] A test shaft was sunk into the limestone bedrock on Stony Island.[15] The preliminary engineering study convinced the railway not to proceed further with the tunnel.

Instead the railway decided to cross the Detroit River using a combination of bridges and ferries.[16] The 1,400-foot channel between the Michigan mainland and Grosse Ile was to be traversed by a railway bridge having a double draw portion which, when opened, would give a clear opening of 150 feet. The 900-foot channel between Grosse Ile and Stony Island would be bridged by trestle. The railway would use a ferry service to cross the main channel of 3,500 feet between Stony Island and Gordon, Ontario, just over a mile north of Amherstburg. The CSR fully expected that the ferry would be placed into service on 25 June 1873.[17] The ferry would have a capacity of 21 freight cars or 9 passenger cars. The bridge was to be constructed by the Detroit River Railroad Bridge & Tunnel Company (a Michigan enterprise), with the CSR and the Chicago & Canada Southern Railway sharing the expenses equally.[18]

The various legal entities on both sides of the Detroit River were consolidated into the Canada Southern Bridge Company between 1873 and 1877. This was the smallest unit of the Canada Southern Railway Line, but the little company held a keystone position. To it was entrusted the

SOUTH.					**DETROIT AND TOLEDO DIVISION.**			NORTH.				
309 Gr. Isle Accom. Ex. Sun.	307 Cin. & So. Exp. Daily.	305 Toledo Express Ex. Sun.	303 Cin. & St. Louis Daily.	301 Tol., Cin. & South. Daily.	Miles	STATIONS.	Miles	302 Cincin. & So. Exp. Daily.	304 Buff. and Det. Ex. Daily.	306 Cin & Detroit. Ex. Sun.	308 Cin. & N Y. Ex. Daily.	310 Gr. Isle Accom. Ex. Sun.
......	4.40P.M.	10.00P.M.	6 05P.M.	1.07P.M.	8 50A.M.	..	Dp .Detroit. Ar	59	7.25A.M.	9.35A.M.	6 20P.M.	10.45P.M.	7.50A.M.	......
......	4.50	10.10	6.15	1.17	9.00	3	West Detroit.	56	7.15	9.25	6.10	10.35	7.40	......
......						4	..South Yard..	55					
......	+4.55					5	.. Woodmere ..	54					7.34†
......	4.57	10.16	6.22	1.22	9.06	6	.....Delray ..	53	7.08	9.20	6 01	......	7.33
......	5.01		6 25†		9.09†	7	..River Rouge..	52		9.17‡	5.58†		7 30
......	5.06		6.30†	1 29†	9.13†	9	...Ecorse ..	50		9.13†	5.53†		7.25
......	5.12	10.26	6 35	1.34	9 19	12	...Wyandotte ..	47	6.55	9.08	5.48	10.12	7.20
......	+5 16		6.39†	1.38†	9 23†	15	...Sibleys ...	45	‡	9.03†	5.42†		7.15†
......	5.20	10.33†	6 43	1.43	9 27†	16	...Trenton ...	43		9 00	5 38	10.02	7.10
......	5.22		6.45			17	.Slocum Junct.	42		8.58	5.36‡		7.08
......	5.32P.M.		6.53P.M.			..	A Grosse Isle D	..					7.00A.M.
......			6.32P.M.			..	D Grosse Isle A	..					
......			6.50†		9.34†	20	...Gibralter ..	39		8.50†	5.29†		
......	10.43		6.55	1.55	9.40	23	So. Rockwood..	36	6.35	8.45	5.26		
......			7.05†	2.05†	9 50†	28	...Newport ..	31	6.25†	8 33†	5.16†		
......			7.10†		9.55†	31	..Stony Creek.	28		8.26†			
......			7.16†			33	..Frenchtown.	26					
......						34	...Warner ..	25					
......	11.04		7.19	2.18	10 02	35	...Monroe..	24	6.13	8.19	5.03	9.30	
......			7.29†	2.28†	10.10†	40	...La Salle ..	19		8.10†	4.56†		
......			7.37†	2.38†	10.20†	45	...Vienna ...	14		8.02†	4 48		
......			7.48†		10 28†	50	...Alexis....	9			4.40†		
......			7.51†			52	.. Toledo Belt..	7					
......			7.53†	2.52†	10.33†	53	West Toledo ..	5	5.45†	7.46†	4.35†		
......			7.56†			54	Wagon W'ks Jc	5		7.44†			
......	11.38		7.58	2.58	10.38	55	Wagon W'ks St	4	5.42	7.42	4.32	8.57	
......	11.50P.M.		8.10P.M.	3.10P.M.	10.50A.M.	59	Ar..Toledo.. Dp	..	5.30A.M.	7.30A.M.	4.20P.M.	8.45P.M.	

Lake Shore & Michigan Southern tickets good on Toledo Division trains.
Parlor car on day trains and Sleeping car on night trains between Detroit and Cincinnati. Train No 304 on Sundays will make stops of Train 310.

Passenger trains on the Toledo, Canada Southern & Detroit line are shown in this Michigan Central Railroad timetable for 18 November 1894.

— Michael P. McIlwaine Collection

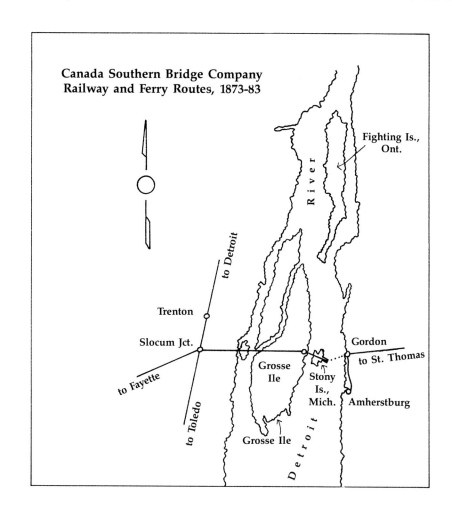

The Ontario and Michigan operations of the Canada Southern Railway were linked by ferry. In this woodcut by W. Moulette the first CSR ferry, Transfer, is portrayed being loaded at the company's slip at Gordon (Amherstburg), Ontario. After loading, the ferry would steam down the Detroit River, sharing the channel with numerous other vessels, and dock at the railway's wharf on Stony Island, Michigan. The side-paddle-type ferry was built in 1873 by Jenkins Bros. of Walkerville, Ontario. The vessel's principal measurements were 242 feet in length, 43 feet in beam and 14.3 feet in draft. The ferry had three tracks and a capacity of up to 21 railway cars, depending on their length. Transfer was registered in Canada, but there was no known number. The wooden hull was declared unseaworthy in 1888, when its steam engines were removed. The remainder of the vessel was sold on December 4 of that year to John Lane of Windsor, Ontario, who used it as a floating dry dock. — PAC C-85348

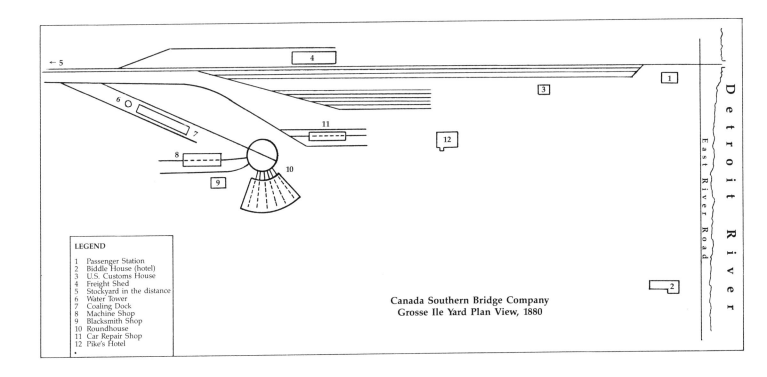

LEGEND

1 Passenger Station
2 Biddle House (hotel)
3 U.S. Customs House
4 Freight Shed
5 Stockyard in the distance
6 Water Tower
7 Coaling Dock
8 Machine Shop
9 Blacksmith Shop
10 Roundhouse
11 Car Repair Shop
12 Pike's Hotel

**Canada Southern Bridge Company
Grosse Ile Yard Plan View, 1880**

This view shows the original Canada Southern station at Grosse Ile, Michigan. Built about 1873, the wooden building provided service for about three decades. The rundown appearance, the overgrown track and the sagging roof indicate that the picture was taken after the heyday of heavy passenger and freight traffic.

— Grosse Ile Historical Society

The rails of the CSR reached Stony Island from Grosse Ile, Michigan, on a wooden truss bridge of the Canada Southern Bridge Company. Note that each side of the bridge consists of three sets of timber trusses reinforced with three sets of vertically oriented iron rods. The bridge had just been completed, and that was cause for a photograph involving officials of the railway and contractor.

— Grosse Ile Historical Society

A first mortgage bond of the Toledo, Canada Southern & Detroit Railway to mature in January 1877.

— Author's Collection

Among the conditions which the town of St. Thomas set for the granting of a bonus was one requiring that the railway establish its principal shops there. Canada Southern completed its extensive passenger and freight car shops in 1872. This photograph was taken within a few years.

— Elgin County Pioneer Museum

Canada Southern passenger train headed by locomotive No. 649 stands beside an imposing station at an unknown location. The picture is a puzzling one. The interlocking letters on the tower could be "CSRR" but Canada Southern did not own such an impressive structure on either side of the international boundary. The author suspects that this union station might have been in Toledo, Detroit or possibly Buffalo.

John Wilson Murray was born in Scotland on 25 June 1840. Following his family's immigration to the United States, the young Murray went to sea, enlisting in the U.S. Navy in 1857. During the U.S. Civil War he uncovered a plot to free 4,000 prisoners on an island prison in Lake Erie. A few years after the war he left the navy and joined the police department in Erie, Pennsylvania. In the early 1870s he moved to St. Thomas, where he served the Canada Southern Railway as head of detectives. His success in railway police work brought him to the attention of Sir Oliver Mowat, the Attorney General of Ontario at that time. In 1874 Murray left the CSR to become Provincial Detective, a position he held until his death in 1906. Murray's detective career was an incredible one. He pioneered work in footprints, the chemical testing of clothing and murder weapons, the cross-checking of alibis and motives, and the reconstruction of crimes. These procedures are quite common today. Though long ignored, he has been the subject of a book and a CBC television series in recent years.

The Michigan Central Railroad station at Monroe, Michigan, was built in 1883 to replace the original TCS&D depot. The MCRR station, photographed in June 1956, was demolished 24 February 1958.

— Everette J. Payette Collection

The Toledo, Canada Southern & Detroit Railway station at Newport, Michigan, is the subject of this postcard view. This station was subsequently operated by the Michigan Central Railroad. Note the triangular train time board which could be backlit. Under MC/NYC operation this station serviced northbound traffic. Southbound traffic was handled over the NYC (ex-LS&MS) line nearby. The NYC System operated the two lines as if they were a double-track route linking Detroit and Toledo.

— Monroe County Historical Commission and Everette J. Payette

international link, which consisted of 1.2 miles of railway from Amherstburg to Gordon, the ferry route of one-half mile, and the CSBC railway of 3.66 miles from Stony Island to Slocum Junction, near Trenton, where a connection was made with the TCS&D and the C&CS railways. The bridge company raised $450,000 in stocks and $1 million in bonds to apply against the original construction costs.[19]

In 1872 the Canada Southern Railway had ordered a wooden side-wheeled railway car ferry from Jenkins Brothers' shipyard at Walkerville, Ontario (now a part of Windsor). The vessel, 244 feet long overall and 74 feet wide over the guards, was rated at 1,222 gross tons. Both ends were equipped with pilot houses and rudders. It was launched on 14 May 1873, underwent water trials for a month, and then was turned over to the railway in time to enter service during July 1873. The ferry's hull was sheathed in metal on those surfaces most likely to be exposed to ice. The vessel was christened the functional but unimaginative name *Transfer*.

Right from the start Canada Southern's railway ferry service was successful, its only weakness being winter ice conditions on the Detroit River. The winter of 1875 proved to be exceptionally severe and the railway was forced to suspend ferry operations for more than a month. Canada Southern was having second thoughts about the accuracy of its engineering study of this portion of the river. The shallow waters and swift currents were conducive to piling up ice. The railway had considered tunnelling beneath the Detroit River at this point, but contemporary technology and engineering skills were not adequate to the challenge. Several additional harsh winters prompted renewed discussions of tunnelling or changing the crossing site entirely.

Despite the uncertainties of winter navigation, Canada Southern's traffic continued to increase over the years, and by January 1878 the ferry was averaging 35 trips daily. Three months later the company had a submarine telephone cable installed to facilitate the dispatching of *Transfer*.[20] Two years later the Gordon terminal was enlarged to accommodate a second ferry, the *Transport*, which had been newly delivered from the Detroit Dry Dock Company of Wyandotte, Michigan.

The increasing traffic had other implications, too. There was a need for increased yard facilities and equipment servicing shops. The Canada Southern decided to build these at Grosse Ile, which by 1881 was a busy railway community. It could at that time boast of a railway yard with 6,000 feet of track, a six-stall roundhouse, a turntable, machine shop, blacksmith shop, water tower, coal dock, stockyard, freight transfer shed and a frame passenger station.

Various factors were forcing the railway to reflect on its western interchange point with American railways. Canada Southern's proposed high-level bridge over the Detroit River was thwarted following the concerted and at times vehement opposition of the Great Lakes' shipping industry. The Chicago & Canada Southern Railway was but a branch line with a very dim future. The TCS&D was feeding its parent by increasing traffic, particularly from Detroit. But this traffic flow was increasingly hampered by ice problems on the Detroit River. By 1880 the Grand Trunk Railway had completed its own line to Chicago and within two years of that had acquired the Great Western, thereby gaining access to Windsor and Detroit. If the Canada Southern were to continue to entertain ideas of being an independent, would-be great railway, then it would have to change its crossing of the Detroit River to improve its financial situation and its services to customers. Time would tell.

Meanwhile, Canada Southern was not idle in the struggle to build its line to Chicago.

Chicago, the Chimerical Railhead

In promoting their railway both Buchanan and Thomson had spoken enthusiastically (and perhaps fancifully) of their line as being part of a grand international bridge route. Two major river crossings and the extension to Chicago were the three projects upon which their railway's fortunes would rise or fall. Reaching Chicago was considered of paramount importance, so much so that Canada Southern would embark upon two routes to this key American railhead. One of these (to be discussed in a subsequent chapter) would traverse central Michigan; the other would cross the southern extremity of the state. Despite the grave financial risks such foolhardy optimism entailed, Canada Southern, with more spunk than money, set out to establish subsidiary companies.

The first of these companies was the Chicago & Canada Southern Railway Company of Indiana, whose Articles of Association were filed on 19 May 1871 with the secretary of that state.[21] The firm was scheduled to construct a railway from the western boundary of Indiana in Worth Township,

Lake County, to the state's eastern boundary in Richmond Township, Steuben County. The route would traverse the counties of DeKalb, LaGrange, Noble, Elkhart, Kosciusko, St. Joseph, Marshall, LaPorte, Starke and Porter, a distance of 144 miles.[22] The company was capitalized at $1.5 million, and of this sum, stock to the amount of $52,600 was subscribed.[23] Its six-man board of directors included Milton Courtright.

A second subsidiary, the Chicago & Canada Southern Railway Company of Illinois, was set up on 27 June 1871 with a capital of $1.5 million.[24] This was actually a consolidation with the Michigan Air Line Railroad Company of Illinois. On 3 July 1871 this company was consolidated into the Indiana company.[25]

A third CSR subsidiary was established in Ohio. The Northwestern Ohio Railroad Company had filed its certificate on 20 March 1871.[26] This company was empowered to build a 30-mile rail line from a point on the northern boundary of Ohio in Gorham Township, Fulton County, to a point on the western boundary of the state in Florence Township, Williams County, being wholly within these counties. The Chicago & Canada Southern and Northwestern Ohio companies then consolidated as an Ohio corporation under the C&CS name, with an initial capital of $3 million.[27-28]

The South Eastern Michigan Railway Company, which had been set up on 19 May 1871 with an authorized capital of $6 million, constituted the fourth Canada Southern subsidiary.[29] The SEMR was empowered to construct a 65-mile railway from the east line of Monguagon Township to the south line of Medina Township in Lenawee County. On 27 October 1871 this company was taken over by the C&CS.

The consolidated Chicago & Canada Southern Railway Company now had a revised authorized capital base of $14 million.[30] The railway was the proprietor of charters which formed a direct and continuous route from Chicago to the Detroit River, a distance of 252 miles.

Construction of the railway was begun in Michigan after the ground had thawed, and by November 1871 the first section, that between Morenci and Blissfield, was ready for trackwork.[31] At this time consideration was given to the building of a branch line from Morenci to Toledo, but financial constraints weighed against it. By late spring 1872 the second section of the line, that between Morenci and the Ohio line, was graded and ready for iron, but the railway suddenly suspended work for three months. Late summer found construction crews clearing and grubbing the third section of road, the 40-mile route between Grosse Ile and Blissfield. By the end of the summer, track had been laid from Trenton, Michigan, to Fayette, Ohio, a distance of 67 miles.[32] The route for a further 18 miles was graded. Although the Blissfield–Fayette portion was completed first, it was not operated until the eastern portion was finished. The line cut diagonally through Monroe County (not far from the TCS&D) and, as the railway was extended, the communities of Scofield, Maybee and Dundee came into being. The Monroe County portion was completed during July 1873; that in Lenawee County was finished the following month.[33]

A 12-mile section in Steuben County, Indiana, was graded in July 1873 by J.P. Parker of Batavia, Illinois, who had a work force of between 200 and 300 men wrestling with much heavy work.[34] Two months later the remaining tracklaying on the section linking Trenton and Blissfield was completed. During October 1873 train service was in effect between Grosse Ile and Fayette.[35] But all was not well.

The backers of the Chicago & Canada Southern Railway found themselves amid the ruins of the earlier shocks as the depression of the 1870s worsened. They lacked the personal wealth to support their railway. With 160 miles yet to be built, the C&CS was nothing more than a branch line. Its arrival at Fayette had exhausted the company's finances, and so in 1873 it suspended any further construction for the remainder of the year. The following spring the trade press confidently reported that the Canada Southern had been financially replenished and construction of its Chicago extension was expected to resume with new vigour.[36] The line would be built almost due west to Porter County, Indiana. From there it would curve its way into Chicago between the lines of the Michigan Central and the panhandle roads. The C&CS line would pass through the towns of Montpelier, Hamilton, Steubenville, Goshen, and Kankakee (Indiana), on the way. At Valparaiso, it would intersect the Fort Wayne & Pittsburgh. Construction of the entire Fayette–Chicago section was entrusted to General J.S. Casement (the "lightning tracklayer"), who had built part of the Union Pacific.[37] Again, financial problems intervened to cancel the publicly announced intentions and the railway had to settle for Butler, Indiana, as its new western terminus.[38] In the summer

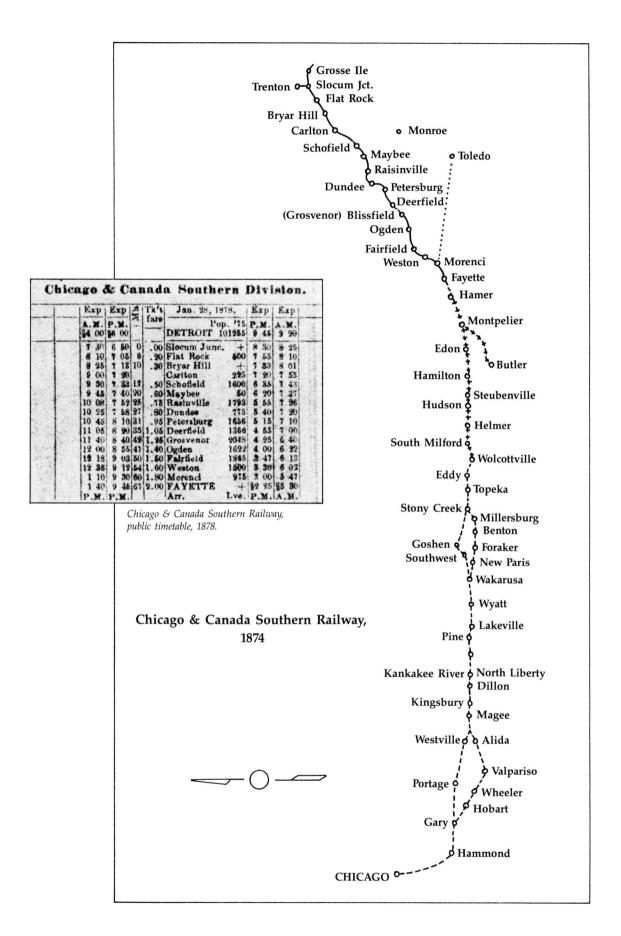

Chicago & Canada Southern Railway,
public timetable, 1878.

Chicago & Canada Southern Railway,
1874

of 1874 arrangements were made to build 35 miles southwestward from Fayette to Butler, where a connection there would be made with the Detroit, Eel River & Illinois Railroad.[39] This company's road ran for another 95 miles to Logansport, Indiana. The DER&I had opened only recently. Organized in 1872, the DER&I was under lease to the Wabash, St. Louis & Pacific Railroad, a line with which the Canada Southern had had some dealings. Instead of pursuing a traffic arrangement to help with the cash flow, the C&CS pressed onward alone. It did manage to complete the grading of its line to Wolcottville, Indiana, just 135 miles from Chicago.[40] What turned out to be the last construction on the C&CS line was the grading of the middle portion, namely, that from Fayette to Butler. The remainder of the line was surveyed.

The economic depression dragged on. The railway wars (which had started in the U.S. shortly after the C&CS opened) continued with unabated violence for years and culminated in the Great Strike of 1877. The financial position of the Chicago & Canada Southern was very precarious. The railway was earning $886 per mile, but it was spending at the rate of $1,214 a mile. The railway had had chances, if not opportunities, to conclude an agreement to establish some desperately needed bridge traffic. But it failed to do so. Meanwhile, its parent company had fallen to Vanderbilt control, Vanderbilt having purchased stock quietly as it became available. So had the Lake Shore line. Negotiations were opened between the C&CS and its archrival, the Lake Shore, and from 10 November 1879 the latter company was to operate the Chicago & Canada Southern. If the latter had invested 30 days' labour to build to Butler, thus possibly gaining some bridge traffic, the company might have survived.

The Chicago & Canada Southern Railway was officially opened on 13 November 1873.[41] Although it was operated by the Lake Shore from 1879, it was not owned by that company. The C&CS survived another nine years, when it was sold under mortgage and articles of reorganization under the name of Detroit & Chicago Railroad Company on 24 November 1888.[42] The C&CS was dismembered and sold. The Lake Shore obtained that portion of the line west from Summit (Dundee) to Fayette. The Wabash Railroad purchased that portion of the line between Montpelier, Ohio, and Hammond, Indiana. The remainder of the built line (Summit to Trenton) survived as the D&C until 23 December 1914, when it was consolidated into the New York Central Railroad.[43]

A once bold scheme to link western U.S. railways with upper New York State via Canada was extinguished.

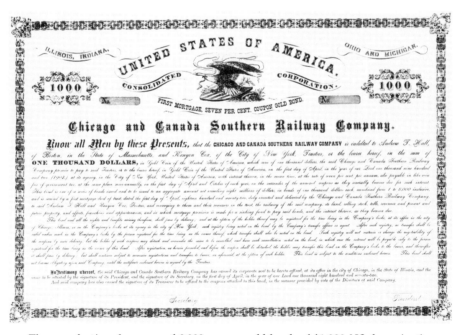

The reproduction shows one of 8,000 coupon gold bonds of $1,000 US denomination issued by the Chicago & Canada Southern Railway Company after consolidation.

— PAC C105956

III

LOOKING WEST AGAIN

Reaching Chicago was considered to be of such importance that the Canada Southern Railway chose to embark on a second main line. From a junction just west of St. Thomas the rail line was projected to traverse the countryside lying immediately to the west, passing through St. Clair, Michigan, and heading directly for the Lansing area. Depending on factors encountered along the way, the railway would then go to Lake Michigan, whence a ferry connection with Chicago would be built, or the rail line would turn southward and head for that city by an overland route.

The St. Clair Branch

Originally, the St. Clair Branch Railway was the Canadian portion of the CSR's second and more northerly route to Chicago. By the 1870s Moore Township was nearing three quarters of a century of history, yet it had no railway. But that was about to change. Moore Township lay directly in the path of the projected CSR line to St. Clair, Michigan. When existing communities entertained a speculative land boom, Canada Southern by-passed them all and chose a point on the river opposite the Michigan town. It named the place Courtright, after the company's president. At the time, it was fully expected that the Michigan Air Line Railway, or some other line, would continue the rail route westward from St. Clair to Chicago.

There was great anticipation that prosperity would follow the development of a through railway and that the towns of St. Clair and Courtright would flourish. Such prospects merited appropriate social recognition, and thus, on 29 December 1869, the advent of the railway scheme was suitably celebrated at Reilly's Hotel in Mooretown with a grand banquet to which many business and political figures from both sides of the border were invited. The joyful proceedings began with a lengthy toast befitting such an occasion in Victorian times.

Before long there were more tangible signs of the proposed railway. By late October 1870 Garber, the divisional engineer in charge of the Mooretown Branch (as it was then called), was on the western side of the Sydenham River, in the midst of surveying the route. By the summer of 1871 nearly one half of the right of way had been secured and several gangs of workmen were already clearing the route. Construction of the 62-mile line was carried out in earnest that year without any major obstacles, until winter put a stop to it. The following spring work resumed and about 18 months later the line was ready. The navvies laid track into Courtright on 25 June 1873.[1] Canada Southern inaugurated service by running an excursion train from Courtright on 1 July 1873.[2]

Construction of a 1,200-foot dock to accommodate the anticipated railway car ferries was by then well advanced. The ferries would serve until the river could be crossed by some other means. From St. Clair the traffic would be routed to Chicago by one of the five railways then building between that city and the St. Clair area.

The first scheduled train over the line ran on 24 January 1874 (some sources say 1873) and it conveyed 60 local residents who had been invited to a celebration in St. Thomas, where CSR officials and townspeople made excellent hosts.[3] So great was the imbibing that of the 60 who had accepted the invitation, only six were thought fit to make the return trip. Their confreres wended their way home in twos and threes as the occasion (and their constitutions) allowed. Whether or not as a direct result, this celebration appears to have been one of few to mark the opening of any portion of the Canada Southern Railway.

The Canada Southern Railway station at Brigden, Ontario.
— Moore Museum

This Hadden photograph shows the waterfront Canada Southern station and dock at Courtright, Ontario. The building on the right was the Customs House. Between the two structures can be seen the small freight shed and in the background the water tank. Originally, Canada Southern had planned to build a bridge or tunnel across the river to St. Clair, Michigan. From there, the company's trains would roll across the state to a suitable port and thence by ferry to Chicago. This scheme was one of many concerning a second main line to that U.S. city. In the early 1870s the railway operated a steam-powered ferryboat, the Milton Courtright, between Courtright and St. Clair. Early in April 1873 the vessel caught fire, drifted downstream and sank near Recor's Landing. This misfortune was one of many which contributed to the ultimate failure of the Michigan Midland route. Only the St. Clair Branch portion of this route would remain viable.

— Lambton County Public Library

This portrait shows Canada Southern's No. 100, likely at St. Thomas, perhaps in 1883. The engine was handsomely appointed and painted, a credit to the craftsmen of the Schenectady works. — Railroad Museum of Pennsylvania

The CSR's freight office and shed was a smart-looking structure. It was frequently a hive of activity, as this photograph from the 1870s shows. Because of the appearance of several CSR personnel and officials, it is thought that the picture was taken on a special occasion, perhaps the completion of the building. — Author's Collection

Such were the early beginnings of the Canadian portion of the projected second route to Chicago. The American portion was entrusted to a separate enterprise.

The Michigan Midland Routes

Among the proposed routes for linking Chicago and St. Clair was one which traced a giant reverse curve between the end points, with Lansing in the middle. From Lansing, there would be a line to Lake Michigan, with Grand Haven being the leading site for the port, from which there would be a ferry and steamer connection to Chicago. This weighty enterprise was entrusted to the Michigan Midland & Canada Railroad Company. Evidently, this company had been formed in 1870, but it was not incorporated under Michigan law until 21 September 1872.[4-5] Colonel John E. Kitton presided over this obscure but ambitious railway. He and Milton Courtright visited several Michigan communities during the winter of 1872 to marshal public and private support for the Michigan Midland project. They canvassed Grand Rapids businessmen and municipal officials, saying that the main line to Grand Haven might not pass through Grand Rapids but rather the village of Holland (about nine miles to the south), as was projected in an earlier conception.[6] Although the businessmen were wary, the city was not. It readily pledged both a right of way and $50,000 towards the construction of the line, and Michigan Midland pledged to build its line through Grand Rapids en route to the lake.[7] Very shortly the entire projected line from St. Clair to Grand Haven, a distance of 200 miles, was under tentative contract. The railway was to be built just as soon as pledges for the right of way and bonuses of $3,000 per mile could be secured.

Kitton predicted that the MM&C would reach a junction with the Peninsular Railway just north of Lansing within the year. In July 1871 Kitton disclosed that there had been negotiations between the two companies towards a possible merger. In view of the stated goal, the acquisition of the Peninsular's completed line between Lansing and Cassopolis, Michigan, would have been particularly advantageous for the Michigan Midland, but Kitton's public comments, rash promises and embellished remarks quickly offended Peninsular officials and the deal fell through. The Michigan Midland was soon scrambling to carry out the grand designs of its loquacious president. The Peninsular Railway extended its line to Valparaiso, Indiana (just 50 miles from Chicago), whence it fell into bankruptcy, only to be acquired by rival Grand Trunk at a foreclosure sale in 1879.[8] Canada Southern's failure to come to terms with the Peninsular Railway would prove to be very costly indeed.

Meanwhile, the Michigan Midland pressed onwards. By the summer of 1871 it was about to survey its route west from Fenton to Three Rivers, Michigan, a point about 20 miles east of Cassopolis. A few months later it was reported that engineers had completed locating the railway line from St. Clair to Fenton, passing a short distance north of Holly, Michigan.

During the spring and summer of 1872 the Michigan Midland & Canada Railroad employed a small work force on the easternmost section of its line, that between St. Clair and Ridgeway (now Richmond). This section was to be completed by mid-September.[9] During October 1872 the Canada Southern Railway agreed to lay the iron and to equip its struggling subsidiary. Early January 1873 saw rails placed along 25 miles of right-of-way, ready to be laid. During the summer the line was completed as far as Ridgeway, where it joined the Grand Trunk and later the Michigan Air Line. As well, the MM&C connected at this point with the St. Clair & Chicago Air Line Railroad, which linked St. Clair and Washington, Michigan, a distance of 22 miles. On 4 December 1873 the Michigan Midland & Canada opened to traffic.[10]

Had Kitton been bluffing after all? By 1876 the ambitious MM&C could boast of a 15-mile main line in service, one mile of sidings, one locomotive, two passenger cars, and seven freight cars and vans (cabooses). Its authorized stock of $400,000 equalled its funded debt, but its stock subscription barely totalled $300,000. A year later its operating deficit approximated $25,000. The future was looking bleaker by the month. Perhaps some other alliance would improve the CSR's fortunes in the state.

The Michigan Air Line Railway Company was one enterprise with which the Canada Southern had hoped to be allied, but MAL was itself deeply in trouble. It had been incorporated in 1868 to construct a line from Ridgeway, Michigan, to South Bend, Indiana. Through a subsidiary it would build an extension into Chicago. These plans fitted well with those of the CSR, but there

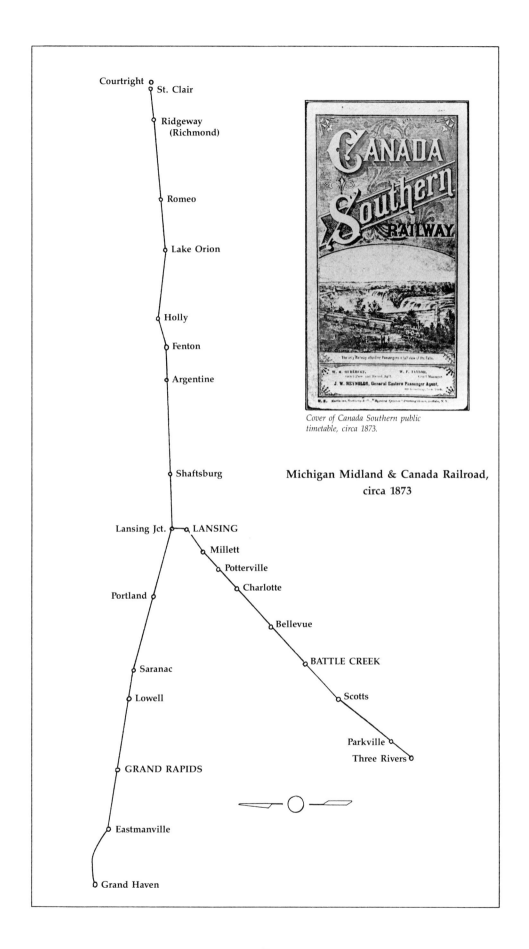

Courtright ○
St. Clair ○

Ridgeway ○
(Richmond)

Romeo ○

Lake Orion ○

Holly ○
Fenton ○
Argentine ○

Cover of Canada Southern public timetable, circa 1873.

Michigan Midland & Canada Railroad, circa 1873

Shaftsburg ○

Lansing Jct. ○─○ LANSING

Millett ○
Potterville ○
Charlotte ○

Portland ○

Bellevue ○

BATTLE CREEK ○

Saranac ○

Scotts ○

Lowell ○

Parkville ○
Three Rivers ○

GRAND RAPIDS ○

Eastmanville ○

Grand Haven ○

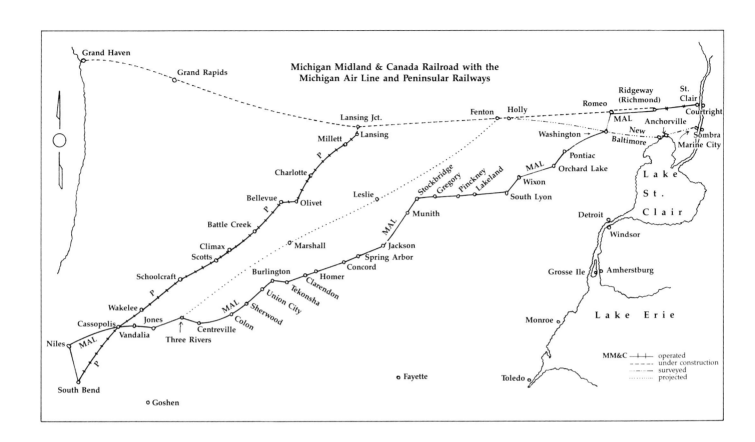

Michigan Midland & Canada Railroad with the
Michigan Air Line and Peninsular Railways

MM&C ┤┤┤ operated
- - - under construction
-·-·- surveyed
········ projected

*Enlargement of proof strike of RR-141,
OC 25/78, used on the CSR's St.
Clair Branch over a century ago.*

— Lewis M. Ludlow Collection

*Passenger service on the St. Clair and
Michigan Midland Branches are shown
in this extract from the Michigan
Central timetable for 18 November 1894.*

— Michael P. McIlwaine Collection

EAST.			ST. CLAIR DIVISION.		WEST.	
84 Mixed. Ex. Sun.	**80** St. Thos. Accom'n Ex. Sun.	Miles	STATIONS.	Miles	**81** St. Clair Express. Ex. Sun.	**85** Mixed. Ex. Sun.
2.30 P.M.	9.30 A.M.	66	A..St. Thomas..D	....	3.30 P.M.	5.00 A.M.
2.10	9.20	62	..St. Clair Jct...	4	3.40	5.18
2.03†	9.16	61	.Air Line Cros'g.	5	3.43	5.22†
1.53†	9.06	57	...Southwold ...	9	3.52	5.30†
1.40†	8.57	54	....Muncey....	13	4.01	5.40†
1.23†	8.43	47	...Melbourne....	19	4.13	5.53
1.09†	8.37	44	.G. T. Crossing.	22	4.19	6.00†
			C. P. R. Crossing			
12.45†	8.20	35	...Walkers ...	31	4.36	6.20†
12.28	8.05	31	...Alvinston....	35	4.47	6 35
12.10	7.54	26	...Inwood....	41	5.02	7.00
11.55	7.52	25	...Weidmans..	42	5.06	7.06
11.45†	7.48	23	...Glen Rae...	43	5.09	†7.13
		18	.Oil City Junc. .	48	5.17	
11.25	7.40	18	...Oil City....	48	5.18	7.50
11.10	7.35	15	.Petrolia Junc. .	51	5.22	8.05
10.55	7.21	10	.....Brigden...	57	5.36	8.25
	7.14†	6	....Kimballs...	60	5.42†	
10.32	7.02	...	.Courtright Jct. .	66	5.57	8.55
10.30	7.00	...	...Courtright...	67	6.00	9.00
10.10 A.M.	6.40 A.M.	....	D...St. Clair..A		6.20 P.M.	9.20 A.M.

EAST.			PETROLIA & OIL SPRINGS DIV.		WEST.	
94 A.M.	**92** P.M.	**90** A.M.	Ex. Sundays.		**91** A.M.	**93** P.M.	**95** A.M.
9.40	.....	.....	12	A....Eddys....D	..	.....	.....	10.20
9.30	5.25	7.15	9	..Oil Springs..	3	7.25	5.35	10.40
.....	5.17	.....	7	...Oil City Jc...	5	.....	.....	.....
9.20	5 15	7.08	7	.....Oil City....	5	7.40	5.44	11.25
9.15	5.10	7.03	5	..Petrolia Jc...	7	7.45	5.50	11.35
9.00	4.55	6.50		D..Petrolia...A	12	8.00	6.05	11.55

EAST.			Mich. Midland Divis'n.		WEST.	
	122 Ex.Sun.	**120** Ex. Sun.	STATIONS.	**121** Ex.Sun.	**123** Ex.Sun.	
.....	6.00 P.M.	10.10 A.M.	A.St Clair.D	7.35 A.M.	4.00 P.M.	.....
.....	5.40	9.45	....Adair...	7.55	4.20	.....
.....	5.20 P.M.	9.25 A.M.	D.Lenox.A	8.15 A.M.	4.40 P.M.	.....

were powerful forces in opposition. From the very start MAL was the object of a bitter battle in the state legislature, denounced by Vanderbilt sympathizers. When the railway finally got under way, beginning at both Ridgeway and South Bend, it quickly found that its capital on hand was insufficient to complete the road. With reference to its northeastern end, MAL built only from Ridgeway to Shelby, a distance just under 21 miles. Of this, it had opened during December 1869 the Ridgeway to Romeo portion, a scant 14 miles.[11]

Spurned by the Vanderbilt interests, courted by Canada Southern, watched by the Michigan Central and coveted by the Grand Trunk, the Michigan Air Line led a most precarious existence. By 1877 it was already in its third incarnation and its main line was still in two scrawny pieces protruding out of South Bend and Ridgeway. By March 1879 its emaciated resources were exhausted as a result of the extension of its line another six miles from Shelby to Rochester, Michigan. It lacked the resources to continue, and its officials were too proud to form a partnership to survive in an altered form. Eventually, its estate was carved up among Canada Southern, Grand Trunk and Michigan Central. But the CSR itself was in no position to benefit fully from the charter provisions so obtained.

With the demise of both the Peninsular and Michigan Air Line railways, the Canada Southern was finally confronted with the stark reality of its will-o'-the-wisp subsidiary. The Michigan Midland & Canada Railroad would languish for years, allowing its physical plant to deteriorate, its financial obligations to go ignored, and its purpose to evaporate. It became little more than obscure footnotes in the state's railway history. Finally, it collapsed. On 23 February 1906 the MM&C was reorganized as the St. Clair & Western Railroad Company, a wholly owned CSR subsidiary.[12] In this form it would survive for a quarter century, but it was nothing more than a paper railway.

The reorganized Michigan Midland had now fully withered, and like a dead branch on a tree, it finally dropped off. Canada Southern's dreams of serving Lake Michigan from the ports of Chicago and Grand Haven had dimmed beyond recognition. The American portion of the route had disappeared, its obscure existence ignored in the pages of history.

St. Clair Branch Revisited

The Canadian portion of the projected secondary line might have suffered much the same fate had it not been for the discovery of a strange, thick black fluid that oozed from tacky "gum beds" in Enniskillen Township. A small commercial oil well and refinery had been built during 1858 in Oil Springs, Ontario, a pioneer village which had sprung up amidst these surface poolings of petroleum. What was perhaps the world's first gusher thundered into service on 16 January 1862, at a time when the well's owner, James M. Williams, seemed to have exhausted his finances, health and hope beyond any point of recovery.[13] With the Titusville, Pennsylvania, oil field dormant during the U.S. Civil War, the world turned to Oil Springs. The population swelled, and soon the township resembled a large pincushion, as primitive drilling rigs thrust skyward.

The area experienced an oil boom during 1864-66, but then tapered off, largely because of inadequate transportation. Shortly after the opening of the Petrolia field, just to the north, the Great Western Railway extended its line. For the early oil industry, however, there was still no benefit. The GWR charged higher prices for refined oil than for crude out of Petrolia, thereby favouring the London refineries. The region's oil industry languished into the 1870s, until the Petrolia oilmen turned to the Canada Southern to request that a branch line be built to serve the area.

The CSR saw a chance to make some desperately needed money and agreed to build the line. For some unknown reason CSR decided not to do this under its own name. It set up the Dresden & Oil Springs Railway Company in 1873 to link the villages in its corporate name. Construction of the line was begun near Oil Springs on 15 March 1875.[14]

In November of that year the railway petitioned the government for a change of name, for an increase in powers to expand northward towards Sarnia and southward to Rondeau Harbour on Lake Erie, for a telegraph service, and for an extension in time. These were granted under legislation passed during 1875-76. The company took the name Sarnia, Chatham & Erie Railway.

Construction of its road continued despite the lack of a guarantee from the Canada Southern and the lack of government bonuses, both of which seemed mired in paperwork. Two miles west of Oil City, the CSR engineers laid out Petrolia Junction. From here the construction crews built

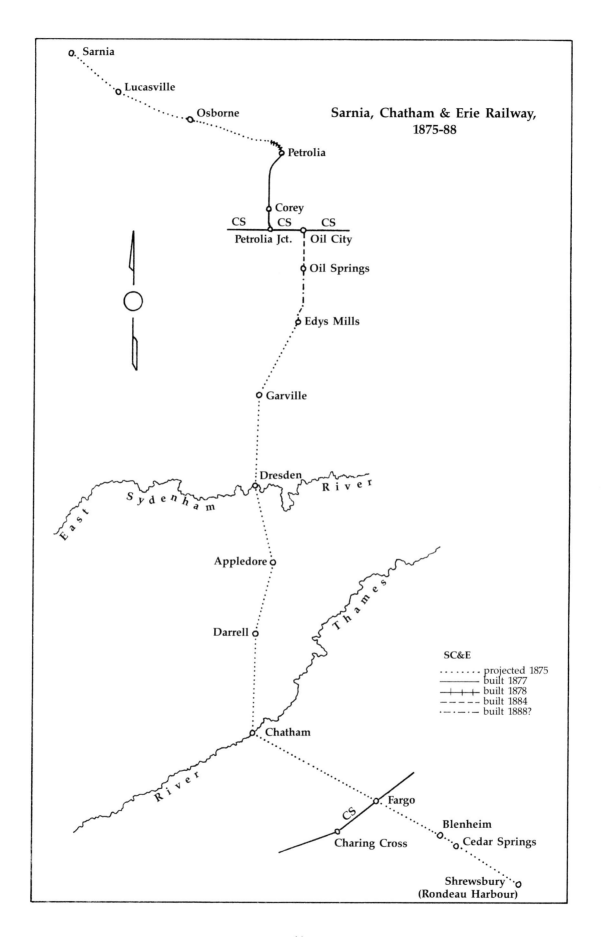

Sarnia, Chatham & Erie Railway, 1875-88

Sarnia

Lucasville

Osborne

Petrolia

Corey

CS   CS   CS
Petrolia Jct.   Oil City

Oil Springs

Edys Mills

Garville

East   Sydenham   Dresden   R i v e r

T h a m e s

Appledore

Darrell

SC&E

.... projected 1875
———— built 1877
+ + + built 1878
– – – – built 1884
– · – · – built 1888?

Chatham

R i v e r

Fargo

CS
Charing Cross

Blenheim
Cedar Springs

Shrewsbury
(Rondeau Harbour)

Oil derricks! Around Petrolia they were everywhere. The high prices the Great Western Railway charged for the shipment of oil to London for refining prompted oilmen to petition Canada Southern to build a branch off the railway's intended second line to Chicago. The CSR found plenty of revenue in petroleum and the tussle over oil traffic became one more front in the prolonged struggle between the two railways. This scene is for the year 1886. — PAC C30225

The former New York Central depot at Oil Springs is perhaps the only Canada Southern station which has been incorporated into a museum. The building forms part of the engaging Oil Museum of Canada at Oil Springs, Ontario. — Kenneth A.W. Gansel

northward through what became Corey and on to Petrolia itself. Grateful that its faltering oil industry would be saved, Petrolia gave a bonus of $15,000 to the Canada Southern.[15]

On 17 January 1878 the Sarnia, Chatham & Erie Railway opened to traffic that portion of their road between Oil City station and the town of Petrolia, a distance of 6.5 miles.[16] The following morning a passenger train departed for St. Thomas with 40 citizens on their way to celebrate. Petrolia hosted a parade, and later in the day the people flocked to the oil wells for a first-hand look. That evening a gala banquet was held.

The railway carried out some additional construction on a small scale at both extremities, but it was destined to reach neither Sarnia nor Lake Erie. As a corporate entity it survived until 18 July 1904, when it was absorbed by the Canada Southern.[17] The St. Clair Branch would lead a quiet, almost unnoticed existence until its eventual abandonment in 1960.

Canada Southern's secondary line to Chicago had failed much the same as had its primary one. Their stories involved some historic names in railway history on the western end of CSR territory. On the eastern end was an even more historic line. This was one of (what is now) Ontario's very first railways and the oldest corporate body to operate flanged vehicles commercially. Its story is next.

This rare turn-of-the-century view shows a Canada Southern passenger train at the Petrolia station prior to departure for Edy's Mills. For many years the CSR/MCRR trains made two trips daily between these communities, to ferry schoolchildren from Edy's Mills, Oil Springs, Oil City and environs to and from the old Petrolia High School. Although the trains and the railway disappeared, the old station survived. It was carefully cut in two and then transported in sections, to be reassembled as part of the summer colony of Bright's Cove, a few miles north of Petrolia. The building, complete with its tower, housed kitchens, parlours and sitting rooms to improve the life of summer residents.   — Sarnia *Observer*

THE MICHIGAN CENTRAL R. R. CO.

INDIVIDUAL
46 RIDE COMMUTATION
SCHOOL TICKET

SERIES 1
No. 7912

BETWEEN

BRIGDEN,

—AND—

PETROLIA

Good only on Trains scheduled
to stop at stations named
hereon.

Form Com. 46 B

HEDSTROM-BARRY CO., PRINTERS, CHICAGO.

In 1924 a pupil's school ticket for transportation between Brigden and Petrolia looked like this.
                    — Moore Museum

This rare view shows a Michigan Central passenger train, powered by 4-4-0-type engine No. 8867, crossing the Black Creek trestle.
— Zeta M. Miller Collection, Willoughby Historical Museum

This Hadden photograph records the result of a wintertime head-on collision between two Michigan Central trains near Alvinston, Ontario.
— Lambton County Public Library

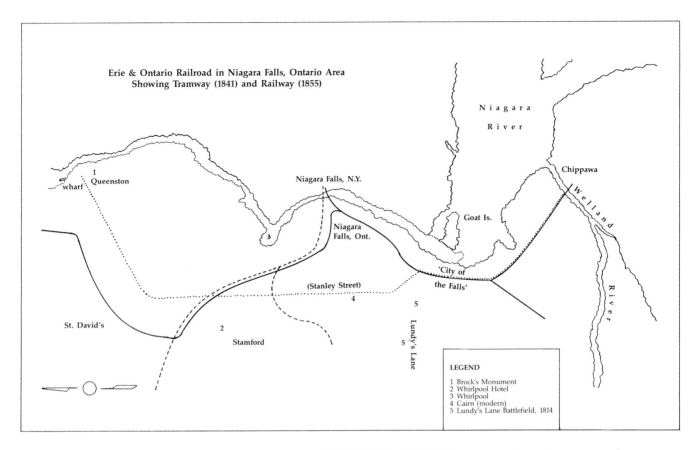

Erie & Ontario Railroad in Niagara Falls, Ontario Area
Showing Tramway (1841) and Railway (1855)

LEGEND

1 Brock's Monument
2 Whirlpool Hotel
3 Whirlpool
4 Cairn (modern)
5 Lundy's Lane Battlefield, 1814

*Erie & Ontario Railroad, notice of
opening, 1854.*

ERIE AND ONTARIO RAILROAD.

OPEN FROM NIAGARA TO CHIPPAWA.

ON and after Wednesday, June 28th, until further notice, Train will run as follows, (Sundays excepted).

FIRST TRAIN will leave Chippawa at 7 25, Clifton House, (Niagara Falls) at 7 45, and Suspension Bridge at and arrive at Niagara at 8 35, a m, in time to take the morning boat direct for Toronto.

Returning, leave Niagara at 9, Suspension Bridge at 9 40, Clifton House at 9 55, and arrive at Chippawa at 10 05, a.m.

SECOND TRAIN will leave Chippawa at 2 25, Clifton House at 2 45, and Suspension Bridge at 3, and arrive at Niagara at 3 35, p.m., in time for the afternoon boat for Toronto.

Returning, will leave Niagara at 4, Suspension Bridge at 4 40, and Clifton House at 4 50, and arrive at Chippawa at 5, p.m.

At Suspension Bridge the Trains connect with the Great Western, Niagara Falls and Buffalo, and the New York Central Roads, making a direct line to and from Buffalo Rochester, Albany, New York and Boston.

Passengers from Toronto by the steamer *Peerless* will reach Niagara Falls in three and a half hours from the time of leaving Toronto, and the same time in returning.

J. SPAULDING,
Engr. and Supt.

Niagara June 26th, 1864.   1312-tf

IV

GETTING 'ROUND THE FALLS

The earliest antecedent of the Canada Southern Railway was, despite its name, a tramway. The Erie & Ontario Railroad Company was incorporated on 16 April 1835 with a capital of 75,000 pounds sterling for the purpose of constructing a tramway from the Welland River (Chippawa Creek) to the Niagara River at or below Queenston.[1] The company was further empowered to build extensions to both Lake Erie and Lake Ontario. In order to retain authority for the interlake extensions, the company had to let the contract for the work before any other company was incorporated for the same purpose. Perhaps it was for this reason that a tramway was selected, since it could be more easily constructed in less time than a steam-powered railway.

Among the tramway's backers were to be found names such as Hamilton, Clark, Street, Thorburn, Grant, Tench, Laing, and Cummings, all prominent merchants in the area. They had proposed the tramway as a means to counter the loss of business in the region on account of the construction and, in 1829, the opening of the Welland Canal. Their efforts had been thwarted for four years by Merritt and fellow backers of the canal company, but that was only part of the opposition. When the Legislature of Upper Canada passed the act to incorporate the E&O, Royal Assent was withheld until the (British) Board of Ordnance's wishes could be ascertained, so concerned were the military authorities that the new light railway might be an avenue to weaken the defence of Canada. Royal Assent was granted only after the Board of Ordnance was satisfied that the country's defences would not be unduly compromised.

Construction began in 1835. Work progressed slowly, however, and in 1840 a time extension was obtained. The line between Chippawa (original spelling) and the City of the Falls (now the Falls view area) was completed that same year, and apparently the line to Queenston was finished in 1841.[2] (The City of the Falls was conceived as a speculative residential city core with peripheral tourist attractions.) E&O's southern terminus was on the Chippawa Creek, where a wharf was constructed to handle a steamboat service to Buffalo. From here the route headed towards Clark Hill (Oak Hill), then the City of the Falls, thence along portions of Stanley Street (in present-day Niagara Falls, Ontario) to the escarpment. It descended the escarpment from the north end of Stanley Street on a northeasterly route to a small depot about halfway down the heights and situated between Brock's Monument and the Queenston wharf. The work was directed from the company's headquarters in the Whirlpool Hotel in the nearby village of Stamford.

Resembling large stagecoaches, the Erie & Ontario rolling stock could accommodate 20 passengers inside and their luggage on the roof. Four horses in tandem could haul as many as three passenger cars and a baggage car on level terrain. Two horses, however, were required to pull a single car up the escarpment. By 1846 the tramway's roster consisted of just three coaches and one cart.

Even in those days tourism was an important business. The Railway House, located at the line's crossing of Ferry Street (in what became modern Niagara Falls), was the depot from which passengers disembarked to visit the Battlefield of Lundy's Lane, the principal tourist attraction of the time. From this same stop, one could also go to the Clifton House hotel or to the foot of Ferry Street to board a ferry to the United States.

Known locally as the Queenston & Chippawa Railway, it handled a lucrative summer business until the costly City of the Falls project failed. From then until 1854 the horse-drawn tramway eked out a precarious existence. The City of the Falls did not operate during the winter months.

For many summers the Erie & Ontario provided the land bridge between the lakes and the steamboat services which linked the tramway with either Toronto or Buffalo.

The tramway simply could not compete with the Welland Canal. The men behind the Erie & Ontario Railroad realized that they would have to secure a charter revision to protect their investment by constructing a steam-powered railway. With the arrival of the Great Western Railway, the need to convert their line became even more urgent. The investors applied to the Legislature for an amendment to their charter. Then, on 10 November 1852, Royal Assent was given to an act to revise the charter to empower the E&O to become a true railway.[3]

The backers, however, did not have the finances to carry out the necessary revisions to the right-of-way, particularly the realignment through St. David's bay area, which would have permitted an easier grade for steam locomotive operation up Queenston Heights. In places the right of way had to be relocated through (hard as it may be to envision today) dense forest between Chippawa and Queenston. In villages such as Elgin and Clifton, a new line suitable for steam traction had to be constructed. Work progressed slowly. The railway needed a man with money and know-how.

Work languished until Samuel Zimmerman, fresh from a contracting job on the Great Western, took over the Erie & Ontario Railroad and expeditiously completed the railway's conversion to steam locomotion. The track was constructed of iron rails laid to provincial gauge (5 feet 6 inches versus 4 feet 8-1/2 inches). The line was extended northward to Niagara-on-the-Lake. Two locomotives, the *Niagara* and the *Clifton*, were purchased.[4] The entire road from Chippawa to Lake Ontario, a distance of 17 miles, was opened to traffic on 3 July 1854.[5] Shortly afterwards the railway's alignment within Niagara Falls was altered to gain access to the Suspension Bridge, as empowered by E&O's amended charter.

Samuel Zimmerman was born in Pennsylvania of humble circumstances.[6] He left school early to become a labourer. By 28 years of age he had become a contractor of some ability. Zimmerman came to Canada to settle in the Niagara peninsula because he saw opportunity there. He soon obtained contracts for four locks and the aqueduct on the second Welland Canal, all of which he found profitable. Following the completion of the canal, he began to look elsewhere and he became energetically involved in railway contracting. There were so many railway schemes being flaunted in southern Ontario that there was no shortage of opportunities to make money. (Although a railway with which he was connected may have gone broke, it is unlikely that Zimmerman himself ever lost money on any of his undertakings.) His first major contract was that for the extension of the Great Western Railway from Hamilton to Clifton, thence to the Suspension Bridge site. He also helped with the construction of that bridge. His acquisition of the Erie & Ontario Railroad in 1854 was the second major purchase in as many years. On 14 October 1853 he had bought the Niagara Harbour and Dock Company for 9,000 pounds sterling.[7] He planned the prompt construction of two lake steamers, the opulently appointed sidewheel-type *Zimmerman* and the more modestly equipped *Clifton*. Both were launched in 1854 and entered into the Toronto and Buffalo services respectively. A year later he established a banking house (named for himself) and further expanded his business holdings by obtaining Thorold flour mills at a mortgage foreclosure. He also purchased two hotels, one being the Clifton House, which he renovated and enlarged to accommodate 1,000 guests comfortably.

Zimmerman was affable, gregarious, hard-working and shrewd. He was willing to take risks, skilled in the social graces of his day and politically astute. Friendship, while important, was frequently a stepping stone to the furtherance of his own ends. Zimmerman died tragically on the evening of 12 March 1857 when the train on which he was travelling home from Toronto plunged through, so it was thought, a weakened (and improperly built) bridge over the Desjardins Canal near Hamilton, killing 59 people in the crushing pile-up of wooden railway coaches in the icy waters. It was later learned that the cause of the accident was a locomotive axle which had broken just as the train entered the bridge.

As an immediate consequence, the Erie & Ontario shelved its plans for an extension to Fort Erie. Another enterprise would build that line.

The second antecedent of the CSR in the peninsula was the Fort Erie Railway Company, which had been incorporated on 10 June 1857 to build from Fort Erie to Chippawa with a branch line to Port Robinson.[8] During April 1862 the railway started building its line, and amid considerable financial, supply and labour problems, it completed the challenge in July 1864.[9] Despite its shaky

Samuel Zimmerman (1815-1857), the founder of Niagara Falls, was a prominent contractor, financier and transportation developer. Among his major contracts were the construction of four locks and an aqueduct on the Welland Canal, and the construction of 120 miles of the Great Western Railway. Smaller ones included a variety of railways. He acquired control of the Erie & Ontario Railroad and converted it from a horse-powered tramway to a steam-powered railway. He owned a bank, extensive land, and promoted railways, shipping and heavy manufacturing. He died in the Desjardins Canal accident, one of the worst in Canadian history.

— J. Ross Robertson Collection, Metropolitan Toronto Library Board.

The Erie & Ontario Railroad was empowered to operate vessels on the Great Lakes, primarily on a route linking Toronto and Buffalo. The steamer Clifton ferried passengers from Chippawa, Ontario, to Buffalo, New York, and saw service from 1854 to 1866 on lakes Erie and Huron. The vessel was the subject of this pen-and-ink sketch by Charles Henry Jeremy Snider.

— J. Ross Robertson Collection, Metropolitan Toronto Library Board.

The pride of Zimmerman's E&O Line was the lavish side-paddle steamer named after him. The vessel plied the waters of Lake Ontario between Toronto and Niagara from 1854 to 1863. This pen-and-ink sketch by Charles Henry Jeremy Snider shows the Zimmerman under steam.

— J. Ross Robertson Collection, Metropolitan Toronto Library Board.

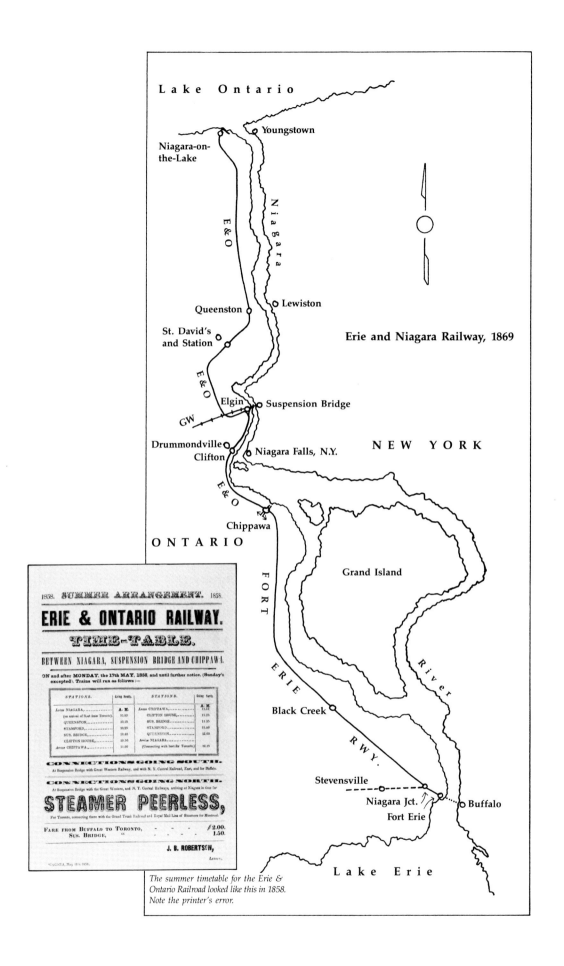

Lake Ontario

Youngstown

Niagara-on-the-Lake

E & O

Niagara

Queenston

Lewiston

St. David's and Station

E & O

Erie and Niagara Railway, 1869

Elgin

Suspension Bridge

GW

Drummondville

Clifton

Niagara Falls, N.Y.

NEW YORK

E & O

Chippawa

ONTARIO

Grand Island

FORT

ERIE

Black Creek

RWY.

River

Stevensville

Niagara Jct.

Fort Erie

Buffalo

Lake Erie

*The summer timetable for the Erie &
Ontario Railroad looked like this in 1858.
Note the printer's error.*

beginning the FER looked to expand. On 15 October 1863 the Fort Erie Railway received authority to acquire the Erie & Ontario line and to change the name of the amalgamated company to the Erie & Niagara Railway. Subject to the laws of New York State, the railway's amended charter empowered it to build from opposite the company's wharf in Fort Erie to Exchange Street in Buffalo, a distance of six miles.[10]

When the backers of the Erie & Niagara decided to lease their railway, the Great Western was quick to conclude a 20-year agreement, operating the line on a commission basis.[11] The GWR continued to operate the E&N until 1872, when an offer to buy the line was made. The deal fell through when the bondholders considered the sum of 75,000 pounds sterling to be inadequate.[12] This development, plus GWR's decision to build a new line from the Welland River to the Suspension Bridge, helped to set the E&N on the way into Canada Southern. Sensing this possibility, Great Western promptly resumed its operation of the E&N on a commission basis — as if nothing had happened — for fear that the latter's lucrative bridge rights might be acquired by the Canada Southern. Meanwhile, the GWR openly courted the Welland Railway and entered into an agreement with it to by-pass the E&N.

On several occasions the Great Western had expressed an interest in buying the line, but the British board always vetoed the recommendation of the Canadian board. When the prospect arose again in 1872, Canada Southern quietly secured statutory authority to acquire the E&N and did so later that year. Once it had done so, the CSR set about to exercise its right of access to the Suspension Bridge. The Great Western vehemently opposed this. The issue ended up before the court, which ruled in Canada Southern's favour.

Summer passenger traffic and excursions were, for many years, a principal contributor of revenue on the Niagara Branch, as the line was officially known. By the late 1890s it hosted a number of freight trains and six daily passenger trains en route to the wharf at Niagara-on-the-Lake. Lake steamers transacted considerable business between this former capital city and the new one, Toronto. For many years the federal government maintained a large army training camp at Niagara, and the CSR line was the only access. Troops, supplies, and heavy equipment all arrived at the camp via Canada Southern. During the summer many military tattoos were held and these required additional military trains as well as extra passenger trains to ferry the civilian visitors.[13]

The Niagara Branch saw increased traffic during World War I, but the reason was not obviously connected with the war effort. Under the exigencies of wartime it was proposed that the Queenston–Chippawa Power Development being contemplated during 1915 should consist of a canal and power plant project with an initial capacity of 100,000 horsepower at a cost of $10.5 million. The huge project comprised an intake structure in the Niagara River at Chippawa; the widening and deepening of the Welland River over the 4.5 miles from Chippawa to Montrose; the construction of an 8.5-mile canal from Montrose to the forebay and screenhouse on the cliff one mile south of Queenston; and the erection of a powerhouse in the gorge immediately below the forebay.[14] It would be the largest hydro-electric generating station of its day. Construction began in earnest in March 1918. The railway was kept busy bringing in supplies and machinery, and taking out rock, earth and debris. The Power Development was officially opened 28 December 1921 with appropriate ceremony.

The Niagara Branch then resumed a less busy life, and shortly afterwards, in 1925, it suffered its first cutback. Michigan Central closed that portion of the line between Chippawa and Fort Erie.

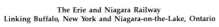

The Erie and Niagara Railway
Linking Buffalo, New York and Niagara-on-the-Lake, Ontario

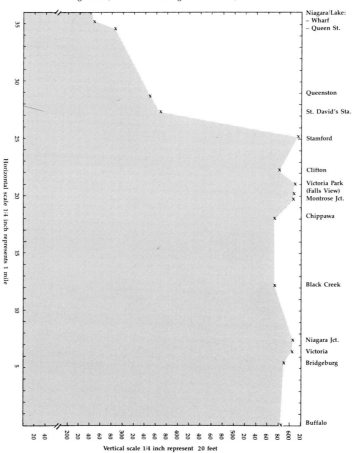

Horizontal scale 1/4 inch represents 1 mile

Niagara/Lake:
– Wharf
– Queen St.

Queenston

St. David's Sta.

Stamford

Clifton

Victoria Park
(Falls View)
Montrose Jct.

Chippawa

Black Creek

Niagara Jct.

Victoria

Bridgeburg

Buffalo

Vertical scale 1/4 inch represent 20 feet

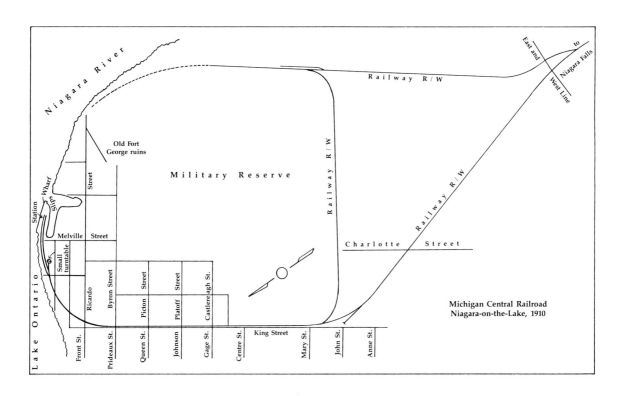

Niagara River

Lake Ontario

Old Fort
George ruins

Military Reserve

Railway R/W

East and
West Line

to
Niagara Falls

Railway R/W

Railway R/W

Charlotte Street

Station

Wharf

Slips

Melville Street

Street

Street

Small
turntable

Ricardo

Byron Street

Picton Street

Platoff Street

Castlereagh St.

King Street

Front St.

Prideaux St.

Queen St.

Johnson

Gage St.

Centre St.

Mary St.

John St.

Anne St.

Michigan Central Railroad
Niagara-on-the-Lake, 1910

The conception, development and construction of the Railway Suspension Bridge over the Niagara River was the masterful work of John A. Roebling. Amid much controversy he pressed forward with his design. There were two stone pylons at either end to support four very stout iron cables. Within a web of auxiliary cables and numerous guy wires, there nested the railway deck. Beneath it was the carriage deck. Following four years of work, the Suspension Bridge was opened on 8 March 1855. As an historic event and engineering feat the Railway Suspension Bridge was without equal until the erection of the Brooklyn Bridge 28 years later. This engraving from the Illustrated London News shows the Railway Suspension Bridge circa 1860. It carried the trains of the Great Western Railway and the Erie & Ontario Railroad. — Courtesy Special Collections, Dalhousie University Library

This old lithograph depicts an early Canada Southern passenger train headed west at Falls View. Note the observation tower for viewing the Falls (extreme right).
— Author's Collection

This postcard provides an overview of the MCRR wharf and station at Niagara-on-the-Lake. Behind the station a short train awaits passengers from the steamboat. On the dock and to the left can be seen a few dozen baggage wagons. During the summer months these would be used for the transshipment of fruits and vegetables, in hamper baskets, between trains and steamers.
— Ross D. Gray Collection

This view, taken on 11 May 1915, shows part of the Canadian Army's Niagara Camp at Niagara-on-the-Lake, Ontario. Looking from the slopes of the ruins of old Fort George, one can see a portion of the military camp. In the centre one can see the slips of the former Niagara dockyard, the Michigan Central passenger station on the wharf, and through the branches, the large warehouse for transshipment between steamers and trains. The Niagara River and the skyline of Youngstown, N.Y., can be seen in the upper right background.
— NAC PA61455

This postcard shows the Michigan Central Railroad station and wharf near Melville Street, Niagara-on-the-Lake, before World War I. The words on the large sign on the roof read: ''Michigan Central The Niagara Falls Route /The shortest and quickest line to Niagara Falls and Utica/where connections are made for all points south, east and west.''
— Niagara Historical Society, Mr. John Burtniak

The scene is Niagara-on-the-Lake in the early 1900s. The Michigan Central passenger train had just departed from the station at the wharf, where travellers from Toronto had transferred from steamboat to train. Locomotive No. 8125, a St. Thomas product, is a ten-wheeler dispatched to handle the train to Buffalo. The train is proceeding west on King Street at the intersection of Queen and Picton streets. A local landmark, Field's Drug Store, is on the left. The locale was popular with photographers, including postcard-makers.
— Niagara Historical Society, Niagara Falls *Review*

210-RAILWAYS-133. N. END OF "Y" BETWEEN M.C.R. AND WABASH. FEB.5.19.

Construction of the hydro-electric generating station at Queenston included excavation for a channel to carry the water to the turbines. This required the relocation of the railways. This view, taken 5 February 1919, shows the power canal on the left and relocation of the north end of the wye between the Canada Southern (used by MCRR) and the Grand Trunk (used by the Wabash). — Ontario Hydro

A Michigan Central passenger train lies in a derailment near Queenston, Ontario, in October 1913. Note the old open-vestibule coach behind the engine. Some of the Canada Southern passenger cars survived into the MCRR period in branchline service.
— Niagara Historical Society, Mrs. Blanche Quinn

Crews unload dump wagons at the MCRR Queenston power development spur, 2 May 1917.
— Ontario Hydro

An advertisement in the 18 September 1874 issue of the Canadian Home Journal *promoted the dining-room service at the Canada Southern station at St. Thomas.*
— Michael P. McIlwaine Collection

An advertisement in the 18 September 1874 issue of the Canadian Home Journal *announced dramatically reduced fares over the Canada Southern Railway.*
— Michael P. McIlwaine Collection

This is a reproduction of a notice in the Canadian Home Journal *of 18 September 1874 concerning the CSR summer passenger schedule.*
— Michael P. McIlwaine Collection

60

V

FROM BAILIFF TO SUGAR DADDY

The previous chapters have outlined the building of the Canadian and American main lines, the secondary route to the west, and the branch line circumventing the great Falls.

Just when the Canada Southern was nearing completion, the company's bonds in the amount of $1.5 million came due. The bonds were endorsed by Kenyon Cox and Daniel Drew, bond and stock brokers respectively, but neither of these men was able to redeem the bonds.[1] The company had been carrying on construction on a broad front in Ontario and across four states. When the depression arrived, the burden proved to be too much and Cox suspended payment on the bonds during September 1873. This precipitated CSR's slide into bankruptcy, the repercussions of which would last for a century. The railway would never recover its independence, though it would remain a legal entity. This was but one effect of the Civil War and of the failure on 18 September 1873 of the Philadelphia banking house of Jay Cooke, financier of the Northern Pacific Railway.[2] With its demise, an era in American history ended. The belief that prosperity was eternal, the shameless race for power, and the life lived in ostentatious grandeur ended abruptly. Railways were at the centre of this misfortune, and in the United States, many of these collapsed into receivership. In Canada the political and economic climate was soon shattered by the Pacific scandal. Another railway was behind this calamity, but the similarity did not end there. Jay Cooke was among the American capitalists who were associated with Sir Hugh Allen in a scheme to build the Canadian Pacific Railway, and this group had endeavoured to secure favours from the government of Canada in return for contributions to the governing party.[3]

The Canada Southern's financial woes and the general economic situation meant that the railway was ripe for the picking. All that was lacking was someone of great wealth. A survivor of the railway misfortunes in the United States now became involved. He was none other than Commodore Cornelius Vanderbilt, the very one who had remained so cold to the mere suggestion that he fund the Canada Southern project. It was he who had used the Michigan Legislature to thwart the Michigan Air Line Railway and its alliance with the CSR. It was he who had blocked the Chicago & Canada Southern's efforts to reach Chicago. Through his influence over the Lake Shore road he had caused the TCS&D to hemorrhage and sap its parent's strength. Ever on the lookout for a bargain, he entered the Canada Southern story as a major player. This grizzled, pugnacious man who had amassed a fortune from steamships had discovered the excitement and wealth to be had in railroading. Vanderbilt was canny and mysterious in his attention to the control of his New York railways, and he became more eccentric as his years advanced. He attended seances, patronized noted American advocates for women's concerns, and then distracted himself with public gifts to charities, religion and even education (something he had despised so openly all his life).[4]

Against this background the Canada Southern endeavoured to conduct business as usual. It proposed that the bondholders themselves fund the coupons which were to mature on January 1 and July 1, 1874, and January 1 the following year. A new three-year bond, bearing seven-percent interest was suggested. But there was no rush to carry this out.

On another front the CSR fared better. For some time it had been battling the Great Western for access to the Suspension Bridge and finally had taken the GWR to court. In the summer of 1874 the CSR obtained a favourable judgment, but when it tried to construct a physical connection, the GWR sent a superior work force to overpower the construction gangs. Canada Southern was expected to counter in kind, but it surprised the Great Western with both an injunction and the arrival of the police, who arrested all GWR employees who had participated. Not only was CSR's access to the bridge confirmed, the court ruled that the GWR's lease of the Suspension Bridge Company was invalid and ordered that railway to pay an additional $5,000 in annual rent.[5] This victory by the Canada Southern further contributed to the combative relationship with the Great Western.

With the securing of access to Niagara Falls, N.Y., Canada Southern, at the issuance of its winter timetable, boldly introduced two daily express trains each way between Buffalo and Detroit/Toledo.[6] These were in addition to the established local trains and reflected a considerable increase in passenger service. This determination was one more reason for Vanderbilt to be interested in the Canada Southern. If its backers could keep it afloat long enough for a major rival to take an interest, Vanderbilt could have trouble on his hands. So he promptly ordered his New York Central & Hudson River Railroad to conclude an agreement for the running of through passenger and freight trains between New York City and Toledo via the Canada Southern. He was concerned that the Wabash Railroad, part of the Gould empire and a road with which the CSR already had friendly dealings, might become Gould's instrument of attack.

Ignoring its bankruptcy status, the Canada Southern pressed for expansion. Traffic with Hamilton was of such importance that the CSR secured running rights over the Hamilton & Lake Erie Railway, which opened on 1 August 1873. Although neither the GWR nor the Grand Trunk was pleased with this development, Hamilton's financial interests were clearly delighted at the prospect of a balancing influence against that of Toronto.

The financial headaches continued, however. By 1875 the Canada Southern and its subsidiaries were mortgaged to the hilt. Their backers had insufficient personal wealth to alter the grim situation substantively. Although it was bankrupt, it deftly managed to avoid receivership. Canada Southern was a bargain in search of a buyer. The Wabash might strike a deal. The Grand Trunk was interested. Over the years Vanderbilt had been quietly buying whatever stock became available. By 1874 or so, he had amassed $10 million in stocks and $1.8 million in bonds. His control of the Canada Southern would be assured.

The Commodore's involvement with the CSR became formalized when at the June 1876 annual meeting the board of directors passed a resolution ratifying the transfer of the majority of the company's stock to Vanderbilt.[7] A new board of directors was chosen and, with his interests protected, Vanderbilt was content to leave matters at that. He transferred these stock and bond interests to his NYC&HR railroad, thus this road gained possession, at a comparatively low cost, of a well-built and well-equipped railway. Vanderbilt's investment was further protected because under Canadian law the railway, although it had defaulted on its interest payment, could not be foreclosed upon. A $40-million property had been acquired for just $11.8 million. The Commodore had purchased the Canada Southern line just as he had purchased the Michigan Central, at bargain rates at the bottom of a depression. These acquisitions had followed the purchase of the Lake Shore & Michigan Southern and served to exemplify Vanderbilt's great wealth, for men of only a few million dollars could not operate in such a manner. In a relatively short time he had gained not one but two trunk lines linking upper New York State with Chicago.

Next, he set about to reorganize the Canada Southern Railway financially. An official announcement on 23 September 1877 disclosed the principal elements of the accord between the CSR and the NYC&HRR. The former would issue $14 million in new bonds to be guaranteed by the latter, with interest to commence 1 January 1878. The interest rate was fixed at three percent for the first three years and five percent for the balance of the 20-year period.[8]

After its reorganization, more traffic was sent over the Canada Southern. Good as it was, the line needed some improvements in its physical plant if it was to compete effectively against the Lake Shore. The problems besetting the Canadian line, it was thought, could at least be partially alleviated by leasing it to the Michigan Central. Canada Southern had unique problems in the form of competition with domestic carriers, extensions for lumbering purposes and the carriage of Canadian immigrants.[9]

There was another twist in the relationship between the two railways. Early in February 1879 it came to light that MCRR president James F. Joy had on more than one occasion during the mid-1870s suspected that the CSR might not honour its traffic contracts with the Michigan Central.

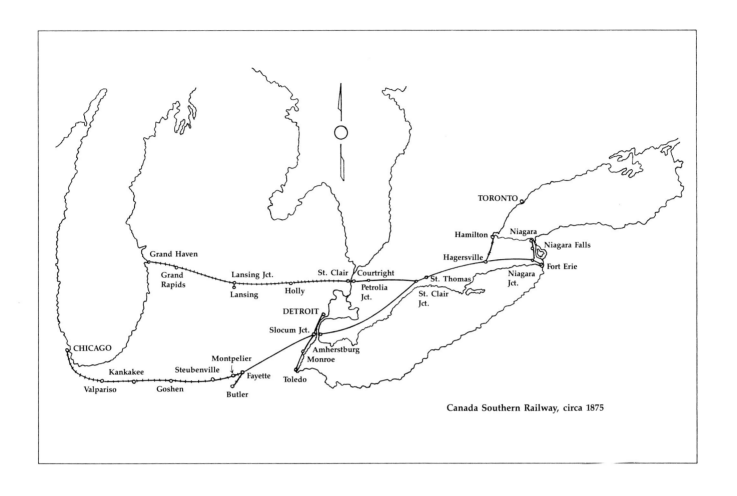

Canada Southern Railway, circa 1875

Table I

CANADA SOUTHERN RAILWAY LINE
REFINANCING SCHEME WITH NYC&HR, 1877
SHOWING DISTRIBUTION AND APPLICATION OF NEW BONDS

CSR First Mortgage Bonds	$8,703,000.00	@ 100%	$ 8,703,000.00
CSR Second Mortgage Bonds	2,044,189.39	31½	643,919.65
CS Bridge Co. Bonds	833,000.00	100	833,000.00
TCS&DR Bonds	1,407,737.50	70	985,416.25
Erie & Niagara Rwy. Bonds	453,000.00	50	226,500.00
MM&C Rrd. Co. Bonds	262,010.00	25	65,502.50
Sub-total to redemption and cancellation			11,457,338.40
Payment of floating debt			1,019,356.49
Equipment purchases			1,000,000.00
Cash			523,305.11
Total Bond Issue			$14,000,000.00

Source: *New York Times*, 13 November 1877, p3

In one instance Joy had hired a spy, who had burgled the St. Thomas offices of the CSR and stole that company's mileage reports. These showed that the Canada Southern owed the MCRR an additional $11,000 for traffic handled during August 1875 and August 1877.[10] When the CSR manager was confronted with this allegation, he matter-of-factly admitted that his records had indeed been falsified, but he made no effort whatever to pay the amount in arrears. It is not known what the Michigan Central did in response, but a commonly held view in those days was that the morality of railway managers was of such low grade that one ought not to expect honesty and faithfulness. Perhaps the manager found himself without a job after the Michigan Central took over the Canada Southern under lease.

During the late 1870s the Michigan Central was a keen competitor with the summer lake boats for heavy bulk freight such as salt and coal. Between 1877 and 1879 this traffic rose by 165 percent.[11] But the MCRR handled considerable passenger traffic as well, much of it originating on the Canada Southern. The reason was the European immigration (mostly British, Icelandic and German Mennonites) to Manitoba. Since the Canadian Pacific had not yet been built, immigrants to the Canadian northwest had to travel by either the Great Western or the Canada Southern to the Michigan Central, thence to Chicago, where they headed north by rail and wagons to the Red River Valley area. Although the numbers of immigrants would not exceed 100,000 until the 1880s, it was welcome traffic.[12]

By the end of the 1870s and the beginning of the 1880s, the Canada Southern was a different railway. Its finances had been placed on a sound basis, its physical plant had been improved, new traffic had been generated, and its future looked bright. Its high iron permitted ever faster trains, and by the end of 1880 it was equipped with 89 locomotives, 61 passenger cars and 2,652 freight cars.[13]

At a meeting on 30 April 1880 two CSR directors resigned. They were William L. Scott and E.D. Worcester. Scott's resignation came as welcome relief for beleaguered Canadian stockholders, who had long suffered his petulant manifestos against Canadian railways.[14] These two directors were replaced by A.G. Dulman and Joseph E. Brown, representing the Amsterdam Syndicate, which was allied with Vanderbilt in controlling the Canada Southern.[15] Sizable amounts of the company's stocks and bonds had been placed in the Amsterdam market.

The various changes and improvements which had occurred in recent years had all been preparatory to making the Canada Southern line the premier routing for passenger trains between New York City and Chicago. There were to be yet other changes. These would see the Canada Southern and Michigan Central advertise themselves as "the Niagara Falls Route" (and not even geography would stand in the way of this objective). Soon promotional literature would appear and the excitement of bridging the mighty Niagara Falls would, through artistic licence, show the impressive bridge considerably closer to the Falls than it actually was.

The building of a short line to Niagara Falls, the construction of the great cantilever bridge, and the acquisition of an important feeder line to Leamington are the subject of the next chapter.

Cover showing Canada Southern RPO cancellation for 7 March 1876 on a letter destined for the Commissioner of Crown Lands. This cancellation design covered the years 1874-86.

— Lewis M. Ludlow Collection

The Main Line of the Canada Southern and Michigan Central Railways
Linking Niagara Falls, Ontario and Chicago, Illinois

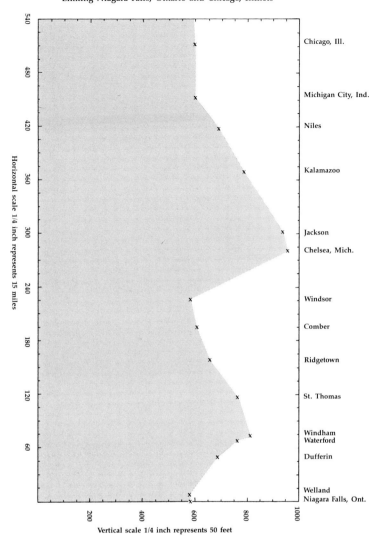

Horizontal scale 1/4 inch represents 15 miles

Vertical scale 1/4 inch represents 50 feet

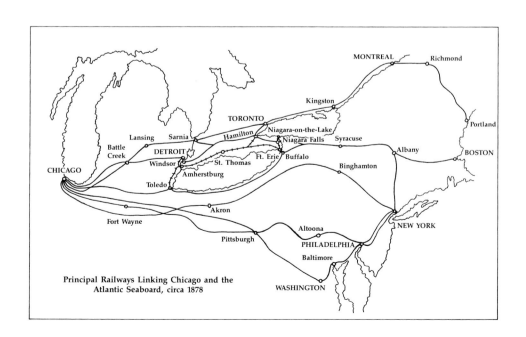

Principal Railways Linking Chicago and the
Atlantic Seaboard, circa 1878

—AND—
TORONTO,
—:: ON ::—
Tuesday, Sep. 2, 1879

To enable Residents on the Line of the St. Clair Branch to visit this Great National Wonder, a Special Train will be run over the

CANADA SOUTHERN RAILWAY

As above, in accordance with the following

TIME CARD:

Courtright	....	....	6.00 a. m.	Walkers	....	8.13 a. m.
Kimballs	....	....	6.10 "	Ekfrid	....	8.28 "
Brigden	....	....	6.20 "	G. W. Crossing	....	8.38 "
Petrolia	....	....	7.00 "	Melbourne	....	8.48 "
Oil City	....	....	7.20 "	Delaware	....	9.13 "
Inwood	....	....	7.30 "	Southwold	....	9.25 "
Alvinston	....	....	7.53 "	Air Line Crossing	....	9.38 "
St. Thomas	....	....	....		.... 10 a. m.	

Arriving at the Falls at 2.30 p. m., and Returning will Leave there at 10 o'clock the same Evening

FARE FOR THE ROUND TRIP: All Stations to Niagara Falls, $1 50 : All Stations to Toronto. $2.00.

Proceeds to be devoted to the erection of handsome and commodious Station Buildings at Petrolia.

Excursionists will have ample time to visit all POINTS OF INTEREST AT THE FALLS by daylight, for which Tickets at greatly reduced rates will be sold on the train ; and to witness the

Illumination of the Cataract ! · Electricity !

in the Evening, a feature but recently introduced, and presenting a that beggars description.

TORONTO EXCURSIONISTS

can have their Tickets made good to return on any regular train up to and including **Thursday, September 4th, 1879,** thus affording them an opportunity of attending the opening of the Great Exhibition by His Excellency the Marquis of Lorne and H. R. H. the Princess Louise. This trip is one of the most delightful on the continent, the route abounding with views of picturesque and historic scenes, embracing the battle fields of Lundy's Lane and Queenston Heights, at which latter point is standing

BROCK'S MONUMENT,

a magnificent free stone column 185 feet high, surmounted by a colossal statue of General Brock.

NIAGARA,

Once the seat of Canadian Government, now a favorite summer resort, lies at the mouth of the river' seven miles below. Here you catch glimpses of old Forts Mississauga and George, among the earliest and most important military posts of their time in Canada, and have a fine view of the American Fort Niagara opposite. Here, also, you embark on a fine Steamer for Toronto, and enjoy a two hours sail across Lake Ontario, a distance of 35 miles.

TORONTO

offers many attractions to Visitors at all times, its Parks, Avenues, Hotels, Residences, Churches, College, University and Government Buildings being among the finest in the land ; but will be rendered particularly attractive at this season by the Provincial Exhibition.

Mr. W. H. Greegor, Traveling Passenger Agent, will accompany the Excursion and attend to the wants and comforts of the party.

W. P. TAYLOR,   M. C. ROACH,   E. P. MURRAY,   F. E. SNOW,
General Manager.   *Passenger Agent.*   *Division Supt.*   *General Pass. & Tkt. Agent.*
St. Thomas, Aug. 2nd, 1879.   [St. Thomas Steam Print.]

This very rare poster concerning the Canada Southern Railway promoted an excursion from communities on the St. Clair Branch to Niagara Falls and Toronto. Then, as today, the illumination of the Falls by electricity was a singular attraction. A visit to the area was incomplete without a side trip to the impressive monument which commemorated the gallantry of Canadian war hero General Sir Isaac Brock at Queenston Heights 13 October 1812. Note that the proceeds of the excursion were to be applied to the erection of a handsome station in Petrolia.

— Michael P. McIlwaine Collection

Harlan and Hollingsworth Co.,

The Harlan & Hollingsworth Company of Wilmington, Delaware, built wooden passenger rolling stock for the Canada Southern Railway, circa 1870. Compare the side-elevation view with coaches portrayed in Robert Whale's paintings.

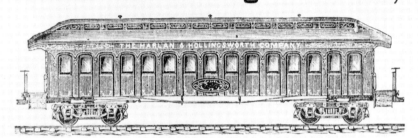

"The Canada Southern Railway at Niagara" is the title of Robert Whale's oil painting on canvas, measuring 23x40 inches. Whale, a native of England, immigrated to Canada in 1852. He took up residence in Burford, near Brantford, Ontario, and consequently many of his works depict the Hamilton-Brantford area. On one occasion he visited Niagara Falls and painted this attractive scene depicting a classic Canada Southern passenger train passing the Falls en route to the Suspension Bridge (in the background). The locomotive, No. 59, is painted jet black with brass, silver and yellow accents. The rolling stock (cars 17, 114 and 103) are portrayed with sides of medium yellow, letterboards and trim in light brown, and the roofs in silver. — The National Gallery of Canada

The Canada Southern crossed the Welland Canal on a wooden swing bridge, as shown in this view taken on 26 July 1872.   — Welland Public Library

The arrival of Canada Southern's locomotive No. 581 at St. Thomas in 1879 created much excitement. The railway's photographer was summoned, and the shop men dropped their tools and came to pose with ''their'' new engine on the turntable. Note the iron bar across the headlight glass for holding the train number (26 in this instance).
                                                                        — Author's Collection

This engraving by W. Schever appeared in the 6 May 1876 issue of Canadian Illustrated News. *The engraver portrayed a Canada Southern freight train accident at Welland.* — Courtesy Special Collections, Dalhousie University Library

The Canada Southern Railway did not subscribe to the practice of naming its locomotives. Apparently, there was just one exception, the Amherstburg. Number 592 was acquired in 1879 from the NYC&HR, where it carried the same number. Note the diminutive turntable in this wintry scene. Perhaps the locomotive, a Schenectady product (s/n 1197), was brought outdoors for the photographer soon after the engine's arrival. The author suggests that the locale was Amherstburg, Ontario, and that the time was the winter of 1880. — Railroad Museum of Pennsylvania

Charles Conrad Schneider was born on 24 April 1843 in Apolda, a town in Saxony, Germany. After receiving his basic education in local schools, he attended the Royal School of Technology at Chemnitz. He graduated in 1864 as a mechanical engineer. Three years later he immigrated to the United States, where he took up residence in Paterson, New Jersey. There he worked as a draftsman for the Rogers Locomotive Works. In 1871 he accepted a position as assistant engineer with Michigan Bridge and Construction Company in Detroit. Two years later he went to New York City to take charge of the engineering office of the Erie Railroad. Following this he worked for about 18 months as a bridge designer for the Delaware Bridge Company. On 1 August 1878 Schneider established his own civil engineering business, specializing in the designing and superintending of bridges and structural work for buildings. Among the projects he tackled in the U.S. were Northern Pacific's Mareut Gulch Viaduct and the internal finishing of the Statue of Liberty. In Canada he prepared the CPR's Fraser River Bridge and the famous Stony Creek Viaduct. For the Canada Southern he designed the renowned Niagara Cantilever Bridge. He also designed the Niagara Railway Arch Bridge for the Grand Trunk. His bridge designs were found in Japan, Mexico, Egypt and other countries. Schneider's work was thorough as it was original. He won many awards for his work. Among them was the Rowland Prize in 1886 from the American Society of Civil Engineers for his paper on the construction of the Niagara Cantilever Bridge. Not one to rest on his laurels, he joined A. and P. Roberts & Company, operators of the Pencoyd Iron Works, and was instrumental in consolidating several bridge works to form the American Bridge Company, of which he became vice-president. On behalf of the Canadian government, in 1908 he conducted an exhaustive study of the tragic collapse of the Quebec Bridge. In 1911 he was appointed to the board of engineers to design and build the replacement bridge. When he died on 8 January 1916 in Philadelphia, Schneider was remembered as much for his lovable disposition as for his tireless dedication to engineering.

James Anthony Bell (1851-1929), a native of the township of Lobo in Middlesex County, had a long association with Elgin County, the Canada Southern Railway and the town of St. Thomas. He received his early education in public and private county schools, during which time he showed interest in maps and planning. He was accepted into a program for surveyors and in 1875 graduated as an Ontario Land Surveyor. The following year, after taking up residence in St. Thomas, he co-established the surveying firm of Ware & Bell. Among his many interests was mapmaking, and in 1879 he was commissioned to prepare the maps for the authoritative Atlas of Elgin County. Three years later the County of Elgin appointed him county engineer, a post he would hold in great trust for many years. His reputation came to the attention of the Canada Southern Railway, which hired him to survey various routes. The more notable ones were the Essex and Welland cut-offs. During the construction of the Niagara Cantilever Bridge, he was appointed assistant engineer of that important project. For the periods 1882-91 and 1896-1911 he was the town engineer for St. Thomas. Bell was deeply involved in the operation of the St. Thomas Street Railway following municipal acquisition in 1902. It was during his stewardship that the town acquired various lands which were eventually developed into what is known today as Pinafore Park.   — St. Thomas Public Library, Author's Collection

70

VI

EXPANSION IN ONTARIO

Canada Southern began the 1880s with a mixture of apprehension and enthusiasm. The railway was now under lease to the Michigan Central Railroad, and CSR employees and minority shareholders were understandably apprehensive as to what this relationship would hold. Their jobs and their investments, however, were more secure than ever before, and there was exciting talk about expansion in the Niagara peninsula and the acquisition of a branch line to Leamington. All this was part of an increasing battle between the New York Central and the Grand Trunk.

The GTR, which had been determined to put through its own line to Chicago, did so during 1880. That railway regarded its Chicago extension as essential if it was to compete with the NYC&HRR for the lucrative freight traffic between the Atlantic seaboard and the Mississippi Valley. Passenger traffic was also important, and Vanderbilt was determined to make the CS/MC link the premier passenger train route between New York and Chicago. The Lake Shore would have to be content with second place, and to protect it, the Nickel Plate Road (another Vanderbilt property, acquired in 1882) would not be allowed any through passenger trains. Surprisingly, the extant agreement between the CSR and the Wabash permitting the latter's sleepers from St. Louis to be routed over the Canada Southern line between Toledo and Buffalo was maintained.[1] Other carriers, particularly the Pennsylvania and the Baltimore & Ohio, kept a close eye on the jockeying for dominance between the New York Central and the Grand Trunk. But as *The New York Times* observed, if a rates battle ensued, only the Grand Trunk was capable of contesting Vanderbilt's strength.

The First Promise, a Great Cantilever Bridge

The Canada Southern crossed the Niagara River at two points, one at Fort Erie and the other at Niagara Falls. Since both of these crossings were single-tracked, they were thought to be rather limited in their ability to accommodate the anticipated large increase in traffic. Another disadvantage was that both bridges were owned by subsidiaries of the Grand Trunk. Both were quite profitable, too. A recent increase in tariffs only quickened the CSR's resolve to fulfil Thomson's first promise of bridging the Niagara River. In itself this would not be enough, for the Niagara Branch was too circuitous and had been built to standards well below those required for a major high-speed line. Thus, a cutoff was conceived. This would leave the existing main line just east of Welland and cut across farmlands and through orchards to the vicinity of Niagara Falls, a distance of approximately 14 miles. A portion of the Niagara Branch, that from Montrose eastward to either of two proposed crossing sites, would be upgraded and incorporated into what would become the new main line. The railway's first choice of a crossing was near the head of Grand Island, but this was abandoned in reaction to the vociferous objections of Tonawanda residents.[2] The second site was below the Falls but upstream from the Grand Trunk's bridge.

Canada Southern employed James Anthony Bell, a provincial land surveyor, to lay out the Welland Cut-Off.[3] The contract for the construction of the cut-off was let to the firm of Fields, Cunningham & Company in May 1883.[4] Construction began shortly afterwards and progressed smoothly during the summer and autumn. By the week of 4 November 1883 there were two construction trains on the more rugged eastern end of the cut-off. Beginning the week of 18 November, track crews were scheduled to lay double track between Niagara Falls and Clifton, whence both tracks would be ballasted.[5] The railway was so determined to have the line finished by mid-December that construction work was continued despite the wintry conditions.[6] Inclement weather and heavy rock cuts slowed the work somewhat and, except for a short section near the convent in Niagara Falls, the grading and the double-tracking were completed as far as Clifton by the middle of December 1883.[7] The rail line was in the vicinity of the site for the bridging of the Niagara River.

Various firms had advanced ideas for bridging the river, and as many as six plans were suggested. The least expensive one was a double-deck bridge of parallel-girder construction. The most expensive one was a single-deck, double-track bridge of the arch type. During October 1882 Vanderbilt interests had contacted the Central Bridge Company of Buffalo concerning the construction of a double-track, single-deck cantilever-type bridge across the Niagara gorge.[8] The bridge was designed by C.C. Schneider, and apparently it was the first bridge to be termed "cantilever."[9] It was a novel concept, one which intrigued the town's residents and engineers alike. Although there were already a few bridges of this type (Schneider had used this principle for the CPR's bridge over the Fraser River in the spring of 1882), never before had the design been proposed to span a distance in excess of 900 feet.[10] This would be the longest cantilever bridge in the world. General George S. Field, the president of Central Bridge, is generally credited with the original idea of using this design. Evidently, he had spoken to Vanderbilt some months earlier. James A. Bell of St. Thomas, who had recently completed some survey work for the Canada Southern, was appointed assistant engineer for the bridge project.[11]

A new company had already been established in 1881 under New York State legislation, with a capital of $1 million.[12] This was the Niagara River Bridge Company of New York. On the Canadian side, a federal statute established the Niagara Peninsula Bridge Company.[13] The acts of incorporation for both companies authorized their subsequent merger as the Niagara River Bridge Company, a Canadian corporation.

Three reasons figured prominently in the selection of the cantilever design. First, the steepness of the gorge left virtually no room for temporary supports and the cantilever design required relatively little in the way of falsework. Secondly, the railway wanted a bridge which would not be susceptible to "wave action", as was the case with the Suspension Bridge. Finally, the railway desired a bridge which would be less costly to construct than the suspension type. The particular design of the great Niagara Cantilever Bridge would not only fulfil these strict requirements, but it would be strong enough to bear the weight of two fully laden freight trains, each hauled by two 76-ton Consolidation-type locomotives. Not only must the bridge withstand the weight of one ton per linear foot, but it must do so during a cross wind of 75 mph, incorporating a safety factor of five.[14]

In order to determine the precise site of the Cantilever Bridge, CSR engineers during January 1883 took river measurements from 200 feet to 1,000 feet upstream from the Roebling-designed Suspension Bridge. The latter spot was selected because the river gorge was somewhat narrower, 850 feet wide, and 210 feet deep. At this point the river itself was 425 feet wide and of a supposed depth of 80 feet. Canada Southern deployed two gangs of workmen, consisting of ten men each, for a fortnight, during which time they excavated the pier foundations. A severe snow and ice storm delayed this work into February.

The Canadian and American governments agreed that all materials to be used for the construction of the bridge were to be free of duty, and customs officials on both sides of the border were so instructed during March. On 11 April 1883 the Niagara River Bridge Company signed the contract with the Central Bridge Company, the primary contractor, and with the Detroit Bridge & Iron Works.[15] The contract contained a clause to the effect that for every day the completion of the bridge was delayed beyond 1 December 1883, the contractor would forfeit $1,000.[16] There were several subcontracts. That for excavations and stonework was let to Dawson, Simmes & Mitchell. The firm of C.H. Turner won the contract for the falsework, while the one for the Beton foundations went to John C. Goodridge Jr. The contract for the steel and iron compression members for the bridge towers was awarded to the Athens, Penn., firm of Kellogg & Maurice (which firm was already overseeing the erection of a cantilever bridge in Saint John, New Brunswick).[17]

Among the innovations used during the construction of this bridge was Beton cement, the invention of Dr. Goodridge of Boston. Once the excavations for the abutments could be cut into the base of the gorge, construction of the abutments themselves was undertaken. This entailed

This view, taken from Suspension Bridge, N.Y., shows the Cantilever Bridge during the construction of the shore-arms.

— G.E. Curtis photo, Niagara Falls Historical Society

the pouring of concrete, a building material which had not been used on such a project before. The concrete was prepared at the top of the gorge and then poured by sluiceway to the work areas far below.

It was a popular pastime to view the construction crew's daily progress. The Niagara Falls area was a population centre and already an established tourist attraction. Engineering news was being made, and the average citizen wanted to be a part of it. Indeed, he believed that he was. Professional engineers, engineering students and dignitaries at all levels of government swelled the parade of bystanders who came to witness this man-made marvel, which was vying with the great Falls for attention.

The cornerstone was laid on the American side on a cold and grey 26 June 1883.[18] Pouring rain delayed the ceremony until about 2:30 p.m. There were speeches, cannon shots and bands. On July 14 the first stone was laid on the Canadian side with typically Canadian reserve.[19] Construction of the great Cantilever Bridge was well under way.

During the construction of the bridge towers and shore-arms, men were suspended on platforms hung by ropes from skeleton structures projecting defiantly from the walls of the gorge. In the building of the river-arms, two travellers were used, one on each side of the river. The entire bridge was erected without the benefit of safety nets. There were only a few accidents and not one of them was fatal. Among the 150 men employed on both sides of the river, only six men suffered injuries during the entire project. The total medical bill was $41. The most spectacular accident involved George P. Rogers, who fell 112 feet and, quite remarkably, broke only an arm and a leg.[20] He recovered fully.

Another engineering novelty was the use of steel pins, a procedure which greatly facilitated the pace and comparative ease of construction. On 22 November 1883 the last pieces were fitted into place to connect the suspended span securely to the cantilever sections. Canadian and American workmen, their faces beaming, approached each other at the centre of the bridge and shook hands. An engineer checked the alignment; the two sections were within one-quarter of an inch.

The Niagara Cantilever Bridge was complete. It measured 910 feet and 1-7/8 inches. it had cost $600,000, and the approaches cost a further $150,000. Excluding the falsework, the total weight of material exceeded 7.1 million pounds; all of this received no fewer than three handlings to move it one-half mile into position. The great bridge had been completed within eight months. It was without doubt a remarkable feat of engineering.

Meanwhile, work on the two approaches continued. The simpler American approach was completed late in November. The more complicated Canadian approach, which entailed a deep rock cut at Niagara Falls and a bridge over Clifton Avenue, was expected to be finished by mid-December.

Before long, it was time for the engineers to begin gross tonnage testing of the bridge, something which proved to be quite thrilling for the general public. The first such test occurred on the morning of 6 December 1883, under the supervision of New York Central divisional superintendent G.H. Burrows. Burrows gave the "proceed" signal and pony engine No. 513 left the security of the American shore at precisely 11:41 a.m. and chuffed gingerly onto the Cantilever Bridge. For two suspenseful minutes the little engine clickety-clacked across the bridge amid the anxious silence of immense crowds on both sides. Upon reaching the Ontario side the engineman gave a joyful tug on the whistle cord. A few minutes later the engine returned to New York. Two more return crossings were made that day, each of them involved strings of flat cars.

The 20th of December 1883 was set as the official opening day. The proprietors of Monteagle House, at the Suspension Bridge in New York, tendered their establishment as the centre for the ceremonies. On behalf of the hosts of Niagara River Bridge, Michigan Central, Canada Southern and Central Bridge, a novel invitation card containing a steel engraving of the Cantilever Bridge was sent to 2,000 prominent railway, engineering, contracting and governmental officials. Special NYC&HRR, MCRR and Canada Southern trains would ferry the guests from the extremities of the Vanderbilt system. The official ceremonies would feature a dramatic bridge test by up to three dozen of the system's heaviest locomotives, two special trains reserved for guests, excursion trains, three bands, lots of food and drink, and generally plenty of hoopla. Guests would dine at Monteagle House and hear speeches; everywhere there would be flags and bunting.

A diminutive Michigan Central passenger train leaves Canada and clatters slowly over the Cantilever Bridge. Meanwhile, the passengers can look upstream (towards the photographer) to admire the Horseshoe Falls in the distance.
                                                                    — Niagara Falls Historical Society

Invitation to the opening of the Niagara Cantilever Bridge.
                    — Niagara Falls Historical Society

"Great Gorge Route" passing under Steel Arch and Cantilever Bridges, Niagara Falls, N. Y.

A tram of the Niagara Gorge Route passes below the Niagara Centilever Bridge (MCRR) and behind it the steel arch bridge (GTR). The tram route would later be reduced to a narrow pathway for those willing to hike.

— Niagara Falls Historical Society

A Michigan Central passenger train having departed the station at Clifton (Niagara Falls, Ontario) rumbles across the Cantilever Bridge and into New York State. In the right foreground can be seen the reinforced wall protecting the International Railway Company's tram line. This electric railway operated on both sides and it afforded a spectacular view of the Niagara Gorge.

— Charles Bierstadt photo,
Niagara Falls Historical Society

Michigan Central's frequent passenger train service contributed to the scheduling of baseball games in the United States. The preparation of the next season's schedule involved a team of men representing both the railways and professional baseball. Thus, it was not unusual for a team from the major leagues to be riding the express trains, and many tales arose concerning the combination baseball and trains. The following anecdote is a sad one. About the turn of the century, an MC train was carrying a baseball team from Detroit to New York via the Canada Southern. Among the players was Ed Delahanty, a man who on account of some personal problems had a difficulty with alcoholic drinks. Whilst crossing Ontario he had become so unruly that the conductor had threatened to put him off the train. The train arrived in Niagara Falls, Ontario, none too soon as far as the train crew was concerned. They forcibly removed Delahanty at the station and the train departed. An enraged Delahanty stormed onto the Cantilever Bridge in hot pursuit of train and crew. Unfortunately he tripped and fell to his death. Delahanty had been a prolific athlete. It had been said that he could hit a ball with such force that it would break. He had been voted into the Hall of Fame, but he did not live to see it. This sketch portrays the Niagara Cantilever Bridge just before the turn of the century. The view looks upstream from the American shore. — Public Archives of Canada C96366

This is an example of an illustration which the Michigan Central Railroad used in its advertising.

Michigan Central promotional literature used a variety of illustrations relating to the Falls. This view appeared in the June 1906 issue of Four Track News.

— New York Central System Historical Society

Thursday, 20 December 1883, dawned bright and cold, but this did not deter people from turning out literally by the thousands. The villages at both ends of the bridge carried few decorations, but the entrances were bedecked in decorations and flags. At 8 a.m. the first official test of the day began when seven heavy locomotives inched out onto the structure. The sky became increasingly overcast as the opening ceremonies drew near, yet people continued to gather. By noon the crowds on both sides of the river were estimated to number 10,000. For those who could withstand the wind rushing through the gorge and who did not mind the occasional icy snowflake in the eye, there was the spectacular view to be had from the Suspension Bridge. The Grand Trunk had co-operated by curtailing railway traffic and by opening the bridge to people on foot. The bridge was packed. The people waited.

At noon an air of expectancy settled upon the crowd as the second test of the day was about to begin. Two trains, each headed by ten locomotives, inched onto the bridge, this time originating on the Ontario side. Each train consisted of ten of the heaviest first-class locomotives and a dozen flat cars laden with gravel. The test trains stopped at predetermined spots until their full weight was distributed across the bridge. The test trains then returned to their starting points and the Cantilever Bridge was opened to the general public, who were cautioned to stay on the broad boardwalks which had been installed for the occasion. Railway officials also reminded people that they had to return to the side from which they had started. The official ceremonies at the bridge were concluded at 3:30 p.m. and the Niagara Cantilever Bridge was declared open. No rail traffic would actually use the structure until the Michigan Central's depot, signalling and additional switchwork at Suspension Bridge, N.Y., was ready sometime during February 1884.

It had been a big day for the two communities of Niagara Falls, and the celebrations continued long after large, soft snowflakes had tumbled from slate-grey skies to dust a tired land. People from the Falls had boasted about the first railway suspension bridge. Now they could boast about the world's longest railway cantilever bridge, too. And they did.

The Test of 'Cantilever'

Lo! Cantilever stands the test,
See! see! it bears upon its breast
Fully twenty locomotives' weight,
Nor bends beneath the heavy freight.
See! twenty engines safely ride
Across Niagara's seething tide —
Across the mystic iron span —
Last product of the god-like man.
'The Cantilever bridge is strong!'
Exultant shout the wondering throng.
Lo! fifty locomotives screech,
Two nations' praise blends each with each,
Resounds the East, resounds the West,
The matchless triumph each attest.
The loud applause — the palm each yields
To Cantilever and to Fields.

James Walton Jackson

James W. Jackson of St. Catharines, Ontario, dedicated this poem to General Fields. Source: *Suspension Bridge Journal*, 10 May 1884.]

Canada Southern's expansion in Ontario consisted, in part, of building a cut-off to link Welland and Niagara Falls and of the erection of an impressive twin-tracked railway bridge across the Niagara gorge. The CSR was also keeping its eye on a small struggling railway which had intentions of linking Lake St. Clair and Lake Erie. The railway cultivated friendly relations with the small line, hoping eventually to bring the town of Leamington into Canada Southern's sphere of influence.

This engraving depicts the testing of the Niagara Cantilever Bridge with ten heavy locomotives.

A diminutive Canada Southern passenger train, consisting of locomotive No. 8, an unidentified baggage and express car, and coach No. 113, chugs by Niagara Falls en route to Fort Erie, circa 1879.

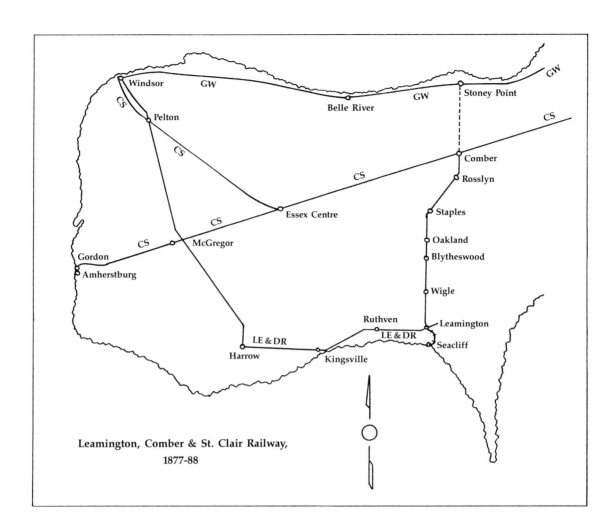

**Leamington, Comber & St. Clair Railway,
1877-88**

Seacliff Park, on the shore of Lake Erie, was a major tourist development on the part of Canada Southern and later the Michigan Central. This view shows the main gate and to the left the pavilion, circa late 1920s.

— Betty Liebrock, Leamington *Shopper*

Onwards to Leamington and Seacliff Park

For the origin of this feeder line, one must go back to 1877, when the Leamington, Comber & Lake St. Clair Railway Company was incorporated under Ontario statute. Under this legislation the railway was empowered to build from Leamington (about two miles from Lake Erie) to Stoney Point on Lake St. Clair. In November 1877 the railway was considering a generous offer from the Great Western, which showed interest in building the line from Leamington to Belle River (a few miles to the west of Stoney Point) for $60,000, including a guarantee on both construction and operation.[21] No decision was made. In 1879 the company's charter was amended to permit the altered route, allow for municipal aid and, mercifully, shorten the name simply to Leamington & St. Clair.[22] Still no construction had taken place and the board of directors, wrestling with the problem of subscription capital, decided to enquire whether the Great Western's offer was still open. This time it was the GWR which remained silent.

At its meeting of 17 May 1880 the board of directors authorized the retention of Alexander Baird, a provincial land surveyor, to conduct a preliminary survey of the company's proposed route. A year later the railway still lacked sufficient capital to commence construction, but the railway employed Baird to undertake a detailed survey in the meantime. The board was preoccupied with the raising of capital. Financial problems persisted and the actual construction of the line remained as remote as Lake St. Clair itself. Canada Southern's board made an offer to build the L&StC line, which offer was discussed on 5 December 1881. A subcommittee then walked the proposed route and reported back to the full board two days later. The L&StC assented to the CSR offer.

By 1885 the Leamington & St. Clair Railway was still little more than a paper charter. Late in 1886 construction crews finally began work, but they accomplished little more than making a start on the station in Leamington.[23] The following spring the clearing and grading were completed. Work crews started to lay track on 3 June 1887 and more or less finished their work later that summer.

On 9 September 1887 the L&StC deemed construction to be complete enough to operate a special excursion train from Comber (on the CSR) to Leamington.[24] But as it would turn out, the railway had actually begun operations prematurely. The railway suffered the indignity of having the steps of several of its passenger cars knocked off by large stumps along the track![25] The L&StC managed to make other memories that excursion day, when it ran over several pigs. The farmer successfully sued the little railway for damages.

During 1888 construction crews pushed the line two additional miles to Seacliff Park and Leamington's wharf on Lake Erie. On 1 March 1889 the Canada Southern took over the operation of the Leamington & St. Clair Railway under a 15-year lease, with an option to purchase the line for $35,000.[26]

Improvements must have been made, for the road is said to have made money and afforded fast-running trains for a branch line. When the railway first opened, the local economy was largely based on forest and agriculture. The community of Staples, seven miles south of Comber, was a shipping point for heavy timber and lumber (as was Comber). Staples also produced staves and hoops for sugar and salt barrels. During the 1890s Blytheswood shipped elm and basswood in great quantities. During one season some 2 million feet of elm logs were shipped out, principally to Wyandotte, Michigan. Cordwood was shipped to Leamington. Blytheswood also produced 150 cars of grain and 25 carloads of dressed hogs annually. These figures give some idea of the commercial importance of the feeder line to the Canada Southern with regard to freight. With the development of the Seacliff Park and the exclusive clubhouse on Pelee Island, passenger traffic increased significantly, particularly during the summer months.

At the railway's annual meeting on 5 June 1895 the stockholders voted to accept an offer from the L&StC to sell to the CSR.[27] The L&StC then became a wholly owned subsidiary. It would retain its separate identity until 1904, when on July 18 it would be merged into the CSR.[28]

The branch line's fortunes rested upon the commercial viability of various crops, and these were dramatically affected by adverse environmental conditions. Dry soil conditions, the lack of snow and the severe cold during February 1899 killed many peach trees in the region. Farmers then gave great emphasis to other crops, such as tobacco, small fruits and vegetables. A tobacco factory was established at Leamington. Two local sorghum mills were kept very busy. In 1908 the town issued $10,000 in debentures to purchase the Henry Ward Tobacco building and turn it over to H.J. Heinz Company, together with the promise of free water, as an inducement to that company to locate its canning factory there.[29] By 1911 tomatoes had become a major crop; the following year the local canneries were operating day and night. This activity generated more freight traffic for the line.

The North-'o-Lake Line

The construction of the Cantilever Bridge at Niagara Falls and the new main line linking it with Welland were part of the preparations the Canada Southern was making to become a key component in the Vanderbilt system, to do battle against other principal carriers in the region. The eventual success of the Leamington Branch contributed important local and export traffic. The story of the main line resumes in the next chapter.

Shipping Order.

LEAMINGTON & St. CLAIR RAILROAD COMPANY

Will please carry the following described property from . . . . to destination, or in case said place of destination is off this Company's line of railroad, then to the place where said property is to be received by the connecting carriers, subject to " Rules Regulating Transportation, as printed upon the back of this sheet.

Leamington Feb 24 1887

MARKED OR CONSIGNED.	ARTICLES.	WEIGHT OR MEASURE.
Order Imperial Bank of Canada advise Bank of Montreal Montreal	*1 Car Dressed Hogs C P Co no 1600 108 Hogs*	*24000 lbs*

Freight consigned to any place where the Company has no Agent, is to be considered as delivered to the Consignee when unloaded, without any further notice, and will be thereafter wholly at owner's risk.

Property consigned to any place off the Company's line of Road, or to any point beyond its termini, will be sent forward by a carrier when there is such, in the usual manner, the Company acting, for the purpose of delivery to such carrier, as the Agents of the consignor or consignee, and not as carriers. This Company will not be responsible for any loss or damage to the property after the same shall have been sent from any warehouse or station of the Company.

NOTICE.— all freight may be delivered to the Consignee named without the production and surrender of shipping receipt, unless otherwise ordered here.

Signature of Shipper, or his Agent   *Allan Bros pr J Mitchell*

A shipping order for the Leamington & St. Clair Railway (despite the spelling error) concerning a shipment of 108 hogs on 24 February 1887.

                — Michael P. McIlwaine Collection

A tobacco farmer stands in his field of tobacco, one of Leamington's major sources of income, October 1923.
— PAC PA31446

The Michigan Central Railroad station at Comber awaits the arrival of the main line train, circa 1920. Standing on the siding is the southbound passenger train consisting of a 4-4-0 locomotive, No. 8875, and a combination passenger and baggage car. The building at the right is the freight shed. The view faces east. — John R. Lee Collection

Boxes of socks await shipment overseas to the 18th Battalion of the Canadian Expeditionary Force. — PA66716

A small 4-4-0-type locomotive has just arrived in Blytheswood, Ontario, with a short passenger train consisting of a combine and a coach. The lack of proper ballast and the presence of an earthen platform suggest that the railway had only recently been opened. Perhaps the occasion for the photograph was the opening of the Leamington & St. Clair Railway. Above the cars of the southbound train can be seen the peak of the freight shed.

The H.J. Heinz Company of Canada pickling and food-processing plant at Leamington. — PAC PA31146

The New York Central's station at Staples, Ontario, as it appeared about 1950. — John R. Lee

This concrete post marks the beginning of the branch line to Leamington at Comber — mile zero. — Kenneth A.W. Gansel

CSR No. 434 heads a passenger train at St. Thomas.

— John R. Lee Collection

The constant quest for speed prompted some people to concoct rather unusual mechanisms. Locomotive engineer Eugene Fontaine of Detroit thought much of his hypothesis that the speed of a steam locomotive could be increased by means of a series of wheels of different sizes connected on their treads. His "friction principle" entailed the linkage of the pistons to a pair of driving wheels (72 inches in diameter) which were surmounted in a frame abreast of the boiler. The treads of these wheels contacted those of a pair of smaller-diameter friction wheels (56 inches in diameter) which were concentrically mounted on the track-riding driving wheels (70 inches in diameter). The pressure between the upper driving wheels and the friction wheels could be varied pneumatically by means of levers. The Fontaine Engine Company held the patent, granted in July 1880, for the unusual design. Three engines were manufactured specifically for the F.E.C. by Grant Locomotive Works during 1881. The Canada Southern Railway accepted F.E.C. No. 2 for road trials for the period of July 1881 to February 1882. Engineer Ike Deyell and fireman George Westfall were among the crews assigned for the testing. Although the eye-arresting locomotive did manage to haul passenger trains quite fast, under favourable conditions, it evidently was unreliable. The engine was simply too light for application to freight traffic. Dubbed "Fontaine's Folly" the locomotive prompted considerable debate as to whether it had any genuine merits. CSR's evaluation team concluded that the engine design held no advantage and returned the engine to the designer. Apparently, Fontaine could find no purchasers and so all three locomotives were rebuilt about 1884 into 4-4-0 types and sold to the Wheeling & Lake Erie.

— John R. Lee Collection

A large MCRR work gang was assembled in front of CSR work car 23297 for this picture. The date and locale are unknown, but it is thought that the picture was taken in Windsor sometime after 1883.

— Hiram Walker Historical Museum

This old postcard shows a westbound passenger train arriving at Ridgetown, Ontario. — Michael P. McIlwaine Collection

A typical title block used by Canada Southern on its maps, circa 1880.
— Author's Collection

The cover of a Canada Southern public timetable, circa 1880.
— Gary S. Daniels

This very old picture shows the main line of the Canada Southern Railway just east of Comber, looking east. Notice the lack of ballast. Crushed stone would later be added. The track on the right beyond the fence is the branch line to Leamington. — John R. Lee Collection

The portrait of Canada Southern sectionmen shows the crews for the main and branch lines on the left and right respectively. Unfortunately, there was no date on this old picture, which was taken at Comber. The main line section crew consisted of Hugh Richardson (foreman), Don (the boy), Jack Thackary, John White and Claude Blackburn. The Leamington branch crew consisted of Tom Wesley (foreman) and George Shaw.

— John R. Lee Collection

A westbound Canada Southern passenger train crosses the newly completed second Kettle Creek Bridge at St. Thomas.

— John R. Lee Collection

VII

ALL TRAINS—VIA THE FALLS

With the dawn of New Year's Day 1883 there was a new railway system in the Lower Lakes area. The Michigan Central Railroad and the Canada Southern Railway had agreed that the former should assume management and operation of the two lines as if they were a single enterprise. This was the implementation date of the covenant which the two companies had signed on 12 December 1882, whereunder the MCRR would lease the CSR for 21 years.[1] The new year saw changes in operating practices, the completion of a new line to Niagara Falls, the erection of a great bridge, the building of a line to Windsor, and the placement of an order for a first-class sidewheel steamboat of iron construction. Another improvement was the replacement in 1883 of the old single-track wooden trestle across Kettle Creek by a double-tracked iron one 1,395 feet in length and standing 93 feet above the creek bed.

There were other improvements to the company's physical plant, too. During 1883-84 the line purchased 36 locomotives, 2 dining cars, 10 first-class coaches and 30 vans at an aggregate cost of $550,830.50.[2] The purchase of the dining cars — the Great Western had introduced them in Canada in 1867[3] — at a time when even the NYC&HRR did not have them, introduced an elegance and convenience few Canadian roads could match. CSR charged its patrons 75 cents a meal.[4] The railway was continuing with its double-tracking program, which had been started in 1882, towards the goal of twinning the main line from Niagara Falls to Windsor.

About 1885 Canadian Pacific was originating traffic for MC/CS, but the MCRR was not satisfied with the division of revenue. As was his style, Michigan Central president Ledyard dashed off a terse letter to Van Horne to apprise him that MCRR was not interested in carrying any freight below cost.[5] The CPR, however, was determined to compete with the Grand Trunk in the latter's back yard. Finally, a working agreement was concluded, and it would last until Canadian Pacific completed its own line to Windsor in 1888-89. Despite the difficult connections at St. Thomas, the Canada Southern link permitted the CPR to share in the trunk-line seaboard traffic.[6]

All did not go well, though. The summer of 1887 was marred by a tragic accident in St. Thomas on July 14.[7] A westbound MCRR freight train was in the process of leaving the yard when a north-bound Grand Trunk excursion train, operating over the London & Port Stanley line, failed to stop. The engineer had applied the air brakes about one-quarter of a mile from the diamond crossing, but the passenger train cut into the freight train, hitting two tank cars, one of which ruptured. The oil inside quickly caught fire and engulfed both trains and nearby buildings. Within 30 minutes the second tank car exploded, hurling fiery debris against more buildings and punching out windows along Talbot Street, a block away. Fourteen people died in the collision and resulting fire. A coroner's jury laid blame partly on the GTR engineer (who was among those killed) for having failed to apply air brakes sooner (the track had been signalled by semaphore fully one mile south of the diamond), partly on the excursion train's conductor for failing to have tested the train's brakes prior to departure at Port Stanley, and partly on the Grand Trunk for operating a defective locomotive. In addition to the fatalities, three people were injured in the collision and 65 were hurt in the fire.

For a while, the Canada Southern Railway was in the hotel business. In 1887 it operated an establishment called the Station Hotel at St. Thomas. A few years later the hotel was sold and the innocuous name quickly replaced by the arrestive title The Devil's Half Acre.[8] Apparently, the name proved to be only too appropriate, and the community was greatly relieved when Canada Iron Foundries purchased the property for expansion of its plant.

Early in July 1889 the Erie & Niagara Railway Company was merged into the Canada Southern.[9]

The Columbian Exhibition in Chicago during 1893 gave rise to much heavier passenger business over the Michigan Central and Canada Southern railways, but neither company substantially benefited, because those revenues were offset by a decline in freight traffic on account of the general depression of the North American economy.

By 1895 Canada Southern owned 151 locomotives, 116 passenger cars and 3,846 freight cars.[10] In Ontario, it owned 381 miles of first line, which had cost $35,439,266 to construct.[11] It had just over 95 miles of double track and could easily boast of being the fastest railway in the country. In times when exceeding cost estimates was commonplace, the CSR was one of three railways for which the actual costs of construction were less than the projected ones.[12]

Ever conscious of its eastern flank, the Canada Southern had renewed running rights over the Hamilton & Lake Erie Railway between Hagersville and Hamilton. Following Grand Trunk's acquisition of this line in 1888, the CSR sought another access into Hamilton. The Brantford, Waterloo & Lake Erie was a locally backed railway which had been incorporated in 1885, and although it did not then go into Hamilton, running rights were secured in 1888 with the expectation that the line eventually would. The BW&LE opened the following year with an ex-TCS&D locomotive, No. 111. Eventually the BW&LE became part of the Toronto, Hamilton & Buffalo Railway, a line with which the Canada Southern would be involved for more than 80 years. Cornelius Vanderbilt was aware of these developments and he realized that securing access to Hamilton, and possibly Toronto, would be of great value in New York Central's battle with the Grand Trunk.

On 13 June 1895 he convened a meeting to conclude an arrangement whereby the TH&B would become a Vanderbilt system member.[13] In this effort he sought and obtained Canadian Pacific as an ally. On July 9 of that year a contract was made among New York Central, Michigan Central, Canada Southern and the CPR for the sharing of the ownership of TH&B in the ratio of 37:18:18:27 for a period of 50 years.[14] Under this arrangement Vanderbilt would strengthen access to the Niagara district and add the Brantford and Hamilton areas. Despite its population of just 11,000, Brantford was rapidly industrializing, and by the turn of the century it would become the nation's largest producer of exports. Hamilton was a steel centre and had a harbour.

As the New York Central system was being strengthened in Canada, corresponding steps were being taken in the United States. As diverse and sprawling as the NYC system was, it was also recognized as one of the best-managed railway empires, and every major component weathered the depression of the 1890s without undue difficulty.[15] One key factor in this situation was the Central's lack of dependence upon any one industry and the broad dispersal of its traffic-originating centres.

As the recession diminished during the late 1890s, freight traffic improved. By February 1897 Canada Southern was handling more eastbound traffic in a two-week period than in the corresponding period for the previous three years. Crews, often working overtime, were handling an average of 50 trains a day.[16] The demand for grain in the East was such that shippers did not wait for the opening of the navigation season on the Great Lakes. During this period grain constituted the main commodity shipped over the CSR. The statistics for 1896 indicated that 691,609 cars were handled.[17] In 1897 the CSR bought 76 additional box cars, bringing its roster to 2,814 such cars.[18]

The heavy increase in traffic had implications for the Niagara bridges and operations. During 1899 three additional trusses were installed, resting on new masonry towers between the existing ones. These strengthened the Cantilever Bridge by at least 50 percent.[19] In April 1900 Canada Southern announced plans for further double-tracking, 100 miles in all. No fewer than four contracting firms were hired to press forward with the work. By June 1901 fully 130 miles of the 227 miles of main line were double-tracked. The benefits were seen immediately, with the running times of both passenger and freight trains improving considerably.

In June 1903 the Michigan Central appointed a committee to negotiate a new contract with the Canada Southern, the existing contract being scheduled to expire on December 1 that year. On 15 August 1903 senior officers of the two railways signed a new lease which would be implemented on 1 January 1904 and which was to endure for 999 years.[20]

The 1890s had seen extensive double-tracking of the main line, the purchases of additional freight cars and locomotives, the erection of new stations, the strengthening of the Cantilever Bridge,

Table II

AVERAGE PASSENGER TRAIN SPEED
AMONG RAILWAYS WITH DOUBLE TRACKS

Railway	Miles of Double Track	Passenger Train Average Speed
Canada Southern	95.25	41 m.p.h.
Canadian Pacific	13.50	28
Grand Trunk	404.50	30
Intercolonial	1.50	25

Source: *Statistical Abstract and Record of Canada*, 1895, p637

Table III

CANADA SOUTHERN RAILWAY LINE
DISTRIBUTION OF MILEAGE BY PROVINCE AND STATE, 1900

Trackage	First Line			Second Line		Sidings			Total
	Ontario	Michigan	Ohio	Ontario	Michigan	Ontario	Michigan	Ohio	
CSR – Main	226.18			95.21		131.03			452.42
St. Clair Br.	62.63					6.05			68.68
Amherstburg Br.	16.83					6.96			23.79
Oil Springs Br.	5.50					0.93			6.43
Niagara Branch	30.60					5.76			36.36
Fort Erie Br. subsidiaries	17.50					12.24			29.74
L. & St. Clair	13.80					4.38			18.18
S.C.&E.	7.00					1.33			8.33
CS Bridge Co.		3.66					1.55		5.21
TCS&DR		47.27	11.65		2.35		47.27	24.48	133.02
MM&CR leased		14.68					0.93		15.61
L.&S. Eastern running rights				1.96					1.96
L&PS	15.00								15.00
Total									814.73

Source: Canada Southern Railway, Annual Report, 1900, p4

and the acquisitions of running rights to serve Brantford and Hamilton. Service to London had been added in 1888 with a 15-year arrangement with the London & Port Stanley Railway and the purchase of the diminutive London & South Eastern Railway for CSR's own terminal facilities in that city. Passenger and freight traffic had doubled over the duration of the initial lease, and both the MCRR and the CSR were real money spinners for the Vanderbilt system. When the sun set on 31 December 1903, it did so on a Canada Southern Railway which had been thoroughly revitalized.

Yet further improvements to the company's physical plant were undertaken. In 1905 an order for 15 locomotives was placed with the Locomotive & Machine Company of Montreal. By the end of that year work crews were engaged in the laying of a second track between Tilbury and Ridgetown, completing the project one year later. Some $900,000 worth of new rail in 100-, 90-, and 85-pound weights was ordered as part of the double-tracking and rail-upgrading program. Additional double-tracking was carried out on the main line between Hagersville and Springfield, and the Fort Erie Branch was upgraded. In 1909 the railway announced that it was planning to build a 25-stall roundhouse and a new passenger station at Windsor. Twenty locomotives of three types were ordered.

During 1910 the railway began upgrading the line between Essex and Tilbury with 100-pound rails on a slightly raised railbed. The same year saw some improvement to employee benefits. Canada Southern employees became eligible for pensions at the age of 70 years. Another improvement for employees came when the railway recognized the need for industrial safety. Two committees were established, one for the of St. Thomas shops and one for the remainder of the railway.

In May 1916 the Michigan Central announced that it would construct new locomotive facilities at its new Montrose yard near Niagara Falls. A 20-stall roundhouse, machine shop, coal house, oil house and sand house would cost over $250,000 and was to be built by the Wallbridge Aldinger Company of Detroit.

The Cantilever Bridge was beginning to show its age. The heavy traffic was such that by March 1917 the railway began studies to determine what it ought to do about the aging structure. In July, following the completion of these studies, the railway announced that it would replace the bridge. It decided to commence work on a two-hinged, spandrel-braced arch bridge over the Niagara River at a site immediately adjacent to the north side of the existing bridge. Construction was carried out expeditiously during 1923-24, and the bridge was opened to traffic on 12 February 1925 without fanfare.[21]

There arose a brief controversy about the railway's intention to dismantle the historic cantilever, but the governing legislation in Canada and the U.S. required this as a condition for permission to build the new bridge. The timber from the old bridge was loaded onto flat cars and shipped somewhere in Ontario. The Michigan Central Railroad saved the tablet (but the newspaper account does not say what the railway did with it). The steel structure was dismantled and shipped to South Africa, where it was re-erected across another gorge.[22]

Another well-known structure was also in need of replacement. A substitute for the aging Kettle Creek trestle would embroil the railway and the town of St. Thomas in protracted and at times acrimonious discussions. The type and precise placement of the replacement structure was finally agreed upon and work begun.

The MCRR line carried one of the fastest and busiest train schedules on the NYC system. The Canadian line carried several units of the New York Central's fleet of 20-hour trains between New York and Chicago. A study of train movements for a 21-day period in the autumn of 1928, covering the 14-hour period from 0530 to 1930, revealed an average daily movement of 36 trains in both directions. The average maximum interval (average of daily maximums based on 21-day sample) between eastbound trains was 3 hours and 13 minutes; that between westbound trains was 2 hours and 15 minutes. Between opposing movements the maximum interval was 1 hour and 46 minutes. Consequently, it was deemed of prime importance that the bridge design be one which, during construction, would be the least disruptive to traffic.

The point of contention was an awkward roadway intersection beneath the bridge, where the railway initially planned to erect a concrete pier in the middle of the road. The issue was finally resolved when the railway agreed to build on each side of the highway a concrete substructure, upon which a steel bent would be built well above the road.

Table IV

CANADA SOUTHERN RAILWAY COMPANY
SCHEDULE OF PASSENGER ROLLING STOCK
BY TYPE AND QUANTITY FOR THE PERIOD 1877 to 1910

Car Type	1877	1880	1885	1890		1900	1905	1910
Passenger, First Class	20	26	37	35	51	54	42	33
Passenger, Second Class	14	12		23	21	21	20	92
Passenger, Smoking			21					
Passenger, Smoking and Baggage								20
Combination Passenger and Baggage	1	1	5	7	7	7	7	0
Baggage & Express	9	15	20	22	26	27	19	0
Baggage, Mail & Express	6	4	4	4	4	4	4	10
Express Box	2	2	0	0	0	0	0	0
Postal						1	0	0
Dining			2	3	3	3	2	4
Buffet				2	4	4	0	0
Paymaster	1	1	0	0	0	0	0	0
Business				1*	1■	0	0	0
Totals	53	61	89	97	117	121	94	159

Note: All CSR passenger rolling stock was integrated with that of MCRR during 1910, thereby losing identity.

Sources: 1877 – CSR AR 1880, p21
1880 – CSR AR 1880, p21
1885 – CSR AR 1885, p16
1890 – CSR AR 1890, p5; *ORER, Jan 1890
1895 – CSR AR 1895 p5; ■ORER, Jan 1895, p35
1900 – CSR AR 1900, p5
1905 – Official Railway Equipment Register, Jan 1905
1910 – Official Railway Equipment Register, Jan 1910, p47

Hamilton's National Steel Car Corporation built many sets of steel underframe and truck assemblies for Michigan Central. These were shipped to the St. Thomas shops, where wooden box car bodies, couplers, brake rigging and finishing hardware were added. This photo is the only surviving record of the sales order P-15/1913.
— National Steel Car Corp.
Author's Collection

95

The erection of the superstructure for the eastbound track was begun on September 16 and it was finished on 30 October 1929. That for the westbound track was started on November 4 and completed on November 29. The new bridge cost $689,000 and, except for some minor painting and hardware, it was finished on 30 January 1930.

The replacement of key bridges, the modernization of the St. Thomas shops, the purchase of new motive power were among the railway's improvements. There were enhancements to both the Montrose and Windsor yards. Nearly $1 million was spent on general track improvements, excluding bridgework. All 105-pound rail, the first of which had been laid in 1917, was scheduled to be replaced with 127-pound rail, which was on order from Dominion Iron & Steel Company of Nova Scotia. This would be the heaviest rail in Canada.

For a number of years the New York Central had been interested in acquiring more direct control of its principal Canadian leasehold line. Towards this end, Michigan Central sought and obtained regulatory approval to dispose of its rights in the Canada Southern Railway. On 21 August 1929 the Canadian federal government approved Michigan Central's plan for subleasing the CSR to the New York Central Railroad for a period of 99 years.[23] On 9 December 1929 the Interstate Commerce Commission authorized the New York Central to merge with its principal subsidiaries.[24] In anticipation of the merger, which was scheduled for February 1930, all subsidiary lines were busy taking inventory during January.[25] Although it would still exist as a legal entity, the Canada Southern Railway was included in the inventory process. For 46 years the Michigan Central had operated in southwestern Ontario, and it had done so in a manner that left an indelible mark on that part of the province. Its name would prevail for many years, despite the arrival of its parent company as the direct operator of the Canada Southern.

Before continuing the story of the rail line under New York Central operation, however, there is one principal enhancement of the CSR which needs to be discussed. That is the story of the construction of the Detroit River Tunnel.

This photograph by Scott & Hopkins of the second Kettle Creek Bridge appeared in the Dominion Illustrated *magazine for 16 February 1889. Completed in 1883, this Canada Southern trestle was 1,395 feet in length and stood 93 feet above the creek. The viaduct consisted of alternating 30-foot tower spans and 45-foot intermediate spans. Although the wrought-iron bridge was double-tracked, trains travelling in opposite directions were prohibited from meeting each other on the structure. Because of increasing traffic and heavier motive power, the Michigan Central shortened and strengthened the bridge in 1902. The girders and towers were covered by heavy fill for some distance at both ends of the trestle, leaving the central 855-foot section as it was. Supplemental steelwork, in the form of three lines of girders and columns, was incorporated into the structure. The timber deck was replaced by an I-beam, steel-plate deck with ballast floor. In this photograph the view is from Fingall Hill, looking to the east.*

Train 23, the Fast Western Express, *thunders across the Kettle Creek Bridge at St. Thomas, circa 1913.*

A grasshopper derrick was used to place 75-foot, 70-ton girder sections in place on the third Kettle Creek Bridge.

Crew and special passengers gather for a conversation beside the cab of No. 380 on a Michigan Central passenger train at St. Thomas in the mid-1880s.
— Elgin County Pioneer Museum

This engraving offers a portrait of Canada Southern compound locomotive No. 338. Built by Schenectady in 1890, this engine had cylinders measuring 20 inches and 29 inches by 24 inches in size and operated under a boiler pressure of 180 pounds per square inch. In 1897 the locomotive was renumbered 450.
— Author's Collection

During the late 1800s the steamer J.W. Steinhoff was under charter to the Canada Southern to assist in ferrying passengers between Windsor and Detroit. Constructed by Jenkins at Wallaceburg, Ontario, in 1874, the vessel was 123.2 feet long, 24.1 feet wide and 8.7 feet in draft. Powered by steam, the wooden ship was registered in Canada (#71101) at 312 gross tons and 209 net tons. After service with Canada Southern, the vessel saw service on Lake Ontario and Lake Huron before being abandoned in 1909 near Owen Sound, Ontario. — Dossin Great Lakes Museum

Mr. Charles Bradburn (1867-1942), born in the township of Dereham, was blessed with an inquiring mind. Self-educated, he could converse intelligently with a host of scientific figures, Thomas A. Edison and Nikola Tessla among them. Bradburn invented electric heaters, electric signals, an internal-combustion engine and a device which eliminated gear shifting in motor vehicles. His interests ranged from electrical and mechanical devices to geology and nuclear isotopes. Some of his work, that for Imperial and Allied Research, remains secret. The Canada Southern Railway line which ran near his home did not escape his seminal thinking. He designed the manual block signalling system deployed by the Michigan Central Railroad in Ontario.

— Mrs. W.R. Crawford and Mrs. Margaret Crawford

Michigan Central Railroad Co.
...
SPECIAL TARIFF
—— ON ——
PETROLEUM OR COAL OIL
IN CAR-LOADS, MINIMUM 24,000 LBS.,
FROM PETROLIA, ONT.
Taking Effect January 1, 1889.

TO	Rates per 100 lbs.
Windsor, *Pelton, Maidstone Cross, Edgars, Colchester, Amherstburg............	16 cents.
Essex Centre, Woodslee, Ruscomb, Comber,...........................	15 cents.
Tilbury, Fletcher, Buxton,...	14 cents.
Charing Cross, Fargo, Harwich, *Weldon, Ridgetown, Highgate, Muirkirk, Taylor,	12 cents.
Rodney, Bismarck, Dutton, Iona, Shedden, *Southwold, *Delaware, **London, St. Thomas,** *Yarmouth, Kingsmill, **Aylmer,**...............	12 cents.
Springfield, Brownsville, **Tilsonburg,**..........................	14 cents.
Cornell, Hawtrey, Port Dover Junction, Windham, Waterford, Villa Nova, Townsend, **Hagersville,** Dufferin, Cayuga, Canfield, *Moorhead, Attercliffe, Wellandport, Perry, Hewitt, **Welland,** *Brookfield, Stevensville, Niagara Junction, Black Creek, Chippawa, *Niagara Falls, Clifton, *Queenston, Niagara-on-the-Lake...	15 cents.
*Melbourne	11 cents.
*Walkers, Courtright,...	8 cents.
Alvinston, Edy's Mills,...	7 cents.
Inwood, *Weidman, *Glen Rae, Brigden,.........................	6 cents.
Oil City, Oil Springs,..	5 cents.

ST. CATHARINES & NIAGARA CENTRAL RAILWAY.
Thorold, Merritton and St. Catharines,
15 cents per 100 lbs.

LEAMINGTON & ST. CLAIR RAILWAY.
Leamington and Blytheswood,
16 cents per 100 lbs.

LAKE ERIE, ESSEX & DETROIT RIVER RAILWAY.
Kingsville, Ruthven, Harrow, Walkerville,
16 cents per 100 lbs.

* No agents.   Freight charges must be prepaid.

A. MACKAY,
General Freight Agent.

JNO. CRAMPTON,
General Eastern Freight Agent.

Matthews, Northrup & Co., Art-Printing Works, Buffalo, N. Y.

With this flyer, Michigan Central announced special tariffs on petroleum and coal oil in carload lots from Petrolia.
— Michael P. McIlwaine Collection

Four crews of sectionmen with their hand cars are shown in this undated photograph taken at Comber, Ontario, likely in Michigan Central days.
— Hiram Walker Historical Museum

Canada Southern box cars were frequently found on affiliate Toronto, Hamilton & Buffalo. One such car, No. 33267, is positioned at the warehouse on Walnut Street in Hamilton in the summer of 1897. This picture affords a rare view of a box car assigned to the service operated under the label ''Canada Southern Line'' (the name printed in an arch above the car number on the side of the car). The far end of the car carries a Michigan Central emblem and a notation that the Canada Southern Railway was operated by MCRR. — Canadian Pacific Corporate Archives

MAIN LINE. GOING WEST.

Mls.	Canada Div.	Mail and Accom. Ex. Sun. 1	Bos., N.Y. & Chi. Spl. Daily. 15	N'th Shore Limited. Daily. 19	Fast West'n Ex. Daily. 23	American Express. Ex. Mon 31	Pacific Express. Daily 37	Windsor Accom. Ex. Sun. 131	Windsor Accom. Ex. Sun. 133			MIXED. Ex. Sun. 41
		A.M.	A.M.	A.M.	A.M.	A.M.	P.M.					A.M.
...	Buffalo E.S.T'e. Dp	6.00	12.45	3.20	6.30	7.55	4.30		Eastern Standard Time			
...	Buffalo C.S.T'e. Dp	5.00	11.45	2.20	5.30	6.55	3.30		Central Standard Time			
24	Ni. Falls, N.Y.				6.13		4.12					
25	S. Bridge, N.Y.	Via Fort Erie Div.	Via Fort Erie Div.	Via Fort Erie Div.	6.25	Via Fort Erie Div.	4.25					
26	Clifton				6.31		4.31					
27	Niagara Falls				6.37†		4.37†					
28	Falls View				6.45		4.44					
29	Montrose Jc.											
30	Montrose											
40	Welland	6.13	12.40†		7.00		5.00					6.40
45	Hewitt	6 21†										6.50†
50	Perry	6.29										7.24
52	Montague	6.33										7.30
58	Attercliffe	6.43										7.44
66	Canfield	6 56										8.01
72	Cayuga	7.08										8.40
77	Dufferin	7.19†										9.00
82	Hagersville	7.25			8.01		6.04					9.15
87	Townsend	7.35†										9.35
89	Villa Nova	7.39										9.40
94	Waterford	7.48			8.22		6.23					11.20
101	Windham	8.00										11.39
105	Pt. Dover Jc.	8.07					6 39†					11.50
106	Hawtrey	8.10										11.54
111	Cornell	8.19										12.07
117	Tilsonburg	8.30					6.55†					12.40
122	Brownsville	8.40										1.00
128	Springfield	8.51										1.18
130	Aylmer	8.57†										1.28
133	Kingsmill	9.02										1.40
137	Yarmouth	9 10										1.55
141	St. Thomas { Ar	9.20 AM	3.05	5.20	9.35	10.05	7.35					2.15 PM
141	St. Thomas } Dp	2.50 PM	3·10	5.25	9.49	10.10	7.50					5.35 AM
146	St. Clair Junc	3.00†										5.53
150	Shedden	3.10										6 05
154	Iona	3.19										6.15
160	Dutton	3.31					8.18					6 35
167	Bismarck	3.45										7.00
171	Rodney	3.55										7.15
174	Taylor	4.02										7.30
177	Muirkirk	4.08										7.40
179	Highgate	4.12										7.50
185	Ridgetown	4.25			10.40		8.53†					8.45
191	Mull	4.37										9.05
196	Fargo	4.48										9.45
198	Charing Cross	4.54										10.00
204	Buxton	5.07										10.35
208	Fletcher	5.15										11.42
215	Tilbury	5.30						A.M.	P.M.			12.25
222	Comber	5.45						7.17	4.05			1.10
227	Ruscomb	5.56						7.27	4.15			1.40
231	Woodslee	6.06						7.36	4.23			2.00
236	Essex	6 20			11.51			7.47	4.33			3.05
240	Maidstone Cr	6.30						7.57	4.43			3.30
244	Pelton	6.40†						8.06†	4.52†			3.44
249	Round House	6.55†										4.00
250	Windsor	7.00	5.50	7.50	12.20	12.30	10.30	8.25	5.10			
251	DETROIT. Ar	7.25	6.20	8.20	12.55	1.00	11.00					
35	Monroe		10.02	10.02	2.18							
59	Toledo .... Ar		10.50	10.50	3.10							
		P.M.	A.M.	A.M.	P.M.	P.M.	P.M.	A.M.	P.M.			P.M.

Westbound main-line passenger service on the Canada Division of the Michigan Central Railroad is shown in this extract from the timetable effective 18 November 1894.

— Michael P. McIlwaine Collection

This substantial structure was the Michigan Central's station in London, Ontario. The brick and stone building was constructed about 1885-87 on Canada Southern property at the southeast corner of Clarence and Bathurst streets. It replaced CASO's diminutive station which had been inherited from the London & South Eastern Railway. The MCRR station evidently was built with the conviction that a secure access to the city would be obtained. But the battles with Adam Beck brought no resolution, nor did various other arrangements. By the early thirties MCRR was fading and about 1936 the station was razed. This photo was taken about 1890.

— London Room, London Public Library

This photo of the reverse of a registered shows two RPO cancellations used on the Canada Southern. The vertical rectangle is of RG-3, a cancellation which is shown more clearly elsewhere. The cancellation to the far right is from 0-308 for the St. Thomas and Fort Erie route, travelling east on 29 November 1890. This RPO cancellation was in effect for the period 1887 to 1898.

— Lewis M. Ludlow Collection

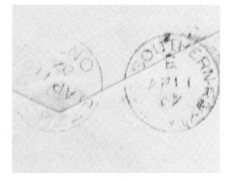

The RPO cancellation #RR-17 East for 11 April 1887 is extremely rare. The only known use was on the reverse of a registered cover from St. Thomas, Ontario, to Straffordville, Ontario. The words on this stamp are "CAN-SOUTHERN-RWY." This cancellation is accompanied by RG-3, the words for which are "REGISTERED/CAN SOUTHN-R."

— Ross D. Gray Collection

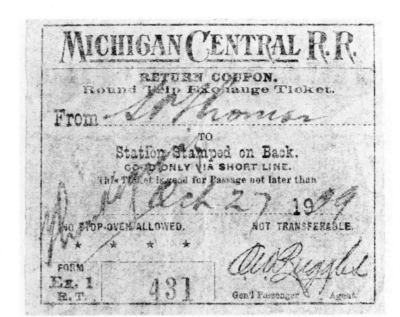

*Obverse of MCRR ticket from
St. Thomas to Courtright and return,
27 October 1909.*

— Author's Collection

The Canada Southern Railway bisected the Murray farm which was along the Grand River. This photo, taken in the summer of 1901, shows work crews building the second track about one-quarter mile west of the Grand River. The contributor's father was grade boss on the project and the railway paid him $2.25 per day. A man with a team of horses was paid $3.50 per day for construction work. The donor is in the picture, too. He's the boy standing just to the right of the man with a horse on the right of the picture.

— J. Douglas Murray

MICHIGAN CENTRAL R·R·
CANADA SOUTHERN DIVISION.
AGENT'S STUB.—NOT GOOD FOR PASSAGE.
COMMERCIAL TRAVELER'S TICKET.

LEAMINGTON
—TO—
WINDSOR

Issued to..

Good not later than..................... 190....

Holding Certificate No........................

291 $ .... Form H.

| Day | 2 | 4 | 6 | 8 | 10 | 12 | 14 | 16 | 18 | 20 | 22 | 24 | 26 | 28 | 30 | JAN. | FEB. |
| | 1 | 3 | 5 | 7 | 9 | 11 | 13 | 15 | 17 | 19 | 21 | 23 | 25 | 27 | 29 | 31 | MAR. | APR. |

MAY JUNE
JULY AUG.
SEPT. OCT.
NOV. DEC.

MICHIGAN CENTRAL RAILROAD
CANADA SOUTHERN DIVISION.
COMMERCIAL TRAVELER'S TICKET.
ONE FIRST CLASS CONTINUOUS PASSAGE.

LEAMINGTON to WINDSOR

Via..
This Ticket is void if any erasures or alterations are made hereon.
It is subject to conditions of, and good for passage only when presented
in connection with
Commercial Traveler's Certificate No............................
GOOD NOT LATER THAN DATE PUNCHED OUT IN MARGIN.
Not Good on Limited Trains.

★   ★   ★   ★   *A. V. Ruggles*,

291 Form H. Gen'l Pass'r & Ticket Agent.

1905
1906
1907
1908
1909
1910
1911

A commercial traveller's ticket for September 1905.　　　　　　— Michael P. McIlwaine Collection

During the St. Andrew's centenary celebration of 1894, there were gatherings everywhere in Niagara-on-the-Lake. The Michigan Central station and wharf were no exception. Note the men's apparel.　　— Niagara Historical Society

This attractive station of stone construction was unique on the CSR. This postcard view shows the Essex station in prosperous days of the 1900s, under MCRR operation. — John R. Lee Collection

The 10th of August 1907 dawned in Essex like innumerable days before. There seemed to be nothing different as the workday began. Shortly after 09:00 there sounded like rifle shots coming from the railway near the station. At precisely 09:50 the earth recoiled and a thunderous sound punched its way through town. People dashed to the MCRR railway station, the apparent source of the noise. The stone structure was in tatters. The freight shed behind it was demolished. Between them lay remnants of a freight train and its switching crew. Beneath part of a box car was a crater 20 feet deep and ten or so feet across. Only moments ago, two men were on or near the box car, which had been laden with 5,000 pounds of trinitroglycerin. One had been riding the car during shunting; the other had been relaying signals to the engineer. The two men were no more. The apparent rifle shots had actually been drops of TNT which had leaked through the car onto the rail only to be detonated by the car wheels. Two men were killed, several people were injured. Some $250,000 worth of property had been destroyed. The town was in a panic. The shock wave knocked plaster from ceilings as far away as Windsor and had rattled windows in Detroit. The load of TNT had been destined for Amherstburg for dredging operations and was being marshalled for the branch line freight train when the explosion occurred.

— *The Three R's of Essex* by Evelyn Couch

Royal trains were extremely rare on the Canada Southern. Only one such train is known to have passed over the CSR and been photographed. This one carried the Duke and Duchess of Cornwall and York from Niagara Falls to Niagara-on-the-Lake in 1901. While the train returned to the Falls, the royal party went by steamer up the Niagara River to Queenston, thence by carriage to the Falls for a visit. The royal party entrained at Niagara Falls for the return trip to Toronto. The royal train consisted of GTR locomotive No. 981 and a mixture of Grand Trunk and Canadian Pacific passenger rolling stock. The engineer for the CSR leg of the trip was John McDermot, who on account of the occasion dressed in Knights Templar regalia! The photograph was taken at the Niagara Falls Grand Trunk station.

— PAC C46987

In 1909, under sales order number Q-111, MLW built a pair of six-coupled engines for Michigan Central's Canadian operations at a cost of nearly $30,000. The engines, Nos. 8590 (shown here) and 8591, were equipped with small tenders which could carry 7.5 tons of coal and 5,100 US gallons of water. — Author's Collection

En route to Chicago, the famous Empire State Express *of the NYC&HR Railroad stopped at St. Thomas, where crowds gathered to admire the train. They venerated the locomotive, too. No. 999 had done an incredible one mile in 31.5 seconds!* — Elgin County Pioneer Museum

Canada Southern No. 8790 was built by MLW in April 1909 under sales order number Q-112. This locomotive was renumbered 8990 in 1912 and 7190 in 1936. This CSR engine, s/n 46267, weighed 274,000 pounds and was the heaviest of the trio of 0-10-0-type locomotives acquired from Montreal (two) and Brooks (one) during the period 1907 to 1910. No. 8790 was assigned to the hump service in CASO's Windsor Yard. In keeping with this duty, the tenders of this group of locomotives carried 8,000 US gallons of water and 12 tons of coal. Note the use of two sand domes.

— R.J. Sandusky Collection

Fresh out of the Schenectady shops in 1904, Canada Southern locomotive No. 499 looked like this. Note the unusual shadow painting of the numerals on the tender. This Pacific-type engine was one of many which the various NYC properties had on hand to ensure that the tight schedules of the limiteds could be maintained.

— Alco Historic Photos

Michigan Central Railroad banner.

MCRR public timetable cover, 1897.

This publicity painting by C. Graham portrayed the railway and Niagara Falls as attractively as one might ever hope to see them. For many years all daylight Michigan Central trains paused at Falls View for five minutes. The Canadian Horseshoe Falls are in the mid-ground; the American Falls are shown in the upper left. The painting was made into a splendid lithograph which the New York Central used extensively in promoting "The Niagara Falls Route."

— Lundy's Lane Historical Museum

John A. Sinclair at work in the station office. — Mrs. Hester Sinclair

Canada Southern 4-6-0-type No. 459 was built by Schenectady in December 1912 (s/n 5656). Michigan Central assigned the locomotive to class S-2. Note the extended piston rods. — Alco Historic Photos

The interior of the locomotive erecting shop looked like this, circa 1925. On the floor is Mikado-type, Brooks-built, class H-7c engine No. 7914 in the midst of being overhauled. The overhead crane was built by Whiting Foundry Equipment Co. of Harvey, R.I., and was designed to lift up to 150 tons.　　　　　　　　— Larry Broadbent

Engine tires were hoop-like structures which, because of their composition, had a greater expansion factor than that of the wheel cores. Following machining, the tires were heated and placed in a mounting jig to be aligned with the wheel core. This view shows a shopman engaged in the ''sweating on'' of locomotive tires. As the tires cooled, they contracted to fit very snugly around the wheel core.　　　　　　　— Larry Broadbent

This ominous-looking machine was a metal planer built by the John Bertram & Sons Co. Limited of Dundas, Ontario.

— Larry Broadbent

This view shows the transfer table of the St. Thomas shops, looking towards the freight shed (roof line in background). The tender at the right is on a track leading to the tank shop. The two-storey structure in the right background housed offices for the shops.

— Larry Broadbent

Judging from the crowd in attendance, this major ball game was a community event. The ball park was on land which the Canada Southern Railway established for this purpose. This view was taken about 1925 from a point near the St. Thomas shops, which are to the right and behind the photographer.
— Larry Broadbent

This view of CSR Mike No. 7943 prompts memories of that ear-piercing sound of jetting steam. At the time, the engine was positioned near the St. Thomas roundhouse. Rising above the tender one can see the top portion of the coaling tower. In fine print on the tender's letterboard are the block letters "M.C.R.R. (C.S.DIV.)." The name on the side of the tender is "NEW YORK CENTRAL LINES."
— Larry Broadbent

Although it did not show, Canada Southern did have some big, handsome motive power. One example was this 4-6-4-type No. 8207, as it appeared outside the builder's works at Schenectady, N.Y., in November 1927. Following a few years of service on CASO, the engine was transferred to Michigan Central in 1931 and renumbered 5352. Note that there was no "CS Div" on the letterboard. The J-class locomotives were the only ones which were not annotated for CASO.
— Alco Historic Photos

This view was taken about 1925 from the coal dock, which straddled the central track in the foreground. The next track on either side of the central one passed outside the coal dock. Moving away from the centre, the next track on either side was depressed in order to serve the cinder pits. Strings of hopper cars can be seen on these tracks. On the extreme right is the oil house (with oil barrels on the platform) and (at right angles) the roundhouse office. Covering the centre background is Canada Southern's 41-stall roundhouse. Two of the stalls contained run-through tracks. One of these gave access to the back shop and transfer table; the other gave access to the yard (to the right) by passing to the right of the nearer water tower. The tall chimney on the left marks the powerhouse. About 12 steam locomotives are visible in this picture. The only identifiable one is No. 7544, a Consolidation type.
— Larry Broadbent

Fully loaded with freight cars, including several dairy reefers, Transport *backs away from the ferry ship. The vessel was built in Wyandotte, Michigan, by the Detroit Dry Dock Company in 1880. The principal measurements of the iron hull were 254.1 feet in length, 45.9 feet in beam and 14 feet in draft. The ship was powered by twin 2-cylinder horizontal condensing steam engines. The deck had three tracks with a capacity of 21 cars.*

— Center for Archival Collections, Bowling Green State University

VIII

THE SECOND PROMISE FULFILLED

An effective crossing of the Detroit River had been a goal from the beginning of international railway commerce. While it was possible for rail traffic to move over the Buffalo & Lake Huron to Stratford, Ontario, thence via the Grand Trunk to Sarnia (the Grand Trunk had been completed in 1859), this longer routing also entailed two ferry links. The first was between Buffalo and Fort Erie; the second connected Point Edward (Sarnia) and Fort Gratiot (Port Huron). Thus, until the Canada Southern Railway was opened in 1873, the Great Western Railway was the only practical railway link through Canada for American railways between Michigan and the Niagara frontier. After the Grand Trunk opened its International Bridge between Bridgeburg (Fort Erie) and Black Rock (Buffalo) in 1873, the struggle for through traffic intensified. Great Western (1854), Canada Southern (1873) and Michigan Central (1883) each operated railway car ferries across the Detroit River. Ferries were used because inter-railway rivalry, a hostile inland marine lobby, and inadequate technology thwarted repeated efforts either to tunnel or to bridge that river.

In August 1882 the Grand Trunk absorbed the Great Western and became the surviving enterprise with considerable resources at its disposal. To counter this competitive edge the Michigan Central leased the Canada Southern, and the combined railways linked Chicago and Niagara Falls. The CSR altered its main line and built an impressive cantilever bridge over the Niagara River. Following these improvements, the MC/CS line regained the upper hand in the ongoing battle between the GTR and NYC&HRR. This advantage was lost in 1891 when the Grand Trunk opened its St. Clair Tunnel, thereby greatly improving the movement of its trains. Although it once again considered building its own tunnel, knowledge of GTR's problems with sulphur and smoke discouraged the Michigan Central sufficiently and no serious attempt was made. For two decades the GTR would enjoy the only crossing of the St. Clair and Detroit rivers without being dependent on the water. In the meantime, the railway car ferries of Canada Southern and Michigan Central — moving like weaver's shuttles — would continue to carry the heaviest waterborne railway traffic in the world, with the possible exception of some New York City services.

Originally, the intention was that the eventual tunnelling under the river would be done at Amherstburg. Various factors changed this. Following the takeover of the GWR, the city of Windsor courted the Canada Southern to build a line there to return competition to the market. The increased commercial importance of Detroit–Windsor meant that the principal crossing of the river would have to be made there. The terrain near Amherstburg was unsuitable for a tunnel.

When Canada Southern announced that it would build into Windsor, the public's reaction was ecstatic. "No event has occurred within the history of Windsor of so much importance to the people as the swinging hither of the Canada Southern Railway."[1] Construction of the Essex Cut-Off, as it was originally known, was begun at both ends. The railway advertised that if offered good wages: $5 per day per team of horses. The work began during September 1882 and the double-tracked, new main line was completed by the last Saturday in November 1882. Erection of the company's roundhouse was complete and five of the ten new yard tracks were also finished. Just before Christmas, the first of two lines to the Windsor waterfront and the ferry slip at the foot of Cameron Street were nearly ready. On December 31 the MCRR inaugurated ferry service between Detroit and Windsor. There was such a dramatic increase in traffic that the railway ordered a new car ferry, *Michigan Central*, for delivery in 1884, and four years later, another ferry, *Transfer II*, was added.

The increase in traffic prompted the Michigan Central to reflect on a more permanent crossing of the river. During the 1890s plans for bridging or tunnelling the river were discussed with both the Grand Trunk and Canadian Pacific. Van Horne said that his road would have nothing to do with a tunnel. He demanded a bridge, but nothing came of it. In 1904 the MCRR and GTR tried again, evidently without the CPR, but the projected costs for a high-clearance bridge and the tremendous disruptions to waterfront properties during construction, to say nothing of the hostile Lake Carriers' Association response, put an end to the negotiations. By 1905 four ferries with an aggregate capacity of 84 cars were handling 1,097 railway cars daily. For a while the Michigan Central even thought of rejuvenating the CSR's plans for a ferry service out of Courtright. The MC/CS route included a substantial and growing passenger service, and a less disruptive means of crossing the river was essential if the full potential of the market was to be realized. Meanwhile, the old Canada Southern idea of tunnelling beneath the river could not be dispelled. Something had to be done.

The idea of a tunnel remained impractical until the occurrence of two technological developments, both in New York City. One was the Pennsylvania's successful tunnelling under the Hudson River to reach New York.[2] The other was the New York Central & Hudson River Railroad's success with electric traction in the Park Avenue Tunnel and Grand Central Terminal.[3] Michigan Central and Canada Southern reflected that Thomson's idea, and promise, just might be possible.

A corporate entity was already established. This was the dormant enterprise known as the Canada & Michigan Bridge and Tunnel Company (its name since 1895), which had been incorporated in 1888 as the Canada & Michigan Tunnel Company and was empowered to tunnel between Windsor and Detroit.[4] The Michigan & Canada Bridge and Tunnel Company was the corresponding American organization. Both were subsidiaries of the Canada Southern, which oversaw their merger on 9 June 1905 to form the Detroit River Tunnel Company.[5]

During February 1905 the railway began property surveys and preliminary plans. Soundings of the Detroit River were made along the proposed route of the tunnel. Variations in water level, and topical and under currents were dutifully recorded. Geological data for the area were compiled and examined. These data formed the basis for the final specifications and plans which were begun by engineers during August 1905.

On 10 July 1905 MCRR president W.H. Newman announced the appointment of William J. Wilgus to the post of chairman of the Advisory Board of Engineers of the Detroit River Tunnel.[6] Wilgus, a vice-president and chief engineer of the NYC&HRR, had just completed the rejuvenation of the Weehawken Yard. He had also been deeply involved in the Park Avenue Tunnel electrification and the second Grand Central Station complex. W.S. Kinnear, assistant general manager of the MCRR, was appointed to the newly created post of chief engineer of the Detroit River Tunnel. Howard A. Carson, chief engineer of the Boston Rapid Transit subway and who had recently completed the East Boston Tunnel under Boston harbour, was secured as a consulting engineer.[7] This three-member advisory board spent the rest of the year considering various options and plans. Wilgus proposed a novel solution: dig a broad trench in the river bed and place into it prefabricated concrete tunnel sections which would be joined together and pumped dry. Carson contributed a variation using steel tubes instead. Cut-and-cover tunnels had already been built in some rivers (the Chicago River for example) but cofferdams were used. The proposal was unprecedented. Everything would have to be done underwater in a river which flowed at a swift current, which carried heavy marine traffic, and which required a subaqueous tunnel of 2,600 feet in length.

The advisory board formulated three variations of this idea, plus a shield-tunnel plan, then they called for tenders in February 1906. The engineering and contracting communities buzzed with ideas. During the intervening years since the construction of the St. Clair Tunnel, both tunnelling methods and contractor expertise had much improved. There was no reluctance on the part of the contractors. The bids were opened on 3 March 1906 and the contract was awarded to Hoff Brothers-Butler Company of New York on 1 August 1906.[8] The choice was Butler's own combination of the Wilgus-Carson variations, using steel tubes which would be sunk in a trench and subsequently lined inside and out with concrete. The tunnel was to accommodate a double-track main line, each track encased in its own tube, with the tubes laid in parallel across the river bed in a trench. What is perhaps most surprising is that this particular solution was also the least expensive of the final designs.

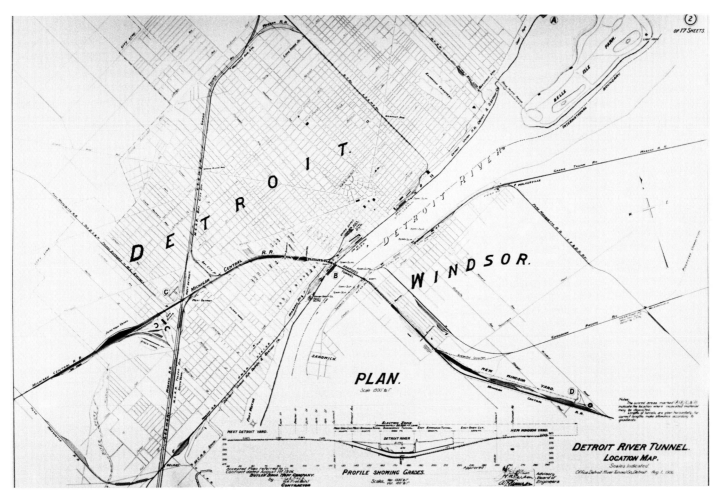

Location map of the Detroit River Tunnel.

— Hiram Walker Historical Museum

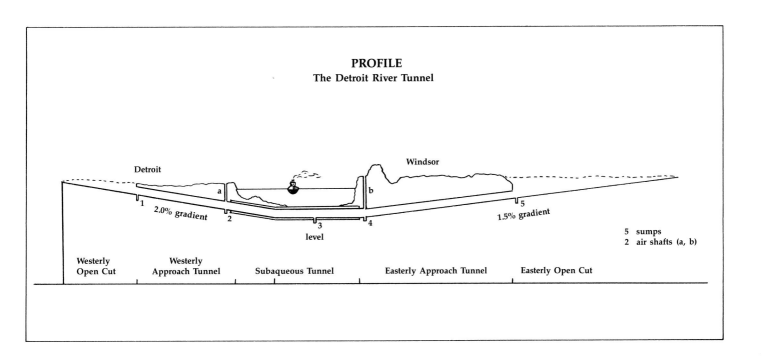

PROFILE
The Detroit River Tunnel

Detroit

Windsor

a

b

1

2.0% gradient

2

3

4

level

1.5% gradient

5

5 sumps
2 air shafts (a, b)

| Westerly
Open Cut | Westerly
Approach Tunnel | Subaqueous Tunnel | Easterly Approach Tunnel | Easterly Open Cut |

*This view shows Section 4 of Hull No. 34
of the DRT under construction on 26 October
1907 at St. Clair, Michigan.*
— Hiram Walker Historical Museum

*A diver is about to make the first descent on
15 July 1907 to perform submarine work on the
Detroit River Tunnel. Each tube or section of the
tunnel has a sleeve at one end which will mate
with the plain end of the previously sunk tube.
Both tubes have flanges which divers will bolt
together after placing a rubber gasket between
them. There is also a similar gasket at the inner
end of the sleeve. (the one towards the middle of
the tube). When the bolting has been completed, a
space of 3x18 inches will be formed around the
tube at the end of the joint. Each space will be
serviced by two small hoses. A grout of cement
will be forced through one tube, fill the space and
exit through the second tube, thus indicating that
the space has been filled.*
— Burton Historical Collection, Detroit Public Library

What lay ahead was the pacification of the Lake Carriers' Association and the obtaining of approval from two national governments. The construction would necessitate having dredges and scows in the channel at uncertain locations for prolonged periods of time, and later there would be the positioning and controlled sinking of floating tunnel sections, to be followed by the submarine connection and completion of the tunnel exteriors. The river was 2,400 feet between harbour lines, and the MCRR proposed to restrict construction to a 600-foot section at any one time, thereby leaving adequate room for navigation. The LCA suggested that the railway provide a patrol boat to serve as pilot to passing vessels, a proposal the MCRR quickly accepted. The assent of the American and Canadian governments was readily obtained. Work on the river portion of the tunnel was about to begin.

The subcontract for the river dredging was given to Dunbar & Sullivan Dredging Company of Buffalo, and their dredges went to work during October 1906.[9] Dredging to a depth of 45 feet below the river bed was done with a dipper dredge, while excavation below that point was carried out with a clamshell dredge.[10]

Great Lakes Engineering Company of Detroit received the contract for the steel tubes, which were to be built at its St. Clair yard, then floated downstream. Ten sections, each 262.5 feet by 64 feet, were fabricated and placed in wooden caissons which were open at the top and bottom but closed on the ends. Each section contained twin tubes 23 feet in diameter and were braced every 12 feet by wide iron diaphragms. These served a dual purpose in that they stiffened the tubes to withstand transit and sinking, and they provided a frame on which the wooden forms for containing the concrete could be affixed. A short closing section brought the tunnel "hulls" to 11 in number. These sections were to fit into a trench, 48 feet wide and 30 to 50 feet deep, across the bottom of the river. Some 700,000 cubic yards of bluish clay had been removed from the trench.

The last excavation work concerned the junctions between the subaqueous tunnel and the shore tunnels. Different methods were used on the two sides of the river. On the Windsor side the shore tunnels were carried close to the shoreline and the trench was dredged into the tunnel without benefit of a cofferdam. This method was inexpensive and it did not pose any problem in making a watertight connection. On the Detroit side, a cofferdam was sunk at the designated junction between the shore tunnel and the subaqueous tunnel. After it was pumped dry, the contractor used dry excavation methods to the point where the subaqueous tunnel sections were to be met.

The tunnel sections were launched sideways with some difficulty; this was subsequently remedied by partially enclosing the leading side and bottom for 15 feet, which allowed the leading side to ride up or float until the trailing side had cleared the slipway.[11] The sections were carefully floated 52 miles downstream to the construction site. As the "hulls" approached the site, four independent air cylinders were surmounted on each section preparatory to a controlled sinking. The tubes were flooded, and while the section floated just below the surface, derricks moved in with seven-ton weighted grillages suspended from their booms. The grillages were then lowered onto the tunnel sections, depressing them. When the derricks hauled the cables up, the grillages were lifted and the caissons floated. In this manner the sinking of the specific section could be controlled. On the river bed beneath the tunnel section there were other great timber grillages (which rested on timber pilings) which would permit concrete to be poured around the tube once it was in place.

The controlled sinking was an exacting challenge; there was no room for error. The twin-tube sections could not be manhandled if they should unfortunately reach the grillages misaligned. The river current pressed against the caisson with a force of 7,000 tons. To counter this, restraining cables were sunk from ships by means of 12-foot-square concrete anchors 1.5 feet thick. Calibrated masts were attached to the top of the section. These were constantly checked as the controlled sinking began and continued to be checked by surveyors' transits on shore until each section had been gingerly lowered to its resting place. Temporary interior semi-partitions built downwards from the top trapped air uniformily so that neither end would sink too quickly. Once the section was properly placed, an underwater crew released the air cylinders. To ensure proper coupling, the sections were made with pins at one end which would mate with holes on the end of the next section. Cables were strung from the pins to the holes, to facilitate ready alignment.

The first caisson was sunk on 1 October 1907.[12] The third one was sunk in June 1908 and the fifth in October of that year. It was expected that the DRT would be ready by about 1 June 1909.[13] (During that year MCRR acquired all the shares of the tunnel company in a manner which minority CSR shareholders would dispute for years.)

After the twin tubes had been secured in place and properly coupled with a watertight sleeve, gravel was deposited in the bottom of the trench to a depth of 18 inches, and outside the forms to a height of several feet. Since gravel was not readily available, Canada Southern hauled the material from its own pit on the Leamington Branch. Scows with concrete plants on board were positioned, and then through canvas chutes the requisite type of concrete was deposited into the wooden forms surrounding the tubes and allowed to harden sufficiently. Afterwards, construction crews moved through the tubes, knocking out the temporary wooden plugs and pumping out the water. They then proceeded to line the tunnels with specially prepared concrete to a thickness of 20 inches and reinforced with one-inch longitudinal rods. On 1 July 1910 the tunnel was declared finished.[14]

The first train to run through the tunnel did so on 22 July 1910.[15] The passing of the first official train through the Detroit River Tunnel occurred on July 26, when a two-car train, hauled by electric locomotive Number 7504, transported William K. Vanderbilt Jr. and his party. The first scheduled freight train ran through the tunnel on Saturday, September 17.[16] Passenger traffic was not routed through the tunnel until Sunday, 16 October 1910, with the honour going to a westbound train, the *Fast Western Express*. The first eastbound train to pass through the DRT was the *Wolverine*.[17]

Since New York Central was so favourably impressed with the General Electric Company scheme for the Park Avenue Tunnel, NYC selected the GE proposal for DC, third-rail operation for the DRT. Detroit Edison would provide 60-hertz, 4,400-volt alternating current to the DRT's substation, which would convert the electricity to 660-volt direct current for third-rail application by means of two synchronous 1,000-kilowatt motor-generator sets. As a precautionary step, the system's back-up was an immense storage battery which in emergency could provide sufficient current for traction and ancillary needs for 30 minutes. This would ensure that a train would not be trapped in the tunnel because of power failure.

The Detroit River Tunnel Company established its shops and yard on the Windsor side as part of Canada Southern's redevelopment. In April 1906 the CSR had applied to the Board of Railway Commissioners for authority to expropriate lands in Windsor and vicinity in order to relocate and enlarge terminal facilities in connection with the tunnel project. The existing yards would be moved back 1.5 miles to the Wellington–Tecumseh Road area in order to accommodate the eastern approach to the tunnel.[18] A subway would be built under Macdougall Street and Marias Road would be closed. The gravel for the Windsor Yard improvement was hauled from the CSR's aforementioned pit. The cost of Canada Southern's improvements was estimated to be $5 million.[19]

The DRT route was 4.5 miles in length, but there were 28.5 miles in total of electrified, under-running, third-rail trackage. With the transfer of all freight and passenger traffic to the tunnel, the Michigan Central discontinued its railway car service and disposed of its ferries to other railways. It was originally estimated that the tunnel would cost between $7 million and $8 million, but its cost now approached $10 million.

As part of the redevelopment of the Windsor properties, during 1911 Canada Southern built a new passenger station to serve the needs of the Michigan Central and the Canadian Pacific. On the Detroit side, the Michigan Central was committed to a mammoth relocation of yards and terminal facilities to the Baker and 14th streets area. The cost of the new yard, the elevated main line, the freight and express structures, and related buildings totalled $4.5 million. The chief attraction of the railway's terminal redevelopment was an eclectic station edifice worthy of the New York Central itself. The hotel-like station, costing $2.5 million was opened in 1913.[20]

Thomson's second promise had now been fulfilled. The Detroit River Tunnel was truly a jewel in Canada Southern's crown. Following the opening of the tunnel, the metropolitan area and Essex County were placed on an arterial east-west railway line that contributed directly to the subsequent commercial and industrial growth of the region. The story of the main line is resumed in the following chapter. The New York Central wanted to imprint its own image on the CSR.

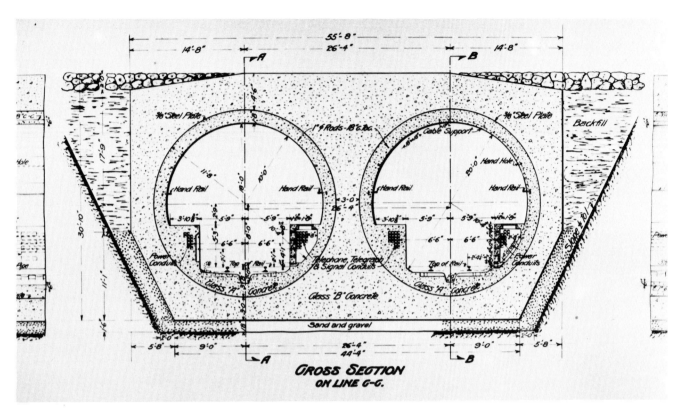

Cross-section, details for the subaqueous tunnel.   — Hiram Walker Historical Museum

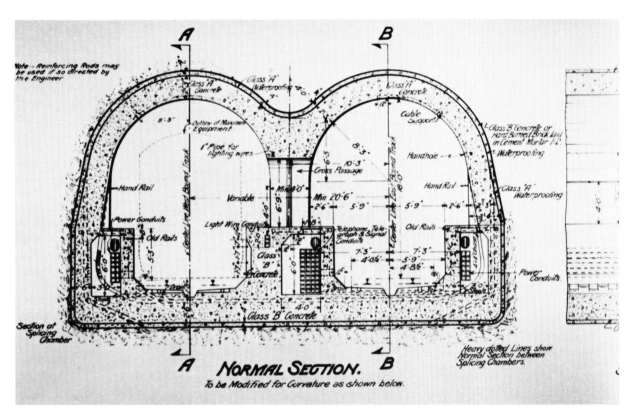

Normal section, details for the east approach tunnel.   — Hiram Walker Historical Museum

A view showing construction of the approach tunnel in the Windsor cut.
— Hiram Walker Historical Museum

The workman in the left foreground of the end of Section 1 provides an idea of the size of the tunnel.
— Hiram Walker Historical Museum

The final section of the Detroit River Tunnel is carefully manoeuvred into position before controlled sinking. — Hiram Walker Historical Museum

Crowds gather on the Windsor shore to witness the controlled sinking of the last tunnel section. — Hiram Walker Historical Museum

This view shows the working decks of the scow Tremie *on 1 October 1908, during construction of the subaqueous railway tunnel.*
— Burton Historical Collection, Detroit Public Library

Train No. 29 of the Michigan Central descends the easterly approach cut at Windsor to make the first run through the Detroit River Tunnel on 18 September 1910. Note that some dignitaries are riding the front of the electric locomotive and that the train consists entirely of baggage cars. Regularly scheduled passenger trains would not be routed through the tunnel until October.
— Burton Historical Collection, Detroit Public Library

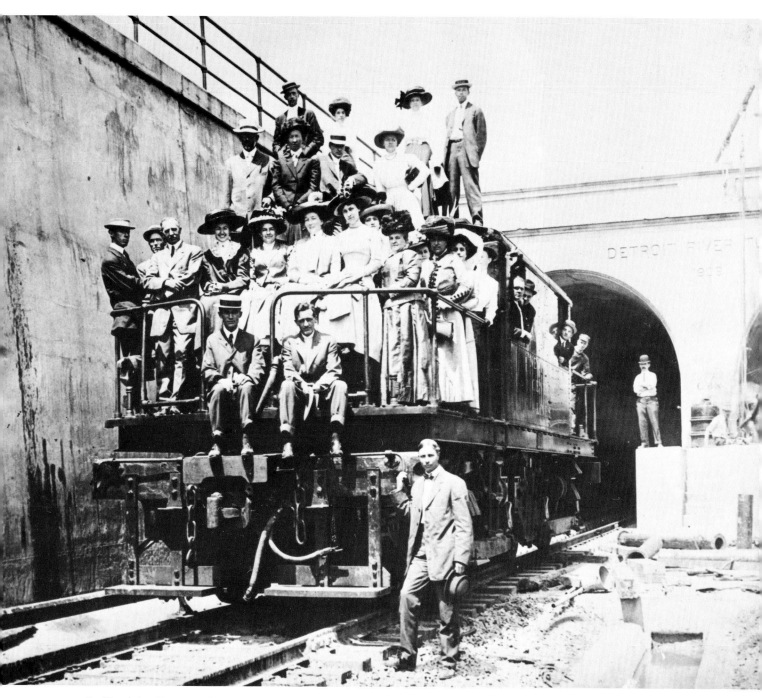

On Dominion Day 1910 the Detroit River Tunnel was declared completed. While some test runs were conducted and finishing touches were applied, plans were made for the official opening. Michigan Central was not noted for marking such occasions, but the engineering achievement was so significant that an exception was made. The first official trip through the tunnel occurred on 26 July 1910, when a special two-car train carrying New York Central, Michigan Central, Canada Southern and DRT officials passed over the line behind a GE steeple-cab locomotive. William K. Vanderbilt Jr. rode the deck of the engine en route. A variety of other officials and their guests rode another engine and paused for their portraits as shown here.

— Hiram Walker Historical Museum

This aerial view shows Transfer (II) *pushing through sheet ice on the Detroit River. Built in 1888 by the Cleveland Shipbuilding Company, the vessel featured a steel hull and was equipped with both paddle-wheel and screw propulsion. The overall dimensions of the ferry were 265 feet in length, 75.2 feet in beam and 12.2 feet in draft. Michigan Central sold the ferry in October 1912 to the Wabash, which operated it until 1938, when it was sold to Pine Ridge Navigation Limited. The vessel was scrapped two years later in Hamilton. The picture shows the vessel plying the Detroit River under Wabash ownership.*

— Center for Archival Collections, Bowling Green State University

The last DRT locomotives were a pair of steeple-back tunnel motors, Nos. 7510-11. They were actually slightly larger than the previous ten locomotives, but they appeared to be smaller. The rather large, 48-inch-diameter wheels created the illusion. Unlike earlier engines the air tanks for these were mounted on the roof rather than being placed within the car body.

— Alco Historic Photos

Tunnel motor 7503 stands outside the heater shed in the DRT's electric yard in Windsor. Note the overhead under-running electric rail protruding from the shed.

— Cyril A. Butcher

The original Canada Southern station in Windsor was built about 1882-83 adjacent to the ferry slip on Cameron Street. The dramatic increase in traffic required the railway to order another ferry and to increase the trackage next to the station. A 1901 newspaper photograph shows four additional tracks on this side of the one shown here. By then the station had become so rundown that residents wondered why Michigan Central had so long kept in operation such a shack in a city of the size and importance of Windsor. MCRR president H.B. Ledyard then announced that the railway intended to erect a new station as part of the milt-million-dollar redevelopment plan.

— Hiram Walker Historical Museum

The brick-and-stone station at Windsor was one of the largest owned by the Canada Southern Railway. This portrait taken in September 1976 shows the east and north faces of the building. The double-track main line leads to the tunnel (to the right).

— Kenneth A.W. Gansel

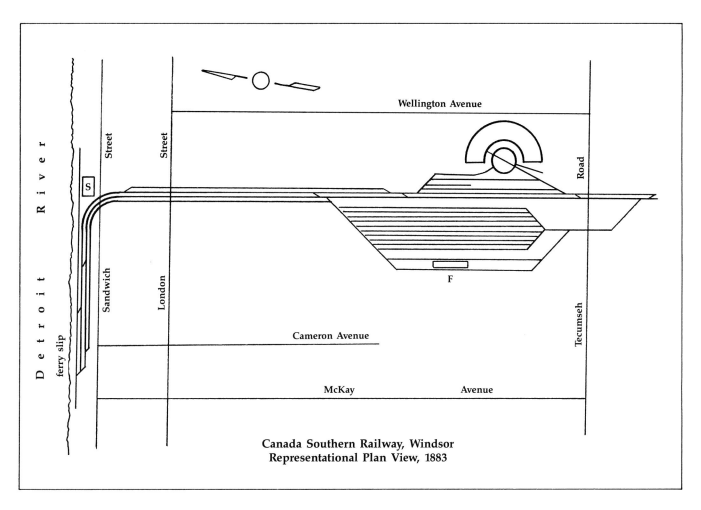

**Canada Southern Railway, Windsor
Representational Plan View, 1883**

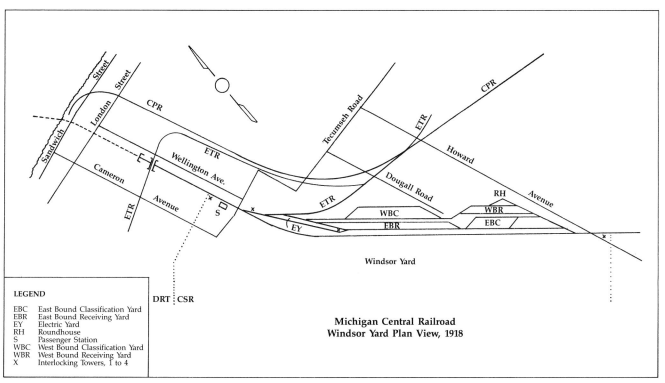

LEGEND

EBC	East Bound Classification Yard
EBR	East Bound Receiving Yard
EY	Electric Yard
RH	Roundhouse
S	Passenger Station
WBC	West Bound Classification Yard
WBR	West Bound Receiving Yard
X	Interlocking Towers, 1 to 4

**Michigan Central Railroad
Windsor Yard Plan View, 1918**

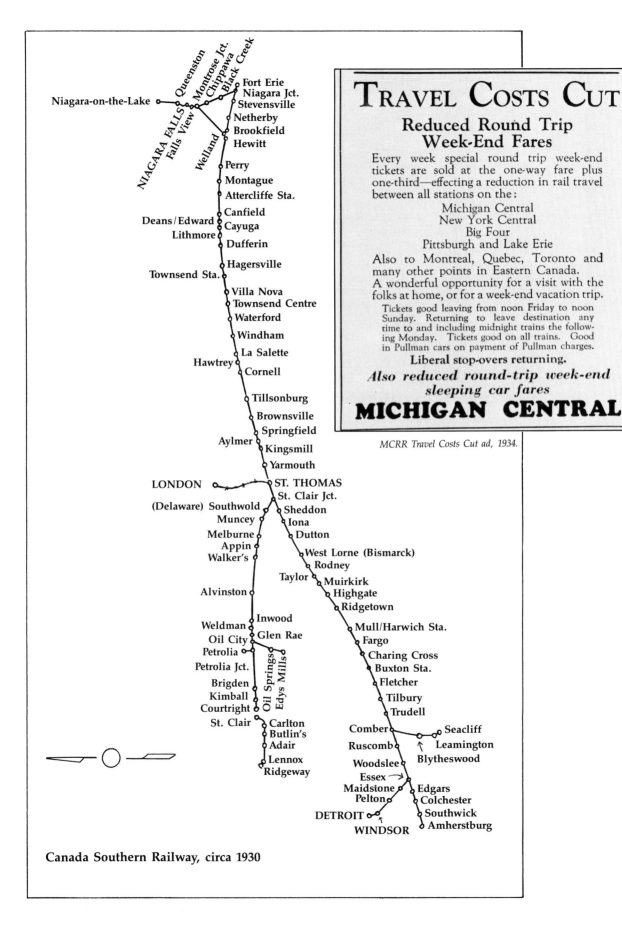

MCRR *Travel Costs Cut* ad, 1934.

Canada Southern Railway, circa 1930

IX

UNDER THE OVAL SIGN

For several years the New York Central Railroad had wished to exercise more immediate control over its principal Canadian line. The Michigan Central Railroad, however, was reluctant to part with its control if it was still to be held accountable for the Canada Southern Railway. The two American railways came to terms during 1929 and signed a sublease agreement. On 1 February 1930 the NYC assumed direct operation of the Canada Southern.[1] Shortly afterwards, the New York Central commenced a far-reaching review of its subsidiary's holdings, operations, equipment requirements, passenger service and freight service. The Great Depression had set in, and pruning for survival was the order of the day.

Canada Division Overview, 1930-1945

In smaller communities such as Waterford, the Depression caused the New York Central to reduce its work week for many employees from six to three days, but the railway did not lay off any of the men. At that time pay for a sectionman was $19.01 for two weeks' work.[2] The railway which had been so well-kept was now maintained at a lower level without jeopardizing safety during the winter months. In the summer the more important track work was carried out with "extra" crews being hired.

The most immediate development in the CSR's physical plant was the modernization of the signalling system and train control. The summer of 1930 saw MCRR (that name would linger for years) arranging a two-year program to replace its automatic semaphore block signal system with automatic coloured light block signals.[3] From September to December 1930 coloured light signals, together with automatic train control (ATC), were installed between Windsor and St. Thomas. During 1931 the coloured light signals were installed between St. Thomas and Niagara Falls and between Welland and Bridgeburg (Fort Erie). The ATC system was extended simultaneously. The signalling and control system was the same kind as was already in use on the Michigan Central Railroad between Detroit and Chicago and on the New York Central between Buffalo and New York City. The total expenditure for the coloured light signals and the ATC program was approximately $775,000. Although automatic train control had gained wide acceptance throughout the world, it had had no application in Canada. As far as is known, its application on the Canada Southern line was the first in this country.[4] This installation on the CSR, however, soon required both the TH&B and the CPR to equip selected locomotives with appropriate devices in order to be included in the locomotive pool which was assigned to operate over the Welland–Buffalo territory.

At the time of the NYC takeover, Canada Southern's motive power roster consisted of 125 steam locomotives categorized as follows: 41 for passenger service, 56 for freight service and 28 for switching service. The company's roster of rolling stock listed 1,038 units consisting of 723 box cars, 150 flat cars, 67 vans, 1 baggage/postal/express car, 2 combination cars, and 95 cars in maintenance-of-way service.[5] New York Central management made its control felt very early, when but two years later it directed the retirement of 13 passenger engines, 11 freight locomotives and 5 switching engines. These annual retirement statistics would remain fairly constant until 1943 for motive power and until 1938 for rolling stock.

During the Depression, passenger traffic declined, and that on branch lines was particularly hard hit. By 1930 passenger service on the Amherstburg Branch was reduced to one train, whereas that on the Leamington Branch had already been reduced to two mixed trains by 1929. The NYC discontinued passenger services on both branches in 1934. (On the Niagara Branch, passenger service had been discontinued by the MCRR in 1925.) Only the St. Clair Branch had some semblance of passenger service.

Passenger service on the main line fared better, but here too there were reductions. In 1930 passenger traffic consisted of eight daily expresses and two locals (daily except Sunday) eastbound, and ten daily expresses and two locals (one daily, one daily except Sunday) westbound.[6] NYC's local service was declining steadily, and with the issuance of its public timetable for 27 April 1941, there was no passenger service for local patrons, a curious situation in view of Canada's being at war. Local passenger train service was provided with a mixture of MCRR and older NYC equipment, dotted here and there by increasingly rarer CSR cars. All through passenger trains were fully equipped with New York Central rolling stock.

The declining traffic and the poor state of repair of the principal passenger station in Niagara Falls prompted the New York Central to seek authority to close and demolish that structure. The large wooden building had been built in 1885, soon after the opening of the Cantilever Bridge, and over the years the station had become rather worn down. The railway argued that the negligible amount of traffic just did not warrant the expense of a new building. The structure was demolished shortly after the receipt of permission to do so on 14 August 1940.

The war years saw some small increases in the number of locomotives for passenger service (replacements) and switching engines (additions) to help with increased freight traffic.

Unfortunately, very little is known about freight service on the CSR following the NYC assumption of operation. The ragtag roster of freight equipment was reviewed and found to be wanting. During 1930 the scrap lines at St. Thomas were kept busy with the scrapping of nearly 500 old CSR box cars. Almost half the roster went to the scrapper's torch. There seemed to be no need to replace the equipment, but a few years later, when Canada was at war, there was a shortage of box cars to carry the nation's war goods.

During the war years there were small purchases of motive power. In 1943 five switching engines were acquired, and these were followed two years later by three more. Three passenger locomotives were bought in 1944 to replace units being retired. There were no increases in nor replacements of the freight locomotive roster.

Post-War Development, 1945-1968

During this period the three most significant changes were dieselization, the rerouting of freight traffic below the border, and the merger with the Pennsylvania. Canada Southern would be altered considerably.

During the late 1940s the New York Central began to introduce diesels on its through passenger trains. For a while the expresses were powered by a mixture of steam and diesel locomotives. The *Wolverine* and *Detroiter* were the first trains to pass over the CSR with diesel power. Occasionally, some of the through freight trains would also be powered by diesels relieving the steam locomotives which were in the shops for routine servicing. In 1949 the New York Central began retiring CSR steam locomotives in preparation for the eventual dieselization of its southwestern Ontario line.

The transition from steam to diesel technology would have a dramatic effect throughout the Canada Southern territory in terms of the impact upon the company's physical plant, train operation, the role of labour and the implications for the economies of communities such as St. Thomas, Niagara Falls and Windsor. Early in 1953 the NYC closed its Windsor roundhouse and permanently laid off 42 locomotive shop workers. Steam locomotive facilities were quickly dismantled, and 19 steam engines were retired, leaving just 55 such locomotives on the roster. That was not all, however. The work force at the Windsor shops was severely cut from 125 men to 43.[7] What angered the employees was not the change in technology as such; rather, it was the suddenness of the conversion and the realization that few of them would have any place in the servicing of the new diesel-electric motive power. Some $10 million worth of diesel power passed through Windsor daily, but none of it was serviced there.[8] St. Thomas fared worse. The car shops were closed forever. Steam locomotive services were reduced. The year 1954 would be the last full year of an all-steam roster on the Canada Southern. Men whose jobs were related to steam,

This aerial view of the St. Thomas shops was taken about 1935. The long narrow building on the left was the freight shed. Going right, the first (closer) large group of buildings consisted of the main machine shop (front portion), erecting shop (rear portion), passenger car shops, another machine shop, and (the building at right angles) the freight car shop. The small building immediately behind the "car" machine shop was the upholstery shop (with the small chimney). The drying kiln can be seen next to the top of this chimney. The second group of buildings (behind the transfer table) consisted of locomotive and car departmental offices, boiler shop, tank shop, flue shop (and behind it the headlight shop), the blacksmith shop (which also extended to the rear), the stores department and the building department. In the background can be seen the roundhouse and power plant. (Refer to the plan view.)

— Larry Broadbent

Table V

PASSENGERS CARRIED IN SELF-PROPELLED CARS BY RAILWAY FOR THE YEAR ENDED 31 DECEMBER 1940

Railway	Passengers
Canadian National	1,160,412
Canadian Pacific	623,289
Canada Southern	172,955
Northern Alberta	131,250
Nipissing Central	102,546
Maritime Coal, Rwy. & Power	98,099
Morrissey, Fernie and Michel	96,266
Canada & Gulf Terminal	40,140
Pacific Great Eastern	25,850
Nelson and Fort Sheppard	24,732

Source: Statistics of Steam Railways of Canada, (for the year ended 31 December 1940) p126

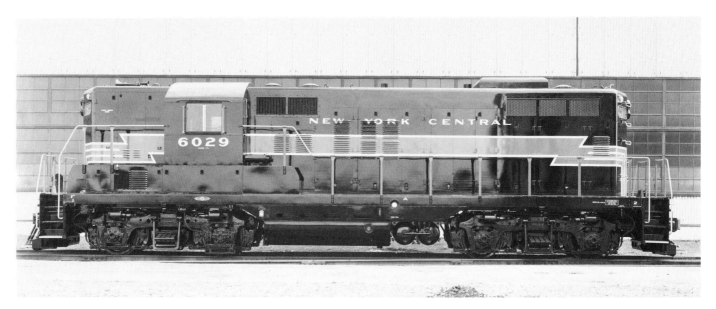

The first new diesel-electric locomotive to be owned by the Canada Southern Railway was No. 6029, shown here in the attractive two-tone grey livery of CASO's sublessee, New York Central Railroad.

— Ron Nelson photo,
General Motors Diesel Limited

This portrait of the nose of No. 6029 shows off the NYC stripes on the car body and the apron. If only the rectangular CASO emblem had been applied...

— Ron Nelson photo,
General Motors Diesel Limited

but who could not be redeployed in dieselization or in light repairs, were permanently laid off. As a consequence, unemployment figures rose significantly in St. Thomas. Similar reductions were made among the employees at the Montrose shops in Niagara Falls. The age of steam was drawing to a close.

One of the first steps towards dieselization occurred in June 1953. On June 16 a pair of aging electrics hauled NYC Hudson Number 5434, her fires banked, through the tunnel from Detroit. The steam locomotive was made ready and coupled to an eastbound train, and in a delightful cloud of smoke and steam, Number 5434 powered the last line-haul steam-powered passenger train over the Canada Southern Railway line.[9] A surprisingly large number of people turned out along the line to wave a fond goodbye to the men and to an era. In community after community, the station platforms, the road crossings and the backs of private properties were dotted with people who took the time to smile and wave. Needless to say, that train was delayed.

In 1956 the New York Central began dieselization with the purchase, on behalf of Canada Southern, of ten diesel-electric locomotives from the Chesapeake & Ohio Railway. These GP7-type locomotives had been built in March 1951 by General Motors Diesel Limited of London, Ontario, as C&O Numbers 5720 to 5729. They were renumbered to NYC 5818 to 5827 respectively and repainted in NYC livery. During 1956, 13 steam locomotives were retired, reducing CSR's ownership to 35 such engines. What turned out to be the first phase of dieselization was completed.

The elimination of steam power was not the only change in motive power on the New York Central's Canadian operations. The NYC was also planning the conversion of the electric railway tunnel to diesel operation. In late June 1953 a ventilation project costing $500,000 was scheduled to begin. This was the first stage in converting the Detroit River Tunnel from electric to diesel operation. The most direct benefit to the travelling public would be the shortening of the passenger schedules upon completion of the conversion program. It was expected to take six months for the installation of the high-velocity air system to the tunnel's existing ventilation fans. Later the electric engines would be withdrawn, the power turned off and the 18.5 miles of third-rail trackage removed. Related facilities would either be converted or eliminated.

The second phase of dieselization began with the purchase of 12 GP9 model diesel-electric locomotives directly from GMD in 1957. These, too, were actually owned by Canada Southern Railway, though they were painted in the smart-looking NYC "lightning stripe" two-tone grey livery. These locomotives were numbered 6029 to 6040 in the NYC series. The last of these units was turned over to the New York Central at a ceremony in St. Thomas on 29 April 1957.[10] The remaining 14 steam locomotives were retired from service and scrapped. Plans were formulated to demolish by the year's end all remaining steam locomotive facilities. The end of the steam era on the Canada Southern Railway had arrived.

The New York Central Railroad made major changes in the routing of freight trains crossing into Canada from the Niagara Frontier. On 19 December 1960 the NYC diverted a number of freight trains away from Fort Erie to Niagara Falls. This change reduced the number of men who worked the Fort Erie's Victoria Yard from 100 to 50.[11]

In the past, the Pennsylvania and the Central had talked about merging, but nothing serious came of these discussions until the early 1960s. Early in May 1962 the Pennsylvania Railroad and the New York Central Railroad, at separate meetings of their shareholders in Philadelphia and Albany respectively, put the issue to a vote. Shareholders of both companies approved the idea. As a result the two companies established teams to co-ordinate their steps towards union, the actual merger being some years away.

This development only added to the growing rumours about a suspected abandonment of the Canada Division. Several unions and a number of municipalities voiced their concerns. The Central's repeated denials, however, were not convincing. The Board of Transport Commissioners (BTC) then announced a series of public hearings on the allegations and denials. On 14 April 1965 the BTC ruled that the NYC was obliged, under the 1878 act governing the CSR, to retain in Canada the principal departmental and other offices as well as its workshops of the Canada Southern Railway. The board further ruled that the CSR, its lessee and the sublessee were equally bound by the act, something the Central had argued against. The board did find that the rumours and complaints suggesting a complete abandonment were essentially unfounded. On the other hand, the New York Central was found to be lax in train inspection, locomotive maintenance and general shop safety. The issue of CSR abandonment was finally put to rest, however.

Meanwhile, the Central gave its attention to developing traffic from northern Ontario. The Adams Mine was being developed near Boston Creek. The iron ore traffic would travel over the Ontario Northland, Canadian National and the New York Central System to Pittsburgh and Aliquippa, Pennsylvania, and Cleveland, Ohio. This was the longest ore run of iron pellets in the world. The railways over whose trackage the traffic would flow were to contribute cars in proportion to the mileage each railway would carry the ore. The Ontario Northland, Canadian National and the New York Central System contributed ore cars in the ratio of 22:40:38. The Central's share was actually composed of ore cars from itself, the Pittsburgh & Lake Erie, and the Canada Southern. The traffic started in February 1965. The ore traffic was perhaps the last bright spot in Central's operation of the CSR.

As the 1960s wore on, the once attractive lightning stripe livery was gradually supplanted by that of a dull grey. It would not be long until the New York Central merged into the Pennsylvania Railroad. What that would hold for the Canada Southern, only time would tell.

It is about midday at Dutton, Ontario, in the summer of 1939. A U.S. Hudson, No. 5213, provides the graceful power on this occasion. — Lorne J. Hymers

The Dutton agent, Mr. L. Patterson, at his post, 1939. — Lorne J. Hymers

Yard goat No. 6992 pauses from chores in St. Thomas in 1938. — C. Gerald Elder

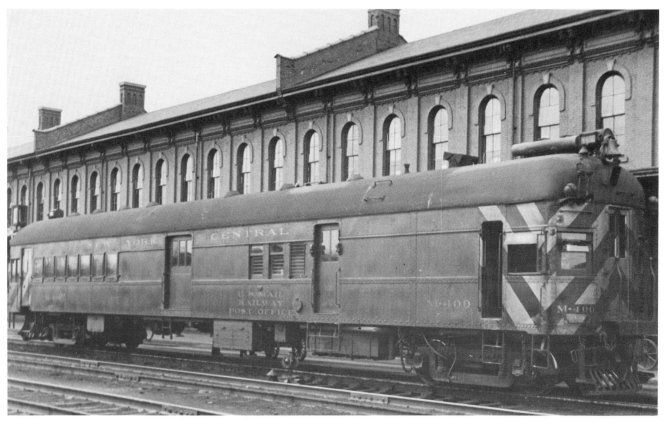

New York Central Rail motor car No. M-400 operated between St. Thomas and Fort Erie from the late 1930s well into 1940s. This 1938 view shows the gasoline-electric car at the base in St. Thomas. — C. Gerald Elder

A track-repair crew are engaged in grinding the ends of rail after the welding process. This scene is near Tillsonburg in 1938. — C. Gerald Elder

Unique in Canada was the deployment of track pans on the Michigan Central for rewatering locomotives while they were moving. This was the scene at Tillsonburg, Ontario, in 1934, looking east from the pump and boiler houses. One can see the water troughs between the rails on each track, the insulated wooden-covered conduit boxes for water (on the extreme left by the base of the telegraph pole) and for steam (between the main lines). Note the extensive use of heavy brick and stone cladding to protect the roadbed. Beneath the odd-shaped boxes at intervals along the track pans were the steam inlet connections. The troughs were one-quarter mile in length, about 18 inches wide and 6 inches deep. Water was injected at two points a quarter of the distance from each end. When the pumpman observed that the water level in front of the pump house was high enough, he shut the water off. During the winter months open steam was bled in at regular intervals to prevent freezing. The build-up of ice along the right-of-way was so severe that a gang of men was continuously employed during the cold season to chip ice away from the rails and other key areas. The marks from the workmen's picks are evident on the ties and steam conduit box. In the distance one can see the station and some maintenance buildings. — C. Gerald Elder

As viewed in April 1945 at Comber, No. 125C was typical of track-inspection cars to be found on NYC lines in Ontario. — John R. Lee

As eastbound passenger train, headed by Hudson-type No. 5228, tops up the tender tank at Tillsonburg track pans on a June day in 1938. New York Central regulations required the engineer to slow his train to 60 mph while lifting water. The scoop was pneumatically operated by the fireman upon direction from the engineer, who gave two short blasts of the whistle. The scoop was deployed for only 10 to 15 seconds. To the passenger there was neither noise nor vibration to alert him to the replenishment of water at speed. But trackside, it was noisy, wet and dangerous. All windows on the pump and boiler houses, even those 30 feet above grade, were protected with heavy screens to guard against pebbles and small stones which were frequently airborne from the pressure of splashing water. — C. Gerald Elder

New York Central ten-wheeler No. 881, in charge of a small way-freight, was photographed at Oil Springs on 10 October 1946. — John R. Lee

Mikado-type No. 2058 reverses under the coaling tower at Waterford in this 1949 scene. — Cyril A. Butcher

Extra East 2048 with 76 cars rumbles through Canfield Junction at 40 mph on 29 May 1948.
— George-Paterson Collection

Pere Marquette Mikado No. 1035 powers an eastbound general freight train along the Canada Southern at Canfield Junction on 29 May 1948.
— R.J. Sandusky Collection

This scene at Waterford, Ontario, on 1 May 1955 shows NYC Mikado No. 2030 pulling a few cars off the interchange track with the TH&B. The bridge in the upper left belongs to the Lake Erie & Northern Railway, which was having its last chartered passenger train movement on this day. Note the overhead wire. The twin track CASO main line is in the foreground. A chance showing of this picture to a fellow in Halifax brought back memories. He said that he frequented the locale as a youth, sometimes with a friend. They would test their adolescent strength and marksmanship by throwing empty soda bottles from the LE&N bridge towards the CASO track pans.

— Robert J. Sandusky

Diamonds aplenty! Here at Welland, southbound Niagara, St. Catharines & Toronto radial car No. 623 traverses three diamond crossings on 3 March 1956 en route to Port Colborne, Ontario. The rear truck is on the TH&B main line to Hamilton (to the left) while the front truck straddles the double-track CASO main line to Windsor (to the left). In the upper left background one can see the TH&B roundhouse. The freight cars in the distance (look above the radial) are on the interchange track between TH&B and NS&T. Notice the extensive interlocking rodding to protect this crossing.

— Robert J. Sandusky

Radial No. 6 of the London & Port Stanley Railway calls at the Canada Southern station in St. Thomas to interchange passengers with the New York Central train (far right). The west end of the station had two stub tracks, one of which was electrified for the L&PS. The other was a storage track for head-end cars. The curving track on the left was the only one behind the station and gave access to the NYC/CPR freight house, which can be seen in the distance. The picture was taken on 30 September 1956, the centennial of the opening of the L&PS. — Robert J. Sandusky

The days for electric operation were numbered when this view was taken in 1953. A pair of Alco-GE products, Nos. 310 and 302, emerge from the tunnel with a New York Central manifest freight at Windsor. — Thomas J. Dworman

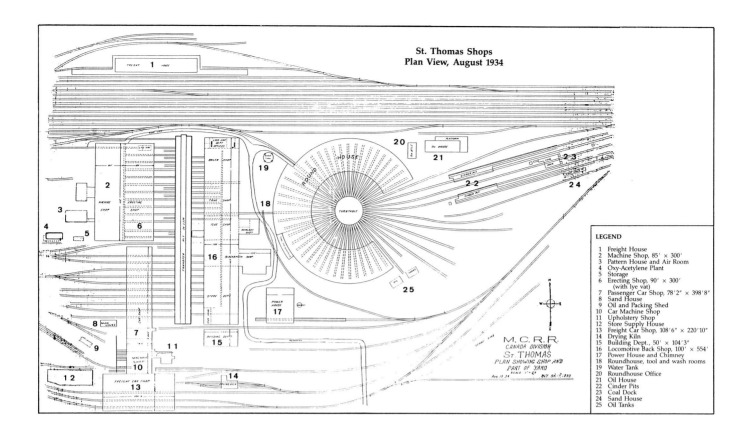

St. Thomas Shops
Plan View, August 1934

LEGEND
1 Freight House
2 Machine Shop, 85' × 300'
3 Pattern House and Air Room
4 Oxy-Acetylene Plant
5 Storage
6 Erecting Shop, 90' × 300'
7 Passenger Car Shop, 78'2" × 398'8"
    (with lye vat)
8 Sand House
9 Oil and Packing Shed
10 Car Machine Shop
11 Upholstery Shop
12 Store Supply House
13 Freight Car Shop, 108'6" × 220'10"
14 Drying Kiln
15 Building Dept., 50' × 104'3"
16 Locomotive Back Shop, 100' × 554'
17 Power House and Chimney
18 Roundhouse, tool and wash rooms
19 Water Tank
20 Roundhouse Office
21 Oil House
22 Cinder Pits
23 Coal Dock
24 Sand House
25 Oil Tanks

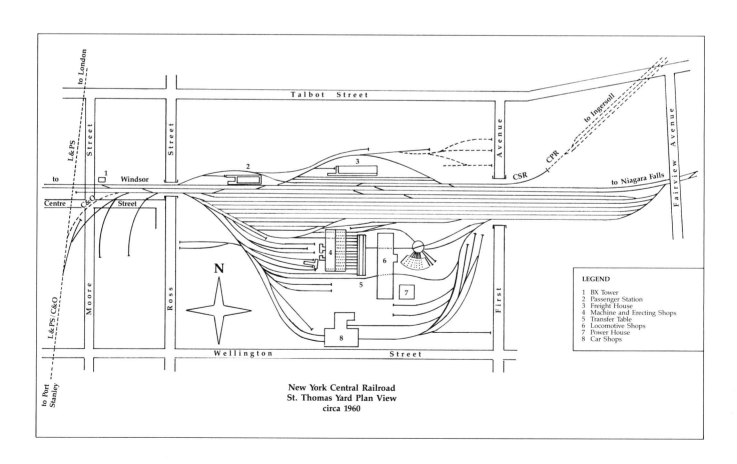

New York Central Railroad
St. Thomas Yard Plan View
circa 1960

LEGEND
1 BX Tower
2 Passenger Station
3 Freight House
4 Machine and Erecting Shops
5 Transfer Table
6 Locomotive Shops
7 Power House
8 Car Shops

146

This 0-8-0-type switcher was transferred to the Canada Division in 1954. No. 7511 was switching in the St. Thomas Yard near the station when this picture was taken. — James Walder photo, John A. Riddell Collection

NYC locomotives 1028 and 1027 power a freight through Comber on Christmas Day, 1948. — John R. Lee

The NYC St. Thomas way-freight rattles and rumbles through Kimball, Ontario, on 6 October 1956. Note the extra tender. For several years all steam-powered trains had auxiliary tenders to ensure a sufficient supply of water for the round trip.

— George-Paterson Collection

NYC No. 2043 heads a train out of Montrose Yard at Niagara Falls, Ontario, on 3 April 1953. Notice that the head-end brakeman is leaning well out of the cab to check the train while it passes through the bridge.
— George-Paterson Collection

Crowned with a billowing plume of smoke No. 2049 powers an 80-car freight train through Stevensville, Ontario on 6 March 1953.
— George-Paterson Collection

Agent's stub for weekend excursion ticket No. 36026, for travel between Windsor and Buffalo on 2 January 1959.

— Author's Collection

This view shows Ed D. Bradt at the control console in Tower No. 3 in CASO's Windsor Yard. Tower three was one of four such structures built shortly after the completion of the Detroit River Tunnel. This tower, which was demolished on 20 October 1959, stood on the site of the yard office. When the tower was opened, it housed one interlocking machine for controlling adjacent switches. When it was phased out, the tower housed three such machines and controlled switches up to one mile away.

— Picture and information from Ed D. Bradt

Canada Southern Railway began its dieselization program in January 1956 with the purchase of ten second-hand GP7-model locomotives from General Motors Diesel Limited. Following several months of operation in C&O blue-and-yellow livery, the locomotives were repainted in the St. Thomas Shops in NYC two-tone grey with lightning stripes. Zebra stripes were added to the aprons. This view shows No. 5820 at St. Thomas in November 1956.

— John D. Knowles

The NYC-operated Canada Southern station at West Lorne, Ontario, as it appeared in April 1967.
— Chris Andreae

NOTICE OF LINE ABANDONMENT

Effective 12:01 A.M. on Sunday, May 1, 1960, all train and other railroad service on the ST. CLAIR BRANCH, including the PETROLIA and OIL SPRINGS SUBDIVISIONS, being those lines of railways of The New York Central Railroad Company, and of its lessor and sub-lessor, The Michigan Central Railroad Company and The Canada Southern Railway Company, respectively, extending from St. Clair Junction, Ontario, to Courtright, Ontario; from Oil City, Ontario, to Eddy's Station, Ontario; and from Petrolia Junction, Ontario, to Petrolia, Ontario, will be DISCONTINUED and ABANDONED.

This action is authorized by ORDER No. 100227, dated January 15, 1960, of the Board of Transport Commissioners for Canada.

A ''Notice of Line Abandonment,'' such as the one shown here, was affixed to all Canada Southern buildings heretofore used for the conduct of railway business on the St. Clair Branch.
— Kenneth A.W. Gansel

This New York Central freight was photographed at Hagersville, Ontario, en route to Niagara Falls on 16 April 1965. Power on this occasion consisted of NYC 2556, CB&Q 942 and CB&Q 153.
— Bruce Chapman

Alco-built No. 1073 commands a lash-up of six locomotives on this westbound New York Central manifest freight. The train is passing BX Tower in St. Thomas and is about to enter the diamond crossing with the CN (ex-L&PS) line to Port Stanley on 30 September 1962. — Robert J. Sandusky

Four NYC Alcos, models RS32 and DL721, race eastbound with their tonnage on 8 June 1963. This scene is facing west at Waterford, just west of the interchange with the TH&B. The state of NYC maintenance on Canada Southern trackage is evident by all the raised spikes on the left foreground track. — Robert J. Sandusky

The Upper Canada Railway Society sponsored a railfan trip over the New York Central System in Ontario on 14 January 1967. The excursion covered the TH&B and the eastern part of the Canada Southern. NYC 7504 and an unidentified TH&B unit provided the power for the railfan special train shown here at Waterford, Ontario.
— John D. Thompson

The drone of five throbbing engines, led by No. 2539, announce the arrival of a lengthy New York Central freight at the swing bridge over the Welland Canal one day in 1967.
— John D. Thompson

The new Penn Central station at Welland in August 1976.

— Kenneth A.W. Gansel

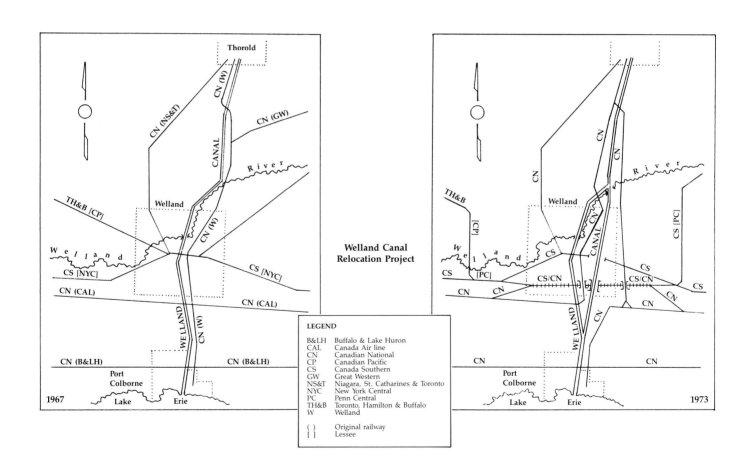

Welland Canal Relocation Project

LEGEND

B&LH	Buffalo & Lake Huron
CAL	Canada Air line
CN	Canadian National
CP	Canadian Pacific
CS	Canada Southern
GW	Great Western
NS&T	Niagara, St. Catharines & Toronto
NYC	New York Central
PC	Penn Central
TH&B	Toronto, Hamilton & Buffalo
W	Welland
( )	Original railway
[ ]	Lessee

X

HUSTLE, MUSCLE AND FIZZLE

On 1 February 1968 the New York Central Railroad Company was merged into the Pennsylvania Railroad Company, and the surviving firm took the name Pennsylvania New York Central Transportation Company. Later this enterprise divested itself of the transportation interests in a wholly owned subsidiary, the Penn Central Transportation Company, and renamed itself the Penn Central Company on 1 October 1969. It was PCT which assumed operation of the Canada Southern, continuing the sublease arrangement inherited from New York Central.

Under Penn Central's stewardship there were some changes made to the CSR physical plant, freight and passenger services, and CSR's investment portfolio. These would not, however, bring the company into the limelight. Rather, it was its corporate manoeuvrings which would awaken minority shareholders from decades of apathy and reticence. As well, it seemed to catch the regulatory authority off guard.

The principal change to the physical plant of the Canada Southern under PCT control was the Welland Canal Relocation Project. This entailed relocating the main line and a new (consolidated) yard at Welland, Ontario. By the early 1960s both water and land traffic had grown to such an extent that the Welland Canal had become a troublesome bottleneck to commerce. Ships were taking as long as 46 hours to transit the canal; at times there were as many as 50 vessels queued up to enter the canal. Railway and highway traffic fared no better, as their movement was frequently punctuated by lengthy waits at lift bridges. The Dominion Marine Association voiced strong protests against increasing congestion and decreasing safety. A railway swing bridge which had been hit as many as six times during a single season drew exceptional criticism. The bridge's central pier limited the 75-foot-wide vessels to two narrow lanes of 92 feet and 102 feet respectively. The railways, truckers, bus operators and motorists (especially tourists) had their own pet peeves. The city of Welland was advocating a four-lane highway tunnel beneath the old canal in order to relieve the traffic congestion at the city's five lift bridges. Two solutions were proposed: a lock-twinning project and a canal by-pass project. The latter was selected and three by-pass routes were studied in detail.

The various Canada Southern, Canadian National and TH&B rail lines were relocated during 1972-73 in a complicated and expensive schedule of moves. The new canal was initially to have been crossed by a high-speed lift bridge, but the construction of a tunnel soon gained favour as a superior solution. In order to have all the relevant railway lines converge at the tunnel site, it was necessary to excavate some 18 million cubic yards of earth and then grade the terrain lying east and west over 2.5 miles on either side of the tunnel site in order to ensure that the gradients not exceed 9 inches per 100 feet. The tunnel measures 1,080 feet in length, 116.5 feet in width and 35 feet in height. On the north side it contains a two-lane highway, and on the south side, a triple set of tracks. Canada Southern and Canadian National each own an outside track, while sharing ownership of the middle one. The Townsline Tunnel, as it is called, was opened to railway traffic in February 1973. It is located approximately five miles west of Welland.

As part of the Welland Canal Relocation Project, Penn Central and TH&B built a new joint yard near Welland during 1971-73, and afterwards they closed their respective separate yards. Wainfleet Yard consists of 18 tracks, a new station and a freight depot. The new yard was primarily used for traffic interchange between the two railways, although the switching trains, WM-2 and MW-1, were based there. There were two Penn Central yard assignments.

The financing of the relocation of the rail lines and of the marshalling yard was borne entirely by the St. Lawrence Seaway Authority, with Penn Central Transportation, Canadian National and TH&B railways providing the engineering work for their respective lines. The WCRP and the Wainfleet Yard were the principal changes to the railway's physical plant.

Turning to freight train operation, PCT scheduled three eastbound and five westbound through freights. Local freight service consisted of 11 trains originating in Windsor, Leamington, St. Thomas, Welland, and Montrose (Niagara Falls). The Montrose Yard was the largest and the busiest on the CSR. The yard consisted of eight classification tracks and five receiving tracks, all to handle eastbound traffic, and a six-track westbound yard. In the latter, two of the tracks were used as a Trail-Van Terminal, the only such facility on the Canada Division.[1] In addition to the PCT traffic, the C&O freights would set off and pick up cars in a small six-track yard which Chessie leased from Penn Central. The TH&B also did some switching here. There were four yard assignments to serve the TOFC ramp, the yard itself, switching in Niagara Falls and the Chippewa spur. At the other end of the division, the Windsor Yard consisted of a two-track interchange yard with the Essex Terminal Railway, a four-track interchange yard with CP Rail, a six-track receiving yard and a 17-track classification yard. The Windsor Yard provided three daily assignments for classification and industrial switching. The oldest and least busy yard was that at St. Thomas, its ten-track yard often being vacant. The locomotive shops, however, maintained 16 London-built captive units and on occasion performed some servicing for PCT American locomotives.

Passenger traffic over the Canada Southern, on the other hand, consisted of an Amtrak train, which made no stops for intra-Canada traffic, and a joint PC-TH&B-CP Rail train using rail diesel cars. The former was Amtrak's *Niagara Rainbow*, which linked New York City and Detroit via St. Thomas. It made its first regularly scheduled runs on 31 October 1974, following ceremonial runs the previous day.[2] The new service through Ontario represented an extension of the *Empire State Express*, which had been operating between New York and Buffalo. The latter, also an international run, consisted of a CP Rail-owned Budd car which was operated between Buffalo and Toronto via Welland and Hamilton, utilizing crews from three railways.

Canada Southern's investment portfolio was the least visible to the observer, but in some respects it would become the object of heated court battles, being one of the railway's few highly successful activities. Just where the money came from and what was the fund's purpose were two unanswered questions. A U.S. court decided that the money was not needed for the railway and so the money was distributed in an extraordinary and controversial dividend. Without the funds, however, rejuvenation of the Canada Southern would be not just more difficult, but that much more unlikely.

Despite the apparent preparations, Penn Central was a premature enterprise. Two short years later it was broke, a victim not of insuperable operational problems, not of horrendous financial complexities — though there were many of both — but of old-fashioned people problems. The problems started right at the top. The senior executives could not work as a team and consequently could not inspire co-operation among subordinates. The rivalry at the junior and middle levels of management was poisonous. Employees throughout the large company still identified themselves as "Central" or "Pennsy" men. There was no planning for the integration of such vital activities as waybill processing and car routings, for example. Even small things like locomotive cab amenities (NYC engines had padded armrests whereas Pennsy engines did not) became festering sores among engine crews and between dispatchers and engine crews. A century of corporate competition was deeply ingrained in both labour and management. There was no attempt to address this; indeed, it seemed not even to have been anticipated.[3] These problems were excrutiatingly real and they disrupted the new firm at virtually every level. The troubled railway giant then filed a petition in the U.S. District Court for the Eastern District of Pennsylvania on 21 June 1970 for an order to authorize the proceedings for the railway's reorganization under Section 77 of the Bankruptcy Act of the United States. The court granted the petition.

On most of its leased railways in the United States the Penn Central had already stopped making payments, but if it were to follow the same practice in Canada, the company would lose its Canadian properties by foreclosure. Penn Central had already missed its October 1970 date for the second semi-annual payment on its lease of the Canada Southern. Since it was insolvent, PCT became subject to Sections 95 and 99 of the Railway Act of Canada. In order to avoid foreclosure

Table VI

**PENN CENTRAL TRANSPORTATION COMPANY
DISTRIBUTION OF HOLDINGS OF CAPITAL
STOCK IN LEASED RAILWAY[1] AND OTHER COMPANIES[2]
IN CANADA, 1973**

Company	Group	Company's Total Stock	Penn Central Directly	Penn Central Indirectly
Canada Southern Railway Co.	1	150,000	18,100	89,163 (a)
Detroit River Tunnel Co.	1	30,000		30,000 (b)
Niagara River Bridge Co.	1	7,000		7,000 (c)
St. Lawrence & Adirondack Railway Co.	1	16,150	16,150	
Toronto, Hamilton & Buffalo Railway Co.	2	54,150	20,120	11,810 (a) 7,525 (c)
Canadian Pacific Car & Passenger Transfer Co. Ltd.	2	1,000	500	

Legend: (a) Michigan Central Railroad Co.
         (b) Michigan Central but disputed by minority CSR shareholders
         (c) Canada Southern Railway Co.

Sources: *Moody's Transportation Manual*, 1973, pp270, 290-92
         Globe and Mail, 29 May 1976
         CSR Minority Shareholders' Association, Submission to Canadian Transport
         Commission, 1976

Table VII

**PENN CENTRAL TRANSPORTATION COMPANY
SYMBOL FREIGHT BRIDGE TRAFFIC, CANADA DIVISION, 1975**

Train	Origination	Destination	Duty	Yard	Direction
MC-4	Detroit, Mich.	Selkirk, N.Y.	PU	WI	E-bd
			CC	ST	
			PU	HA	
			SO	MO	
TF-2	Toronto, Ont.	Buffalo, N.Y.	SO	MO	E-bd
TV-16	Kalamazoo, Mich.	North Bergen, N.J.	CC	ST	E-bd
BM-7	Rotterdam Jct., N.Y.	Elkhart, Ind.	CC	ST	W-bd
FMA-9	Framingham, Mass.	Detroit, Mich.	CC	ST	W-bd
FT-1	Buffalo, N.Y.	Toronto, Ont.	PU	MO	W-bd
			SO	WE	
			CC	WE	
ML-9	Little Ferry, N.J.	Detroit, Mich.	PU	MO	W-bd
			SO	ST	
			CC	ST	
TV-15	North Bergen, N.J.	Detroit, Mich.	SO	MO	W-bd
			CC	ST	

Legend: Duty   Yard
        CC Crew Change   HA Hagersville   WE Welland
        PU Pick Up   MO Montrose   WI Windsor
        SO Set Off   ST   St. Thomas

PCT paid attention to the details of the act and consequently managed to continue running its Canadian properties.

Meanwhile, Penn Central Transportation began looking for a buyer and sounded out both Canadian National and Canadian Pacific, but neither was interested. Nor was anyone else.

It was about this time that Penn Central thought of consolidating its Canadian holdings into one new subsidiary, the Canada Connecting Railway Company, upon whose behalf PCT made application to the Canadian Transport Commission for a certificate of public convenience and necessity to operate a railway. A further application was made, this time to the federal Department of Consumer and Corporate Affairs, for a charter to form a railway and purchase the relevant assets from PCT. In the United States the company sought court approval to establish such a subsidiary and further requested a decision by 8 January 1976 in order to enable PCT to comply with the U.S. government's deadline for disposal of properties if they were not to be transferred to Consolidated Rail.[4]

This prompted a group of Canada Southern's minority shareholders to announce that if Penn Central were to proceed with this proposal, they would intervene at the requisite governmental hearings. A leading spokesman for this group, Albert Segal, pointed out that the Canada Southern could be used for the purpose of "parking" PCT's Canadian properties until a decision could be rendered. He even suggested that Canada Southern buy out Penn Central's interests and resume operation in its own right.

Penn Central went ahead with its proposal to set up the Canada Connecting Railway Company, into which would be folded the "Little Four" (CSR, DRT, TH&B and St. Lawrence & Adirondack), which PCT claimed to be worth $132 million! The hearings were held and the CSR Minority Shareholders' Association argued forcefully against the proposal. The CTC agreed with much of the minority shareholders' evidence and consequently found against Penn Central Transportation early in January 1976. The Canada Connecting Railway Company was dead, but the battle for Canada Southern's future had only warmed up.

On 5 March 1976 Canada Southern surprised minority shareholders and stunned Conrail with the announcement of a $60 extraordinary dividend to be paid on March 30, two days before the rescheduled takeover by Consolidated Rail. This sent Conrail lawyers scurrying before a U.S. court to obtain an injunction to prevent PCT-controlled Canada Southern from paying the dividend. The New York Stock Exchange suspended trading of CSR stock. Congressional Representative William Walsh (Rep., N.Y.) barked his objection that CSR's proposed dividend payment was a "blatant attempt to loot the line's coffers for the enrichment of the trustees of Penn Central."[5] The U.S. court rendered a decision in favour of Penn Central on 26 March 1976, and on April 23 Canada Southern paid out $9 million (US) in extraordinary dividends to shareholders on record as of April 9. Cash-starved Penn Central had secured some desperately needed funds, but they were not enough.

So Penn Central conceived another plan whereby it could obtain further funds by selling not only its own shares in the Toronto, Hamilton & Buffalo Railway, but Canada Southern's as well. During May 1976 the trustees of PCT, the trustee of the Michigan Central Railroad, and officials of Canadian Pacific Limited signed a conditional agreement whereby CP Rail would acquire 31,930 shares of TH&B for approximately $5.4 million. Canadian Pacific would then hold 46,625 shares of the 54,150 shares outstanding. The remaining shares were held by CSR. Later in the month the Canada Southern Railway struck a deal with Canadian Pacific whereby the latter would obtain the CSR-held shares in the TH&B. Canada Southern, however, would do so without informing minority shareholders and without seeking their consent. Minority shareholders saw yet another asset of their company, one directly affecting their investment, being disposed of without their participation.

With Consolidated Rail in control, the only immediate difference was that for the first time in 93 years the word "Central" would be absent in a lessee's corporate name. Some would think that Penn Central's involvement with Canada Southern had ended, but with the trading of litigation threats (which were later exercised), such proved not to be the case. Perhaps purchase of CSR stock in the marketplace might prove the simplest means to minimize any unfavourable judgement which might arise from the Canada Southern's pressing the issue of alleged breaches of the lease. Only time would tell whether the Penn Central would deem it wise to become a shareholder again.

Consolidated Rail Corporation was now the new principal shareholder. A new chapter in Canada Southern's story had begun.

Table VIII

CANADA SOUTHERN RAILWAY COMPANY
SCHEDULE OF FREIGHT ROLLING STOCK
SHOWING TYPE AND QUANTITY FOR THE PERIOD 1875 to 1975

Type of Car	1875	1880	1885	1890	1895	1900	1905	1910	1915	1920	1925	1930	1935	1940	1945	1950	1955	1960	1965	1970	1975
Box – general	692	1932	2328	2500	2738	3203	1660	1423	1586	1388	770	723	717	331	296	291	256	108	3	0	0
Blue Line							1	0	0	0	0	0	0	0	0	0	0	0	0	0	0
CS Line							104	0	0	0	0	0	0	0	0	0	0	0	0	0	0
Carriage							3	0	0	0	0	0	0	0	0	0	0	0	0	0	0
Flat	198	501	424	427	473	327	111	113	62	19	3	150	150	148	146	144	115	0	0	0	0
Gondola							59	71	46	17	1	0	0	0	0	0	0	0	0	0	0
Hopper			69	73	66	156	118	38	8	0	0	0	0	0	0	8	15	3	3	3	1
Reefer					34	34	0	0	0	0	0	0	0	0	0	0	0	0	0	0	0
Stock	73	153	158	299	314	276	82	26	2	0	0	0	0	0	0	0	0	0	0	0	0
Tank		8	40	34	42	35	35	34	22	6	1	0	0	0	0	0	0	0	0	0	0
Van	24	54	95	78	80	85	73	75	69	65	69	67	67	61	64	64	59	52	14	9	0
Totals	987	2648	3114	3411	3747	4116	2246	1780	1795	1495	844	940	934	540	506	507	445	163	20	12	1

Sources: 1875 – estimate based on CSR AR 1877
1880 to 1900 – CSR AR
1905 to 1925 – Official Railway Equipment Register
1930 to 1950 – Statistics of Steam Railways of Canada
1955 to 1975 – Railway Transport

Note: The figures for hopper cars for 1950 onwards should be treated with caution because of discrepancies in sources.

The Penn Central operated some unusual equipment in Canada. On a chilly day at the end of November 1971 this ex-NYC self-propelled Rail Detector Car, No. X-6015, was caught working the eastbound main track at Ridgetown.

— Michael P. McIlwaine

Westbound PC symbol freight train BM-7 pulls 100 cars past the 665-foot-high Panasonic Tower in Niagara Falls, Ontario, on 16 November 1975.
— Gary S. Daniels

Penn Central freight CL-1, the Leamington Local, crosses a road south of Comber, Ontario, on 26 July 1975.
— Gary S. Daniels

The Chippawa Local departs Montrose Yard with one hopper car which is destined for the nearby Ford Motor Company of Canada plant. The picture was taken on 15 November 1975.   — Gary S. Daniels

This scene at Comber in September 1976 shows Conrail crews interchanging cars between train WX-2 (on the main) and train LC-2 (on the siding).   — Kenneth A.W. Gansel

This July 1976 view shows the abandoned and extensively vandalized E&O tower as seen from the CASO tracks. The name comes from the Erie & Ontario Railway, which was chartered in 1914 to build from Port Maitland to Smithville, Ontario. It was acquired by the TH&B.
— Kenneth A.W. Gansel

The only component of the CSR for which there is some commemoration is the Erie & Ontario Railroad. In October 1931 the Stamford Township Council erected an attractive stone cairn on Morrison Street, at its intersection with Stanley Avenue in Niagara Falls, Ontario. The cairn is adjacent to Oakes Park.

An August 1972 view of the Penn Central station in Tillsonburg showing the west and south faces of the building.
— Kenneth A.W. Gansel

CASO Interlocking Tower WX stands guard at the intersection of the company's main line and that of TH&B at Welland, Ontario. Note the train order stand. The upper hoop would hold the orders for the engineer. The lower would hold those for the conductor.

— William R. Linley

Many a station along the CASO line had a sign like this one affixed to it.

— Kenneth A.W. Gansel

THE
FREIGHT AGENT FOR THIS STATION
IS LOCATED AT
ST.THOMAS, ONTARIO
FOR FREIGHT INFORMATION
Phone ZENITH - 74440
" TOLL-FREE "

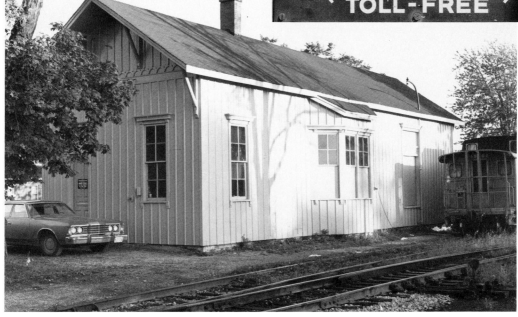

This diminutive structure is the CASO-owned, Conrail-operated station in Leamington, Ontario. Train crews would occasionally lay over in the van.

— Kenneth A.W. Gansel

On occasion the St. Thomas shops performed work for PC's American operations. In 1971 the shops rebuilt this Penn Central switcher, No. 8849, for Detroit. — Larry Broadbent

This Chessie freight train, powered by units 3039 and 3538, has just come off the International Bridge from Buffalo. The train has moved to the north side of the yard throat to enter CASO trackage in Fort Erie en route to St. Thomas, where the train will access C&O trackage. — William R. Linley

These proud shopmen stand beside No. 7438 for this informal 1972 portrait photographed by a co-worker.

— Larry Broadbent

A southbound van hop with TH&B Geeps 76 and 403 crosses the diamonds with the Canada Southern on 31 July 1976.

— Kenneth A.W. Gansel

The Niagara Rainbow, *Amtrak train 64, exiting Canada by the Niagara River Bridge Company's double-tracked steel-arch bridge on 29 December 1978. In the left background one can see a trio of RDC being passed by a CN freight which also is bound for the U.S. over the CNR bridge (the grey band to the right of the Amtrak locomotive).*

— Kenneth A.W. Gansel

XI

AN UNCERTAIN FUTURE

Black and Blue Railroading

On April Fool's Day 1976 Consolidated Rail Corporation assumed operating responsibilities for the Canada Southern Railway. As the manager and principal owner, Conrail gradually introduced changes in operations and physical plant which effectively contributed to a downgrading of the line. The minority shareholders regarded such downgrading as a devaluation of their investment and they were quick to allege that Conrail was not exercising fiduciary responsibility. Conrail let it be known that it wanted to consolidate its Canadian holdings into a wholly owned subsidiary, something which minority shareholders stridently opposed. It was all so familiar. The battle lines were drawn and before long there would be a resumption of the protracted public hearings and extended discussions with the regulatory authority, a struggle the likes of which had not been seen in Canadian railway regulation history. The short-term result was that the CTC directed Conrail to operate CSR under interim orders, make certain changes and report back to the Canadian Transport Commission, which would review the matter and make a final decision.

Before long, there seemed to be a new and disturbing pattern to train traffic over the Canada Southern. Traffic was decreased, rerouted or cancelled. Passenger train operation consisted of two Amtrak conventional-type trains and two rail-diesel-car-type trains operated jointly among Conrail, TH&B and CP Rail.

The first change in the former occurred during 1978, when the stop at Fort Erie for the *Niagara Rainbow* was eliminated. After the states of Michigan and New York had announced that they were going to eliminate subsidies (which were covering over 50 percent of the operating costs), Amtrak announced that it would discontinue the service. On Wednesday, 31 January 1979 the *Niagara Rainbow* made its last run.[1] Some claimed that the lack of advertising in Ontario had contributed to the train's demise, but that was perhaps a moot point. The Canadian government paid no subsidy towards the cost of operating the train in Canada since, as an Amtrak spokesman revealed, the CTC regarded the service as merely linking U.S. points. On the occasion of its final run, only two passengers boarded the train at Windsor. The *Niagara Rainbow* was dead at the young age of four years and two months.

Later in 1979 it was learned that the U.S. Department of Transportation had recommended that the *North Shore Limited* operate through southern Ontario.[2] Subsequent to that recommendation, however, a study disclosed that the original running-time goals could not be achieved over Canada Southern's line on account of the inadequate trackwork. The rerouting of that train via Ontario was postponed indefinitely pending the successful negotiation of a contract with Conrail and the development of the requisite trackwork.

Long-distance passenger-train traffic over the Canada Southern had lasted just over the century. Trains serving a portion of the CASO route seemed to face an equally bleak future. The CTC had yet to deliver its decision of the PCT-TH&B-CP Rail application to discontinue the RDC train. Then it came. The railways could discontinue the service in the spring of 1981. On Saturday, 25 April 1981, following 90 years of continuous service, the Buffalo–Toronto train made its last run.[3] The curtain had fallen on the nation's longest-running existing international passenger train and, with it, passenger train service over Canada Southern rails had come to an end after 108 years.

In the meantime, freight train traffic was faring no better. Between April 1976 and June 1977 abolitions and reroutings of Conrail freights had reduced Canadian jobs for locomotive drivers and firemen by 38.[4] In July 1979 Conrail cut its last through freight train from the CASO route, choosing instead to run the train through the United States.[5] These developments led to renewed charges by minority shareholders of breaches of the lease. Local freight service consisted of a western section train shuttling between Windsor and St. Thomas, the Leamington Branch train to service the big Heinz plant, and a shuttle train between St. Thomas and Hagersville in the eastern section. There was some industrial switching based in the Montrose Yard, and there was just the hint of service between Buffalo and Fort Erie.

The only long-distance trains to be found on the Canada Southern were those of the Chessie System, which held trackage rights from St. Thomas eastward.

In order to further reduce its operating expenditures in Ontario, Conrail planned to reduce the western division of the line between St. Thomas and Windsor to a single-track secondary line which would be unsignalled west of St. Thomas. The westbound main was already "temporarily" out of service and portions of it were used for the storage of freight cars (the very same thing the New York Central had done with the E&O line prior to abandoning it). The remaining line, i.e. the then present eastbound main, would have the zone speed reduced from 60 to 30 mph.

Concerns for the future of the Canada Southern were now beginning to be voiced by Conrail's Canadian employees, who were fearing for their jobs. The suspicion lingered, and the rumours persisted, that Conrail wanted out of its rail properties (but not the real estate holdings), which the CSR owned. At home, Conrail was being pressured to save money, save U.S. jobs and use U.S. taxpayers' money to generate or at least safeguard American employment. It did not need the headaches that this little-known foreign railway was generating. So obscure was the Canada Southern Railway that even the Ontario Securities Commission at first denied (later retracted) the existence of such a company. But this obscurity was not to last.

Canada Southern's annual meeting in 1976 was a bitter and stormy event. Admittedly, Conrail officials had had only 63 days — and the new board less than a month, having taken office on May 17 — to familiarize themselves with the contentious problems which had been 63 years in the making. The meeting catapulted the 108-year-old firm into the limelight with the Canadian Transport Commission, the daily newspapers, the financial press and railway enthusiasts. The grievances, real or perceived, had been decades in the making and they had developed because of stockholder acquiescence, deficient securities legislation and understaffed regulatory supervision.

Conrail had made application in March 1976 for a certificate of public convenience and necessity in preparation for setting up Consolidated Rail Corporation of Canada Limited, a wholly owned subsidiary. This firm would acquire Conrail's various Canadian holdings, but it would really acquire only those assets which Conrail chose to impart. The parent company could insulate itself from any liabilities which the subsidiary might encounter pending developments of minority shareholders' allegations. In addition, Conrail would have to obtain approval from the Foreign Investment Review Agency in order to set up a Canadian subsidiary which would be acquiring Canadian assets.

For the most part, the elimination of passenger service involved other carriers and did not affect the company's lease. But the reduction and subsequent termination of international freight traffic had serious legal implications for Conrail's retention of the Canada Southern. It contributed to labour problems with its Canadian employees and fostered ill will in some communities. What is more, it did not seem to follow the company's initial commitment to improve the roadbed and certain other facilities. In fact, during 1977 Conrail had spent nearly $7 million (US) on tie replacement for 58 miles, replacing rail on 3 miles of line and resurfacing 128 miles of track. This upgrading activity continued into 1978, when the railway spent $4.7 million for the resurfacing of 33 miles of track and installation of over 19,000 ties covering 25 miles of track.

Meanwhile, Canada Southern concluded an agreement with Canadian Pacific to sell it the 7,525 shares of the TH&B which the CSR owned. The price was $156.54 per share and the sale was completed on 19 April 1977.[6]

The public hearings, which had been ordered in response to Conrail's application to set up a subsidiary, were completed with the usual sparks between the majority and minority parties. But several years had passed in the process. In 1980 the CTC handed down its decision. It had decided not to make a final determination! Conrail was permitted to continue operating the CSR

Diagram I

SCHEMATIC DIAGRAM OF CONRAIL'S INHERITANCE OF
FINANCIAL INTERESTS IN CANADA SOUTHERN RAILWAY, 1976

Source: Based on diagram in CTC Decision 14 March 1980 re Conrail and Canada Southern

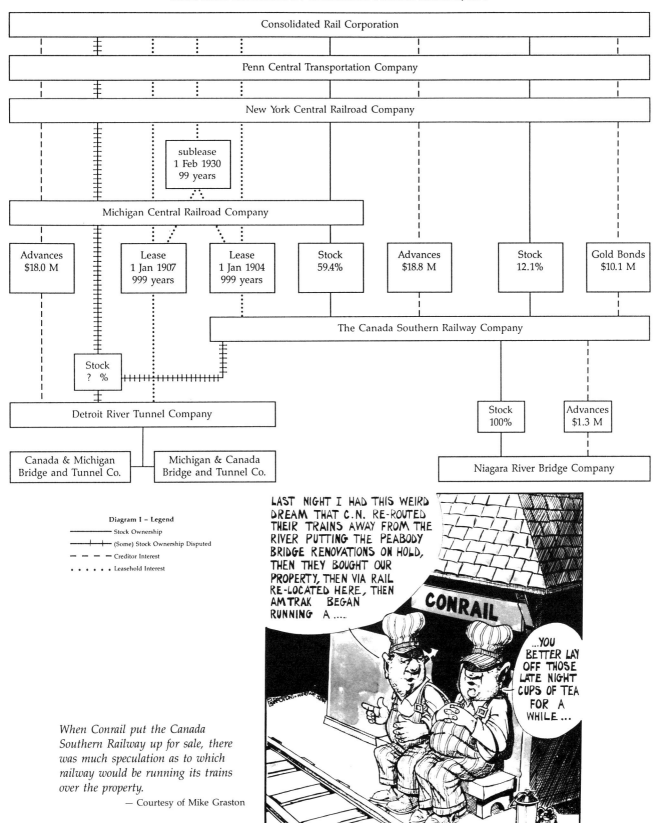

Diagram I – Legend

————	Stock Ownership
—+—+—	(Some) Stock Ownership Disputed
– – –	Creditor Interest
• • • • •	Leasehold Interest

When Conrail put the Canada Southern Railway up for sale, there was much speculation as to which railway would be running its trains over the property.
— Courtesy of Mike Graston

Photographed entering Montrose Yard at Niagara Falls on 1 February 1979, this train was a return movement for the equipment of the last westbound Niagara Rainbow *on the previous day.*

— Kenneth A.W. Gansel

Amtrak's Canadian service lasted four years and two months. The Niagara Rainbow *made its last trip on Wednesday, 31 January 1979, but two passengers boarded the train at Windsor on that day. The last passenger was Father Thomas Mailloux, who is shown here boarding amidst chilling sleet.*

— The Windsor *Star*

(its bridge subsidiary, the tunnel company and the unrelated St. Lawrence & Adirondack Railway). It was required to submit a plan of operation for the Canada Southern, and it was to submit within 90 days a written plan to ameliorate the operations and accounting practices for the CSR, together with a projected time frame within which the required changes could reasonably be carried out. Conrail requested and was granted a 60-day extension within which to file its response to the CTC's interim decision.

On 13 August 1981 the Canadian Transport Commission delivered its long-awaited decision. Conrail could not acquire the properties it wanted until it satisfied the Commission's concerns about employees, shippers, accounting practices, unresolved negotiations with the St. Lawrence Seaway Authority and other public interests. In an unusual parting broadside, the Commission declared that it would not countenance nor permit the possible demise of the Canada Southern in favour of speculative real estate gain. This criticism had probably arisen out of the CTC's unhappiness with the reduction of train service despite Conrail's earlier formal assurances to the contrary and because of the startling discovery that, contrary to what Conrail was stating, its Canadian properties, with the sole exception of the CSR, were in fact making money. The CTC's stinging criticism included such words as "inaccurate," "improperly prepared," and "unrepresentative" with reference to the financial reports for the Detroit River Tunnel Company, the Niagara River Bridge Company, and the StL&A. The Commission stated that CASO, too, would have been profitable if overhead trains had not been diverted.

Another area of concern was that of income tax. During the investigation and analysis, it was ascertained that since 1963 none of NYC, PCT nor Conrail had paid federal or Ontario income tax, a breach of the lease agreement. Yet during this same 20-year period, all four railways had been profitable.

If it had not been clear before, it certainly was now: Conrail would have to make significant changes to how its subsidiaries conducted their business affairs and make substantial commitments in money and manpower to upgrade the Canada Southern, or it would have to sell its interests in these properties. Mindful of its pressing obligations at home, Conrail decided to seek buyers for its Canadian properties.

A Railway for Sale

On 27 August 1981 the Canada Southern Railway disclosed to its minority shareholders that it had begun discussions concerning the sale of its rail properties.[7] Canadian National and Canadian Pacific were known to be possible purchasers, but there were others. Via Rail Canada and the Grand Trunk Corporation had been contacted, but discussions evidently did not proceed beyond a preliminary stage.[8] Generally it seemed most probable that the Chesapeake & Ohio Railway, which had been an intervener in the original hearings, would be a serious purchaser. Chessie had trackage rights on the eastern portion of the CASO line, and acquisition would be a logical step to buttress its own interests. There was the possibiiity, at least for a while, of Guilford Transportation Industries (GTI) being a contender. The CSR would have been a logical extension of GTI's Delaware & Hudson, whose through trackage rights reached Buffalo. Guilford, however, did not have the financial resources to battle either of the two large Canadian roads, and when they indicated that they were more interested, Guilford bowed out.[9] The owners of Essex Terminal Railway, Conrail's Canadian employees, the Government of Ontario and CASO minority shareholders were mentioned, if only briefly, as potential buyers. A key question was just how serious might any of these be? And were there any other potential buyers who for the moment were content to remain out of the limelight?

In the midst of much conjecture the *Toronto Star* reported in mid-September 1982 that Conrail had struck a deal with CN and CP jointly, subject to shareholder and regulatory approvals. But as of December 1982 Canada Southern had still not apprised its own shareholders of any deal, conditional or otherwise, for the sale of the company.

Early in 1983 there was a U.S. Reorganizational Court ruling concerning the extraordinary dividend of $60(US), the funds for which were being held in escrow. The parties were given six months to obtain a ruling under Canadian law as to whether any of CSR's claims were appropriate for disposal. The Ontario Supreme Court heard the case promptly and ruled late in December

1983 in favour of Canada Southern.[10] This development served to heat up the battle between Conrail and Penn Central.

Autumn 1983 brought a surprising development. The Penn Central Corporation set up under Delaware registry a wholly owned subsidiary known as CSR Holdings, Inc. On 11 October 1983 CSR Holdings made an offer to purchase non-Conrail shares of Canada Southern Railway at $220(US) per share (approximately $271(CDN) at the 6 October 1983 exchange rate). That offer was scheduled to expire on November 8, but on that date the offer was extended until November 22. It had been conditional upon the securing of 28,000 shares, but CSR Holdings quickly wrestled away 32,314 shares, or 21.5 percent of CASO's capital stock, from jittery minority shareholders. The stated objective was to improve Penn Central's position in negotiating with Canada Southern Railway the protracted lease litigation and auxiliary proceedings.[11]

Meanwhile, the required public hearings had been delayed until 1984 on account of the unusually high level of public interest. Despite the agreement, it was still possible for another purchaser to come forward at the hearings and be successful.

Under the agreement between Conrail and CNCP, the former was to cause the Canada Southern to be continued under the Canada Business Corporations Act (CBCA) rather than the Railway Act. The objective was to deal out those minority shareholders who could not be bought out. Under the CBCA the shareholder who purchases 90 percent of a company can foreclose on the holders of the remaining 10 percent. The CSR board passed the resolution in March 1984 and the company received its Articles of Continuance from the Department of Consumer and Corporate Affairs the following June.

That same month the Montreal Stock Exchange announced the suspension of trading in the company's stock pending an important announcement. On 8 August 1984 Canada Southern reached a tentative agreement with Penn Central and Conrail. On August 22 the company announced that it had concluded an understanding with Penn Central, Conrail, Canadian National and Canadian Pacific whereby the parties intended to settle litigation and related proceedings as part of the corporate reorganization process.[12]

Penn Central proposed the purchase of the remaining seven percent of shares outstanding for $500 each and Canada Southern proposed to reclassify those extant shares as preferred shares and then redeem them at $500. Shareholders would be given a choice between the two proposals, depending upon the tax implications for each shareholder. Various administrative difficulties delayed the requisite documentation to implement the settlement and deferred the calling of the special shareholders' meeting as well.

Canada Southern's obscurity combined with deficient legal research to create a classic land deal problem. The St. Lawrence Seaway Authority was anxious for Canada Southern's tangled affairs to be sorted out so that the Authority might receive title to a chunk of Welland River waterfront land. The Crown corporation had paid about $1 million to Penn Central for the land which was needed to straighten out a sharp bend in the river, as part of the Welland Canal Relocation Project. When the Authority tried to obtain title, it was very surprised and upset to discover that the lands were registered with Canada Southern, not Penn Central. But Canada Southern had not even been consulted about the sale of its property![13] The railway filed a claim against the Seaway Authority for compensation of $1.1 million (plus interest) arising out of the 1971 relocation of the company's railway line as part of the WCRP.[14] The St. Lawrence Seaway Authority has thus far not been able to get a Fundamental Agreement document signed with Penn Central, Michigan Central and Canada Southern because of the bankruptcies of the two American railways and the formation of Conrail.[15] The Seaway Authority petitioned the CTC to render a conditional decision which would bind Conrail or any other successor to honour the Fundamental Agreement, but the CTC declined to do so, saying it had no such authority. The litigation between CASO and the two American railways added to the tangle.

Whether there would be a future for the Canada Southern Railway remained very much in doubt. It appeared that abandonment or absorption would be the more probable outcome awaiting this historic international bridge line.

Table IX

THE CANADA SOUTHERN RAILWAY COMPANY
APPROXIMATE HIGH AND LOW ANNUAL MARKET VALUES OF
CAPITAL STOCK FOR THE YEARS 1963 to 1983

Year	High	Low	Year	High	Low
1963	55	50	1974	34	$30^5/_8$
1964	55	$49^3/_4$	1975	$43^3/_8$	$36^7/_8$
1965	57	$53^3/_4$	1976*	$70^1/_3$	$32^1/_2$ to 30 Sept.
1966	57	53		39	$33^3/_4$ from 1 Oct.
1967	$61^3/_4$	$54^3/_4$	1977	$40^5/_8$	$36^1/_8$
1968	$68^3/_8$	$55^1/_8$	1978	44	36
1969	64	50	1979	120	41
1970	52	32	1980	90	55
1971	40	33	1981	85	64
1972	43	33	1982	115	61
1973	$34^3/_8$	$30^1/_2$	1983	265	95

*Amounts are in U.S. dollars until 30 Sept. 1976, and in Canadian dollars thereafter.

Sources: *Moody's Transportation Manual,* 1973
Canada Southern Railway, Annual Reports, various years

Ever since railway box cars and chalk found each other, there has been no shortage of graffiti. When Consolidated Rail Corporation was established in the wake of Penn Central Transportation, a trackside pundit pronounced his verdict on a freight car. The car was photographed on the Canada Division.
— Herb MacDonald

Despite the lack of snow, it's wintertime. The Niagara Rainbow *arrives in Windsor on a cold December day in 1977 en route to New York City. Amtrak No. 462 leads a four-car consist past an audience: the photographer and a youth with his bicycle.* — Byron C. Babbish

Amtrak's train 64 stops at the St. Thomas Station on 29 July 1976. — Kenneth A.W. Gansel

Amtrak train 64, the Niagara Rainbow, *rolls eastbound on the Canada Southern on 7 October 1977 behind locomotive No. 405. The location is the Grand River Bridge at Cayuga, Ontario.* — Robert J. Sandusky

Amtrak train 64 with a five-car consist zips along spritely en route to Buffalo. The Townline Tunnel near Welland can be seen in the background. The outer tracks are owned by either Canada Southern or Canadian National; the middle track is jointly owned. This photo was taken on 27 May 1977. — Kenneth A.W. Gansel

An overhead crane suspends Conrail locomotive No. 7435 during intermediate overhaul in the St. Thomas shops during December 1977.
— St. Thomas *Times-Journal*

Conrail Geep 5826 awaits heavy repairs to its prime mover in the St. Thomas shops. — Michael P. McIlwaine

This interior view of the St. Thomas shops shows a Penn Central road-switcher locomotive undergoing repairs.

— Kenneth A.W. Gansel

Freshly painted Geeps 5823 and 5824 stand outside the St. Thomas shops by the transfer table on 5 January 1981.

— Greg McDonnell

The former CASO station at Fargo, Ontario, has been relocated to a farmer's field near the Conrail line and given a new life as shown in this October 1976 picture.
— Kenneth A.W. Gansel

The former Canada Southern Railway station at Amherstburg as it appeared in September 1976. The building has been converted to an arts and crafts shop.
— Kenneth A.W. Gansel

This once magnificent brick structure housed the headquarters of the CSR, the St. Thomas Station, and an elegant dining room. When this October 1976 view was taken, the building, partially used, housed the station and the divisional offices of Conrail.
— Kenneth A.W. Gansel

The second Canada Southern roundhouse in St. Thomas was demolished during October 1978.

— St. Thomas *Times-Journal*

This interior view of BX Tower on 29 July 1976 shows the operator watching the approaching train to which he has given information. In the foreground is a battery of levers, each one of which is connected to rods which radiate from the building at ground level. — Kenneth A.W. Gansel

Penn Central locomotive No. 5824 enters a short siding to fetch a car for interchange with the Canadian Pacific. The freight shed at the right is an original CASO building. On the far side the CPR line (ex-Credit Valley) leaves the CSR and heads (left) to Ingersoll, Ontario.
— Kenneth A.W. Gansel

Conrail train CP-1 headed by ex-PC No. 6143 charges out of the Detroit-Windsor tunnel on 27 September 1976.
— Kenneth A.W. Gansel

On a cold day in February 1978, C&O train 41 accelerates out of Montrose Yard behind a trio of Chessie locomotives.
— Kenneth A.W. Gansel

This modified Jordan spreader was on the front of a Conrail work train at Rodney, Ontario. — Kenneth A.W. Gansel

On 9 June 1984 the Bluewater chapter of the National Railway Historical Society conducted a railfan trip from Detroit to St. Thomas. Two Chessie System B&O Geeps, No. 6504 leading, bring the Royal Canadian *excursion train up the 1.4 percent grade from the Detroit River Tunnel to a stop at Conrail's Windsor Station.*

— John D. Thompson

XII

BLOWING THE WHISTLE

The Suitors Queue Up

Both Canadian National and Canadian Pacific had held discussions with Conrail late in the 1970s, but these talks proved to be fruitless since neither of the major carriers was really that interested. Virtually all the Canada Southern trackage represented a duplication of their own lines. Five years later, however, both big railways were becoming quite interested. Neither could risk the other acquiring the Canada Southern; that might cause some competition. An independent and aggressive CSR might cause even more competition. During June 1982 CN and CP joined forces to commence formal negotiations with Consolidated Rail Corporation. CNCP pressed very hard for concessions which bordered on deal-breakers. Later in the summer, after the outstanding issues were resolved, CP Rail issued word from its Toronto regional office that it had formed a partnership with CN under the name CNCP Niagara–Detroit, which was to be headquartered in Toronto. Through the partnership they would acquire the Detroit River Tunnel Company outright and controlling interest of the CSR. This agreement was subject to Conrail and CSR entering into a mutually acceptable agreement, subject to CSR stockholder approval, and subject to American and Canadian regulatory approvals. If they were successful in acquiring Canada Southern, they would expect that all existing obligations and carry-over liabilities would be discharged. Perhaps these were the very matters over which the deal had nearly failed.

The issue which had brought CN and CP to the bargaining table for Canada Southern was the impasse in the negotiations with the city of Windsor. The key issues during the extended negotiations were the waterfront lands and the Powell Siding dispute. The city of Windsor had been adamant on certain issues which it considered essential for its own future development. The principal points of contention had been CN's waterfront yard (26 acres), CP Rail's Crawford Yard (also on the waterfront), the Peabody Bridge, and the long-standing and extremely divisive Powell Siding issue. During June 1983 the two railways told the city that it must pay $3 million and accept the re-opening of the Powell Siding issue as the price for the removal of railway tracks from the eastside waterfront. If the city should refuse, the railway yards would simply stay put and the old Peabody Bridge would have to be replaced at considerable expense. There would very definitely be no land available from the railways for subsequent development into municipal parklands. But the Windsor city council voted unanimously against trading off the Powell Siding problem for the waterfront property. There the impasse remained. The railways looked at their options. The Sarnia option provided for the continuation of the status quo in Windsor and the concentration of future railway development in Sarnia. The Windsor option involved a variety of scenarios based on relocating railway yards in the greater Windsor area, but these had already been examined and they were not mutually acceptable. The two Canadian railways bristled with objections and with threats to stay where they were, and basically told the city to forget any dreams of riverside parklands. The railways and the city simply could not agree on how to resolve the problem.

It could not have come at a better time. The region's third major carrier was vacating the area. It had a well-situated but under-utilized yard in Windsor. The solution to the Windsor enigma now seemed obvious: simply buy the Canada Southern. This was the thinking behind the formation of the partnership.

The partnership agreement was dated 18 April 1983.[1] On the very same day CNCP concluded a purchase agreement with Consolidated Rail Corporation.[2] CNCP would acquire the Detroit River Tunnel, Conrail's interest in CASO, various leasehold interests, certain debts, assorted equipment (but excluding any rolling stock or locomotives), supplies, contracts and licences. The agreement included stringent provisions for mutual indemnification.

The CNCPND (CNCP Niagara-Detroit) proposal lends itself to discussion as three segments. The western segment was made up of the tunnel, the CASO Windsor Yard, and the main line between Windsor and Fargo. There was initially no intention of enlarging the tunnel in order to accommodate large dimensional equipment such as high-cube box cars and TOFC cars. Canadian National proposed to spend $16.3 million on its share of rejuvenating, enlarging and enhancing the Windsor Yard. This work would consist of the east and west classification yards, the Sarnia international traffic tracks, transfer of the Walkerville intermodal facility, conversion and expansion of yard signalling, and the provision of necessary roadways and service facilities. CN further proposed to construct $9-million locomotive and car shops to maintain 24 locomotives and service 14,500 car repairs.[3] Improvements to the Windsor–Fargo main line would cost another $5 million. CNR's projected capital investments to CASO property totalled $31.6 million. In addition, there would be CP Rail's share of the CASO yard project of $7 million, all for assorted trackwork.

In connection with the CN/GTW Toronto–Cincinnati fast freight service proposal, Canadian National planned extensive trackwork enhancement at both Fargo and Chatham, costing an estimated $2.2 million. At the latter point, CN planned to build a 1,700-foot connecting spur between McGregor's Creek and Park Avenue area to link with the C&O line. A similar short track would be required where the north-south C&O line and the CASO line intersect. These connecting tracks would permit CN to route westbound traffic into Windsor over the Canada Southern line. Eastbound traffic would go to Fargo on the CSR line, thence north to Chatham, and from there eastward on the CN line, by-passing St. Thomas. Consequently, the middle portion of the CASO line would not be required, and it can be expected to be abandoned after a reasonable grace period.

The main line between Fargo and Hewitt (Welland), the St. Thomas shops, and the Leamington Branch comprise the middle segment. This portion of the CSR generated the least traffic, and what traffic was generated was largely concentrated in the St. Thomas area. The St. Thomas Yard would be maintained. Originally, the St. Thomas shops were to have been closed,[4] but CN has since decided that it will use them as the new location for its Work Equipment repair shops, which were previously housed in congested and inadequate facilities at Danforth in Toronto. CN proposed to transfer 64 people from that location to the new one, but in itself such a move would not benefit former Conrail employees who worked in the St. Thomas shops. The Leamington Branch would be abandoned and the town would be served via the C&O line from Fargo under an agreement which had already been concluded.[5] For the near future, CNCP planned to maintain the way freight service, based in St. Thomas. Much of the existing traffic was already interchanged with either CN or CP, both of which had separate access to the town. There appeared to be no plans for the old CSR headquarters building and so, presumably, despite its architectural significance, it faced the prospect of demolition.

The eastern segment consists of the modern Wainfleet Yard (a joint property with TH&B), the branch line between Welland and Fort Erie, the main line between Welland and Niagara Falls, the Montrose Yard, and the international railway bridge. There were no major capital improvements envisioned for this portion of CASO property.

During April 1984 there occurred two significant developments. On Tuesday, April 17, CP Rail dramatically announced that it would move its Powell Siding conditional upon the city withdrawing its opposition to CP being party to the acquisition of the Canada Southern and conditional upon the purchase of the CSR. The very next day the federal government announced that the Department of Public Works would exchange land in Ottawa with Canadian National in Windsor. The Peabody Bridge was scheduled to be removed, subject to funding from the Regional Transportation Assistance Program (assuming Cabinet approval). These prospects also depended upon CN being successful in acquiring the CSR.

The awaited public notice on the final hearings concerning the Canada Southern appeared in the *Globe and Mail* on 26 May 1984. Initially, there were to have been four days of hearings,

Mr. David Flett poses beside the control consol for the Detroit River Tunnel inside the Windsor Station.

— The Windsor *Star*

The Canada Southern Employees Association held a news conference on Monday, 29 November 1982 in St. Thomas with regard to the sale of the CSR. Robert Beer (left), local chairman of the United Transport Union-Trainman, Dorval C. Fox (centre), local protective chairman of the Canadian Division of the Brotherhood of Railway, Airline and Steamship Clerks, and Charles Beckett (right), office chairman for the American Train Dispatchers Association expressed concerns that a sale to CNCP would entail closure of the St. Thomas shops and a reduction of the overall level of employment on the CSR line.

— St. Thomas *Times-Journal*

Resplendent in their blue-and-white livery, a trio of Conrail locomotives power their westbound local freight across the Kettle Creek Bridge on 9 July 1982. — Byron C. Babbish

The crossing of the Welland River provided the locale for this dramatic night shot of the westbound Conrail freight headed by No. 7438 at 20:30 on 22 December 1981. Four type 2 flashbulbs were used to take this picture. — Greg McDonnell

but the issues proved to be so complex and contentious that several additional hearing dates were added. The Railway Transport Committee took the unusual step of conducting a lengthy pre-hearing conference on Tuesday, 29 May 1984, at the Elgin Auditorium in St. Thomas, in order to set out the guidelines for the hearings themselves and to address other issues.[6]

By this time, CN and CP were not the only firms expressing interest in the Canada Southern Railway. Among the companies who were suitors, none had a backer quite like that of Cantunn, Inc. Its name a contraction for "Canada Tunnel," Cantunn was the brainchild of flamboyant Detroit businessman Albert Atwell, who had been involved in various transportation companies in the United States. Atwell had sold Intermodal Systems, Inc. in order to finance the preliminary stages of Cantunn.

Originally, Cantunn was backed by Penfund Management Limited, which was prepared to provide 80 percent of the requisite financing. Penfund was to lend Cantunn $35 million. Of this amount, $30 million would be used to buy the Canada Southern and related properties; the remaining $5 million would be used to extricate Atwell from various personal debts relating to other businesses.[7] Penfund controlled assets of some $14 billion, principally pension plans of the Ontario and Alberta governments. Another backer was thought to be the Ford Motor Land Development Company (FMLD), but a spokesman for that firm denied the rumour. His company was interested in advancing a proposal with Cantunn for the development of certain Canada Southern lands. The Cantunn/FMLD proposal called for the construction of some warehouses for various commercial undertakings and a number of highrise apartment buildings on 1,000 acres of CASO land in Windsor as part of CASO's 4,000 acres of developable land between Niagara Falls and Windsor.[8] The other major financial backers of the $125-million scheme to buy and revitalize Canada Southern were an insurance company and a bank, both unnamed.

The "new" Canada Southern would have its head office in Detroit, as part of the scheme to meet the U.S. Railroad Retirement Board (RRB) qualifications.[9] This was a gamble that the RRB would rule favourably on the retention of pensions to Canadian citizens who worked for a U.S. business, a ruling which would have helped Cantunn's proposal find greater acceptance among Canadian Conrail employees. As it would turn out, however, the RRB ruled against the idea. The operational centre would remain in St. Thomas. This office would look after all administration, payroll, accounting, engineering and operations. The old St. Thomas shops would be rejuvenated and modernized to handle not only CASO's own requirements, but servicing contracts from other railways as well. The Cantunn proposal called for development of the Montrose Yard into a major TOFC facility for trucks entering Canada from the northeastern U.S. A small yard in Buffalo would be obtained under a lease arrangement with the State of New York.[10] At this point there would be a connection with the Delaware & Hudson Railway.

As if these ideas were not interesting enough, Cantunn advanced some radical thinking about the Detroit River Tunnel. This suitor intended to enlarge the tunnel's interior to accommodate TOFC equipment, cylindrical hoppers and tri-level auto racks. The Betchel Engineering Company studied detailed drawings of the tunnel and determined a method of removing the bottom two feet of the concrete liner without compromising the structural integrity of the tunnel.[11] Cantunn planned to lay new tracks and then add a paved roadway (flush with the railhead). Access roads were to be built in Detroit and Windsor, which would allow the tunnel to become integrated with the Michigan and Ontario highway networks when it was not being used for trains.

Atwell's group had already invested some $3 million in engineering studies, regulatory documentation, lawyers' fees, consulting charges and promotion. That figure was expected to double by the conclusion of the delayed public hearings. Cantunn planned to invest $100 million in upgrading the Canada Southern. Market studies showed that the potential for both local and bridge railway traffic was there. Cantunn apparently was able to satisfy stringent CTC regulations that it had sufficient financial resources to operate the CSR for three years without any revenue.

The time had come to take the plunge. Cantunn made an offer of $27 million(US) for CSR and the DRT, $2 million more than CNCP. Conrail surprised some people by turning down the offer with the terse remark that it was not in its "commercial interest" to accept it. Secretly, Conrail, Canadian National and Canadian Pacific had already worked out a deal which would accommodate their respective problems. An independent, viable Canada Southern backed by the financial resources of Cantunn simply had too many good ideas which, if implemented, would give the three big roads some real competition. In addition, it did not solve their own problems. The city of Windsor had already endorsed the Cantunn proposal.

Atwell's proposal engendered considerable and impressive support. It was clearly superior to the offer prepared by CNCP, who were failing miserably on the public relations front. CN and CP officials held a brainstorming session on how they might stop Atwell. As a result, they hired some private detectives to assist in compiling a dossier on Atwell. The work of the detectives and others paid off. They gathered a number of documents and other information, all of it quite critical of Atwell's past business practices. The Atwell dossier included records which had been filed in courts in Michigan, Texas and Washington, D.C., on matters ranging from tax liens from the U.S. Internal Revenue Service to defaults on payments.[12] The dossier was then distributed to a number of politicians between Windsor and St. Thomas and was also filed with the Interstate Commerce Commission. Among Atwell's alleged debts were sums due the Wayne Disposal Company, Alliance Shippers, the St. Thomas Sheridan Inn, and the creditors of a defunct shipping company.[13] The dossier and subsequent news stories eliminated Atwell's chances of securing principal funding and caused the loss of municipal support. Both of these were essential to the success of the Cantunn proposal. Few would disagree with the project's merits, but Atwell's checkered financial background proved to be unacceptable. The Cantunn proposal fell much like it had risen, a colourful meteor tracing a brief arc in the heavens. The intended purpose of the Atwell dossier soon bore fruit. Penfund, the publicity-shy manager of pension funds, suddenly withdrew its support of Cantunn in May 1984 without any explanation. Municipal support for Cantunn evaporated. A troublesome potential competitor had been dealt a mortal blow.

Surely, Canadian National and Canadian Pacific could proceed. But while CN and CP Rail had busied themselves playing a kind of business chess with Windsor and Cantunn, others had organized themselves to buy Canada Southern. The first of these companies, Erie Express Holdings Corporation, turned out to have a familiar promoter. It was déjà vu.

Albert Atwell had also set up Erie Express Holdings Corporation (EEH) for the purpose of acquiring Canada Southern if for some reason his Cantunn company should fail. On 11 August 1983 EEH applied to the Department of Consumer & Corporate Affairs under the Railway Act, on behalf of a proposed subsidiary, for the requisite certificate. Erie Express was granted the certificate of public convenience and necessity to acquire and to operate Conrail's Canadian railway holdings in southern Ontario. Shortly afterwards, a wholly owned subsidiary, Erie Express Railway Corporation (EER), was established, and it was invested with the railway operation certificate for which EEH had done the paperwork. EER would be the operating company for the sought-after Conrail properties.

New players entered the game when a consortium of St. Thomas businessmen, together with two or three businessmen in London, purchased control of Erie Express Railway from Atwell. On 17 July 1984 the St. Thomas consortium concluded an agreement with Atwell for 80 percent of the stock of Erie Express Railway. Under the new owners, EER proceeded with plans to acquire the CSR and the DRT, and to launch an $86-million railway improvement plan and a $14-million tunnel enlargement plan. EER apprised the CTC of its intention to offer to purchase the Canada Southern group and public hearings were subsequently scheduled.

Erie Express Railway still lacked a significant financial backer. Discussions were held with Magna International Limited, a major automotive parts company, but these talks proved to be inconclusive. EER requested and was granted an extension to secure adequate financial backing. Eight weeks elapsed. Canadian Corporate Funding Limited of Toronto was spearheading the gathering of a group of automakers and trucking companies to pool funds, but the mere presence of Atwell as an owner, albeit a minority one, proved to be a principal stumbling block to the participation of reputable firms. Erie Express, which had been so free in its criticism of other suitors regarding their lack of financial preparation, was itself still unprepared financially. Six time extensions were granted, and still the almost-available financial package proved to be as elusive as the gold at the end of the rainbow. At the final hearing on 3 October 1984 the company's solicitor informed the RTC that sufficient funding had not been secured and that EER would not request a further extension.

Lawyers for Canadian Pacific, Canadian National and Conrail pressed the RTC to declare the EER ineligible to purchase Canada Southern, but the CTC chairman ruled against that request,

*Robert V. Wadden, the last president
of the Canada Southern Railway,
served the company from 1975 to 1985.*
— Consolidated Rail Corporation

Diagram II

**SCHEMATIC DIAGRAM OF ERIE EXPRESS RAILWAY
OWNERSHIP AND PROPOSED INVESTMENTS**

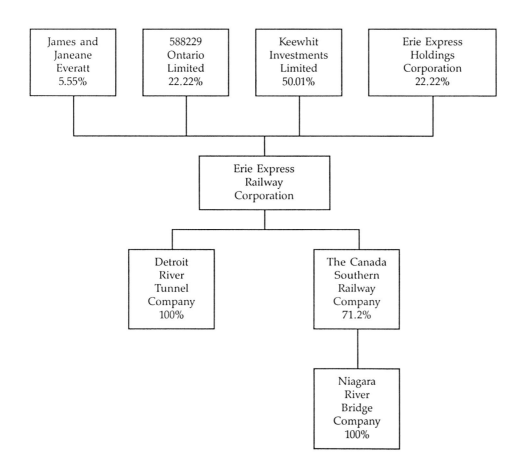

Conrail track crews and equipment carry out an oak tie replacement program in Niagara Falls, Ontario, during April 1981.
— Ron Roels

Diagram III

**CORPORATE ORGANIZATION
TRANS-ONTARIO RAIL HOLDINGS**

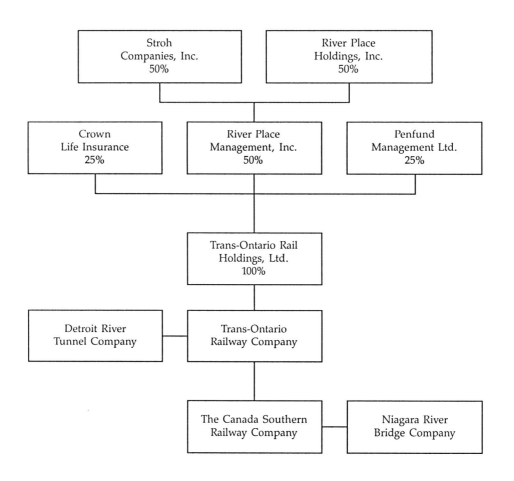

saying that the EER could still be considered upon written request attesting to the presence of adequate funding. Few expected that Erie Express would be heard from again, but on 24 October 1984 EER made a surprise announcement that it had indeed secured adequate financial funding from the Toronto-Dominion Bank following the purchase of controlling interest by Keewhit Investments Limited of Toronto.[14] Armed with a loan of $45 million Erie Express rose phoenixlike from the financial ashes to again become a serious contender. A public hearing in mid-November allowed examination of the plans and resources of EER's new controlling shareholder. Erie Express's plans emphasized TOFC service, but the challenges by CN and CP lawyers revealed quite inadequate homework with regard to market studies, among other shortcomings. On top of this, Conrail repeatedly declared that after taking three difficult years to conclude an agreement with CNCP it was not about to open the door to anyone else. Be that as it may, the EER lawyer argued that the fact of the matter was that so far the CTC had not ruled as to who may acquire the Canada Southern. There was still another party to be heard from.

It had come in at the proverbial eleventh hour and it was getting off to a noticeably shaky start, but the Stroh Companies, Inc. were interested in acquiring the Canada Southern. The Stroh firm, owned by members of the Stroh family, was a Delaware corporation with its principal office in Detroit. Among the many enterprises which the Stroh family owned were River Place Holdings, a Michigan investment firm, and River Place Financial Corporation, a private bank. Following concerns which the city of Detroit had expressed about the acquisition of Canada Southern by two very powerful Canadian corporations and the uncertainty as to what plans there might be for CASO's Detroit property, the Stroh family business felt obliged to enter the picture in response to the city's request to help out. It was thought that the two Montreal-based corporations might not have Detroit's interests at heart. The Strohs were already aware of Cantunn's proposal and there even had been numerous discussions with Atwell regarding his participation, but they simply could not agree on some fundamental points, and so they parted ways. The Stroh bid contained much the same objectives for operating and developing the Canada Southern which, in view of all the joint work, the Cantunn proposal outlined.

Initially, the Stroh firm had filed an objection to the takeover bid by CNCP. Later the Strohs decided to submit their own proposal to acquire Canada Southern. They established in Ottawa, Ontario, a firm under the name Trans-Ontario Holdings Limited. This company was owned 50 percent by the Stroh group and 25 percent by each of Penfund Management Limited and Crown Life Insurance Company, both of Toronto. River Place Management would hold the Stroh interest with 50 percent equity by each of Stroh Companies and River Place Holdings. Trans-Ontario Holdings would be financed by loans from River Place Financial, Penfund and Crown Life, together with equity financing by all three of at least $1 million each.[15]

Trans-Ontario Railway Company, a wholly owned subsidiary based in St. Thomas, was incorporated to operate CSR and DRT. In September 1984 T-OR obtained its certificate of public convenience and necessity. If deemed necessary during the startup stage, Trans-Ontario would be operated by DeLeuw, Cather & Company.

Trans-Ontario planned to bid $114.1 million to acquire and to rejuvenate the Canada Southern Railway and its related properties over a five-year period. The sum of $25.2 million was allocated for the purchase of CSR, NRB and DRT. The sum of $30.7 million had been allocated to rejuvenate the Detroit River Tunnel. The amount of $43.4 million had been budgeted for the restoration of CSR and the Niagara River Bridge. The remaining $14.8 million would be used to equip Canada Southern with new locomotives, rolling stock and other material.[16]

As previously, the Windsor problems figured prominently during the presentation and cross-examination of all applicants. Trans-Ontario's submission was no exception. Again, Canadian National threatened the city of Windsor to concentrate future railway development in Sarnia. For its part, CP Rail was known to want access to Sarnia, and there was the possibility that, rather than build its own line, it might acquire Chessie's line between Chatham and Sarnia. The repeated references to the "Sarnia option" raised questions about the alleged vital importance that the acquisition of CSR really held for CN and CP plans for Windsor.

Trans-Ontario proposed to enlarge only one of the two tunnel tubes, the one which would be designated for westbound traffic, and to install an enhanced train-control communications system. The railway planned to construct permanent intermodal terminals in Detroit and Buffalo (the latter in co-operation with the D&H). T-OR also proposed to rehabilitate the CSR main line to handle considerably increased tonnages and at high speed. The plan called for extensive upgrading of the bridges over the Grand and Niagara rivers as well. The Leamington Branch would in effect be completely rebuilt.

Trans-Ontario's plans seemed to focus primarily on extensive TOFC traffic. The Stroh-backed group forecast the movement of 129,792 loaded trailers annually, more than Conrail's then current traffic on the Toledo–Detroit–New York route by an incredible factor of 7.6.[17] T-OR's projections were quite unrealistic. An expert witness for CNCP lost no time in discrediting Trans-Ontario's figures, which were based solely on computer modelling. There were no field interviews whatever. Its proposal included nothing about sales or marketing. There was no assessment of how the diversion of TOFC traffic from trucking could occur, nor was there any attempt to analyze how the other railways might respond to increased competition from an assertive Canada Southern.

There was another problem with the Stroh proposal. The Railway Transport Committee noted that the working capital in Trans-Ontario's most recent projections was quite small. This prompted the Committee to conduct its own analysis, and it concluded that by the fifth year of operation the railway would be very seriously undercapitalized by $26 million. Despite its impressive financial backers, Trans-Ontario failed to carry out some basic homework on a number of matters, and this failure did not go unnoticed by the regulatory authority.

This concluded the list of formal applicants for the purchase of the Canada Southern Railway and related properties. Throughout the summer of 1984 there were repeated references to a mysterious bidder for the CSR. The low-profile suitor was Centra, Inc., a Delaware-based holding company. It was no stranger to CASO territory, for it had major investments in lower Michigan and southwestern Ontario. Centra owns the Ambassador Bridge linking Detroit and Windsor. It is also deeply involved in regional trucking, through Central Transport of Warren, Michigan, and McKinlay Transport of Toronto. Apparently, Centra was interested in forming a "Southwestern Railway" with 51-percent Canadian ownership. Centra did not make an application, nor did it participate in any way in the hearings. Rather, it was quietly preparing information which would be used in submitting a bid and application in the eventuality that the CNCP proposal should be disallowed.

There it was. An entire summer and autumn had been consumed by protracted public hearings. The railways, their supporters and their detractors had pitched their tents where it had pleased them at the moment. If advantage could be had, or could be thought to be had, by changing tents or location, there was no obstacle. Now the public hearings were over. It was time for the referee to rule.

Blowing the Whistle on the Suitors

The Railway Transport Committee (RTC) surprised many people by sidestepping many of the contentious issues and instead focussing on Section 27 of the National Transportation Act, highlighting a criterion which a proposed acquisition must satisfy. The Committee was empowered to disallow a proposed acquisition if, in its opinion, that acquisition might unduly restrict competition or would be prejudicial to the public interest. The RTC concluded that none of the proposed acquisitions transgressed either of these aspects of the criterion and therefore did not disallow any of the applications.

On 13 December 1984 the Canadian Transport Commission sanctioned the CNCP-Conrail agreement which in effect eliminated the "Third Railway Option" in one of the very few Canadian markets where such a possibility could have been viable.

Controversy surrounded the Canada Southern Railway as much in 1984 as it had in 1868. The complexity of the issues, the convolutedness of the discussions, the polarization of interests, and the cunning with which plots and subplots were revealed and allegiances reversed would impress the most ingenious author of espionage novels. All this for a few acres of railway!

EPILOGUE

In the battle for the acquisition of Canada Southern, the year 1985 dawned with CN and CP Rail clutching all the aces. The appeals to the federal Cabinet were dismissed almost impatiently. Then, on 2 April 1985, the Cabinet granted its perfunctory endorsement for the takeover. Canada Southern's fate was sealed. The purchase proceeded without further challenges and the timetable for the transfer was quickly formulated. On 30 April 1985 representatives from Canadian National, CP Rail and Conrail sat at a table in a Toronto office to affix their signatures to documents transferring the 72 percent controlling interest in Canada Southern from Conrail to CNCPND. The Niagara River Bridge was part of the assets being acquired. Also included in the deal was the transfer of 100 percent of the capital stock of the Detroit River Tunnel Company, CASO's "lost" subsidiary. The partnership paid Consolidated Rail Corporation $25.2 million(US). Conrail had been preparing for this day when at last it would be rid of the headaches and turmoil which had plagued it ever since April Fool's Day 1976. In the Niagara Peninsula that "exit day" Conrail crews prepared to run the last Conrail train over the Canada Southern Railway. That train was the *Montrose Turn*. It departed Montrose at 22:35 on April 30 and it arrived at St. Thomas at 10:00 the following day.

For the first time in more than a century the CSR was returned to Canadian ownership and management, albeit in the hands of a powerful partnership. Some thought the cost to have been too high socioeconomically. It amounted to the willful foregoing of revitalizing competition in one of the very few regions of Canada where a third railway option could have been viable. The sole concession to those minority shareholders and other interest parties in opposition was the Governor-in-Council's order which prohibits CNCP from abandoning Canada Southern between 1 May 1985 and 1 January 2005. According to a story in the *London Free Press*, the federal government knowingly gave up an estimated $200 million in industrial development and 26,000 future jobs by permitting the sale to CNCP, as opposed to directing Canada Southern to be returned to independent operation. All that is now safely academic. The Government of Canada, which had so stridently advocated competition, has ensured that the Canada Southern Railway will not be an instrument to healthier competition in southwestern Ontario.

According to the terms of the agreement among CN, CP, Conrail and Penn Central, the latter would tender its stake in the CSR (about 21 percent) through CSR Holdings. This was done early in June 1985. The remaining individual investors, holding about seven percent, were forced to surrender their shares. The shares from these two groups were acquired during June 1985 at a cost of $8.6 million.[1]

Utilizing the plan which had been formulated prior to the purchase, the reorganization of Canada Southern's property proceeded quickly. The railway was divided into three sections. The western section, operated by Canadian National, comprises the trackage between Fargo and Windsor, plus the Detroit River Tunnel. The central section, also operated by CN, consists of the line between Fargo and Hewitt (Welland). The eastern section, operated by CP Rail, comprises the trackage between Brookfield (Welland) and Fort Erie and between Hewitt and Niagara Falls, plus the Niagara River Bridge. The co-owners share the tunnel.

The Chessie System, which had been downgrading its own Lake Erie & Detroit River Railway route, increased its involvement with Canada Southern. On 1 June 1985 Chessie transferred its Buffalo–Detroit freight trains to CASO trackage for their Windsor–St. Thomas journey.[2] As a result, the C&O unit of Chessie, now CSX, utilizes CASO tracks for the entire trip across south-

Diagram IV

SCHEMATIC DIAGRAM OF INVESTOR GROUPS
IN CONRAIL'S FORMER ONTARIO PROPERTIES
AT TIME OF TRANSFER OF CONTROLLING INTEREST

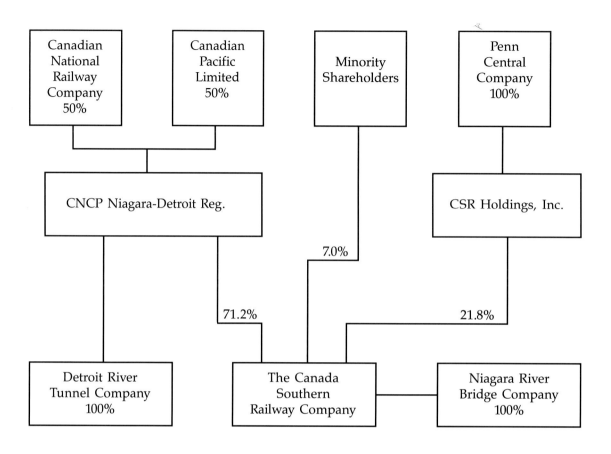

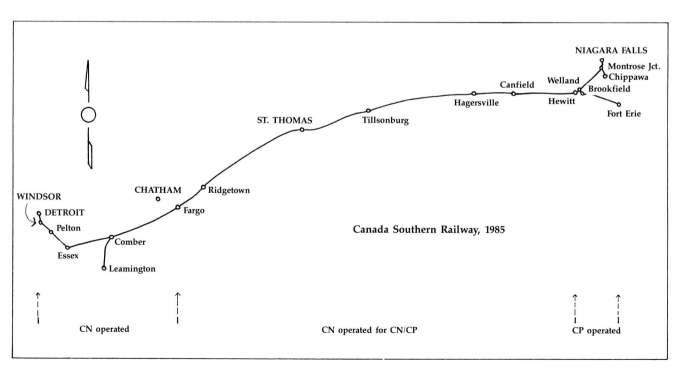

Canada Southern Railway, 1985

More than two years after the signing of the purchase agreement, the final papers conveying prinicpal ownership of the Canada Southern Railway from Conrail to CNCP Niagara-Detroit were endorsed on 30 April 1985. The railway officers are (left) Allan Schimmel, Conrail; (centre) George A. Van de Water, Canadian National; and (right) D'Alton Coleman, Canadian Pacific. The signing marked the return of control to Canadian interests after an absence of 102 years. — Canapress Photo

On 27 November 1985 Canadian National and Canadian Pacific hosted a public display and information centre at the CASO station in Windsor. CP Rail Dayliner No. 91 contained a variety of exhibits concerning the CNCP acquisition of controlling interest of the Canada Southern Railway. The two major railways sought to win public support by showing how, in their view, the railway problems in Windsor would be addressed to the mutual benefit of the public and CNCP. — Michael P. McIlwaine

western Ontario. Chessie next made the obvious move of relocating its regional office from its old St. Thomas roundhouse to freshly renovated quarters in the CSR station and office building elsewhere in town. That move took place about mid-December 1985.[3]

Canadian National, which had run its first train on CASO on May 1, began extensive trackwork at Fargo for a connection between the C&O and the CSR. The cost of the Fargo connection was approximately $1,016,000.[4] CN commenced main line operation on CASO high iron between St. Thomas and Pelton in mid-December 1985.[5]

International freight service was to be enhanced by both major Canadian carriers. CP Rail and the Soo-Milwaukee System (as it was briefly called) concluded an agreement with the Chessie System for a rapid through train service linking Montreal/Toronto with Chicago. Known as the Railrunner, the new service has halved the transit time between the terminal points.[6] The first CP/Soo train traversed the tunnel on 1 August 1985.[7] Canadian National and Grand Trunk Western introduced their Laser train service to Detroit and points south on 27 January 1986.[8]

Throughout the public hearings the concerns of labour were a contentious issue. These resurfaced in 1986, when Canada Southern Employees Association protested the release of six men from their jobs in St. Thomas and alleged that CN had reneged on their promise regarding employment. One of the conditions of the takeover was that CN and CP would not reduce employment during the first five years following acquisition. The unions have been successful in persuading the Minister of Transport to investigate their complaint. Similarly, CNR had promised to relocate its Danforth (Toronto), Ontario, shops for the maintenance and repair of MOW equipment to the St. Thomas shops, but the transfer has yet to occur.

Meanwhile, the partnership continued to integrate the CSR property with that of its parents. As of 12 January 1986 the CN portion of Canada Southern officially became known as the CASO Subdivision and the former Windsor Yard was officially renamed the Van de Water Yard (in tribute to the late George A. Van de Water, who had spearheaded the acquisition of Canada Southern).[9] The eastern section of the railway, known as CP Rail (CASO), and the Toronto, Hamilton & Buffalo Railway were integrated into CP Rail's London Division effective 1 January 1987.[10] The railway was now fully integrated into the CN and CP systems.

The Canada Southern Railway had been conceived to be a great international bridge route linking upper New York State and Chicago via Ontario and Michigan, but after more than a century of struggle the railway has been diminished to a pair of international connections. It had taken a long time for the dreams of Buchanan and Thomson to turn to gossamer but turn to gossamer they did. Canada Southern country was all but a memory.

This oval emblem for the CSR appeared in 1985.

The date is 4 May 1986. The locale is trackside near the eastern portal of the Detroit River Tunnel. Emerging from the darkness is Soo Line/CP Rail train 500 out of Chicago en route to Toronto with plenty of COFC traffic in 79 cars. The motive power on ''Railrunner'' is Soo SD40-2 No. 6616 and CP SD40's 5519 and 5698.

— Byron C. Babbish

Abbreviations Used in the Endnotes

AR	Annual Report	MG	*Montreal Gazette*
BRAC	Brotherhood of Railway, Airline and Steamship Clerks, Freight Handlers, Express and Station Employees, Canadian Division	MRCR	Michigan, Report of the Commissioners of Railroads
		MRR	Michigan Railroad Returns
CSR	Canada Southern Railway	NFG	*Niagara Falls Gazette* (US)
CTC	Canadian Transport Commission	NFR	*Niagara Falls Review*
CR&MW	*Canadian Railway and Marine World*	NYT	*New York Times*
C&CSR	Chicago & Canada Southern Railway	OH-L&PS	Ontario Hydro — London & Port Stanley Railway
DFP	*Detroit Free Press*	OPUC	Ohio Public Utilities Commission
Dorman	*A Statutory History of the Steam and Electric Railways of Canada, 1836-1937,* compiled by Robert Dorman.	OSP	Ontario Sessional Papers
		RG	*Railroad Gazette*
		RSP	Railway Sessional Papers, Ontario Archives
FMB	First Minute Book, Leamington & St. Clair Railway	R&LHS	Railway & Locomotive Historical Society
FP	*Financial Post*	R&MW	*Railway and Marine World*
G&M	*Globe and Mail*	R&SW	*Railway and Shipping World*
HCH	*Halifax Chronicle-Herald*	SBJ	*Suspension Bridge Journal*
HMS	*Halifax Mail-Star*	StTTJ	*St. Thomas Times-Journal*
JC	*Journal of Commerce*	STWD	*St. Thomas Weekly Dispatch*
LFP	*London Free Press*	TS	*Toronto Star*
MDOC	Michigan Department of Commerce	WS	*Windsor Star*
MDOT	Michigan Department of Transportation		

Endnotes to Chapter I

1. Walter Neutal, M.A. thesis, "From 'Southern' Concept to Canada Southern Railway, 1835-1873," University of Western Ontario, (November 1968).
2. M.L. Magill, "James Morton of Kingston — Brewer," *Historic Kingston*, No. 21, March 1973, pp31-32.
3. Gustavus Myers, *A History of Canadian Wealth*, p199.
4. Neutal, op. cit., p107.
5. Ibid., p111.
6. *St. Catharines Constitutional*, 6 February 1868, p2.
7. Ontario statute, 31 Victoria, Chapter 14.
8. Neutal, op. cit., p116.
9. Richard C. Overton, *Burlington Route*, p30.
10. Ibid., p37; a footnote in the bibliography identifies the line as the Canada Southern Railway.
11. *St. Catharines Constitutional*, 1 August 1867, p3.
12. Gustavus Myers, *A History of Canadian Wealth*, pp189-90.
13. Neutal, op. cit., p122.
14. Ibid.
15. *RG*, 16 July 1870, p365.
16. Ibid.
17. Biographical typescript from Erie County Library System, re Milton Courtright.
18. J.M. and Ed Trout, *The Railways of Canada*, p136.

19. Thomas C. Cochran, *Railroad Leaders*, p172.
20. *Herapath's Railway and Commercial Journal*, 25 June 1870, cited in A.W. Currie, *The Grand Trunk Railway of Canada*, p200, footnote 41.
21. Charles Ames, *Pioneering the Union Pacific*, p148.
22. Ibid.
23. Ibid.
24. *Nelson's Biographical Dictionary and Historical Reference Book of Erie County*, p546.
25. Ibid., p547.
26. Ibid.; biographical typescript on Milton Courtright aforementioned.
27. Robert Fogel, *The Union Pacific Railroad*, p76.
28. Trout, op. cit., p135; E.G. Goodwin, "Canada Southern Railway Company," p6.
29. Memorandum dated 2 July 1872, certified by R.G. Scott, in Railway Sessional Papers, AO, RG8, I-7-B-3, Box 1.
30. CSR, *Prospectus, Report and Other Documents*, 1872 edition, p5.
31. *RG*, 18 March 1871.
32. *RG*, 25 November 1871, p356.
33. Neutal, op. cit., p127, fn 61; *RG*, 13 January 1872, p20.
34. *STWD*, 1 February 1872; *RG*, 10 February 1872, p67; *RG*, 30 March 1872, p142.
35. *RG*, July p330.
36. *STWD*, 1 August 1872.

Endnotes to Chapter I (cont'd)

37. *STWD*, 31 October 1872.
38. *RG*, 3 August 1872, p343.
39. *RG*, 10 August 1872, p354.
40. *STWD*, 24 October 1872.
41. *STWD*, 31 October 1872.
42. *RG*, 14 December 1872, p535.
43. *STWD*, 19 December 1872.

44. *STWD*, 15 May 1873.
45. *STWD*, 26 June 1873.
46. G.R. Stevens, *Canadian National Railways*, Vol. I, p131.
47. Ibid., p132.
48. *RG*, 15 October 1870, p59.

Endnotes to Chapter II

1. State of Ohio, Public Utilities Commission, letter of 24 January 1979 from Railroad Department to author, hereinafter cited as OPUC.
2. State of Michigan, report of Commissioner of Railroads, Annual Report, 1872.
3. OPUC
4. OPUC
5. State of Michigan, Department of Transportation, letter of 2 April 1979 from Modal Planning Division to author, cited hereinafter as MDOT.
6. *RG*, 19 October 1872, p458.
7. Talcott E. Wing, *History of Monroe County Michigan*, p234.
8. James F. Joy, "Railroad History of Michigan," in Michigan Pioneer and Historical Society's *Historical Collections*, Vol. XXII, 1894, p295.
9. *RG*, 18 January 1873, p28.
10. *RG*, 31 May 1873, p224.
11. *RG*, 22 November 1873, p474.
12. Wing, op. cit., p239.
13. Canada, Department of Transport, *A Statutory History of the Steam and Electric Railways of Canada, 1836-1937*, compiled by Robert Dorman, p182, cited hereinafter as Dorman.
14. Ibid.
15. *RG*, 15 March 1873, p113.
16. CSR, AR 1873, p8.
17. Ibid.
18. Ibid.

19. George Kuschel, "Canada Southern Bridge Company," *Western Ontario Historical Notes*, Vol. 10, No. 3, September 1952, p94.
20. George Hilton, *The Great Lakes Car Ferries*, p28.
21. OPUC
22. *RG*, 27 May 1871, p104.
23. Ibid.
24. *RG*, 1 July 1871, p164.
25. OPUC
26. Ibid.
27. Ibid.
28. *RG*, 1 July 1871, p164.
29. MDOT: MRCR, AR 1872.
30. *RG*, 4 November 1871, p322.
31. *RG*, 25 November 1871, p357.
32. Wing, op. cit., p238.
33. MRCR, AR 1873.
34. *RG*, 26 July 1873, p305.
35. *RG*, 4 October 1873, p406.
36. *RG*, 30 May 1874, p208.
37. *Ibid*.
38. *C&CSR, Prospectus*, p3.
39. *RG*, 12 September 1874, p359.
40. Charles R. Petcher, "The Canada Southern Railway Company," *The Michigan Railfan*, April 1982, pp8-9.
41. Wing, op. cit., p239.
42. MDOC
43. MDOC

Endnotes to Chapter III

1. Jean T. Elford, *Canada West's Last Frontier*, p159.
2. Isabella Finlayson, "Railroad Built to Courtright to Aid U.S. Line," typescript in Lambton County Public Library, p2.
3. *Chatham Tri-Weekly Planet*, 29 January 1873.
4. *RG*, 8 July 1871, p172.
5. MDOT
6. *RG*, 10 February 1872, p67.
7. *RG*, 16 March 1872, p123.
8. A.W. Currie, *The Grand Trunk Railway of Canada*, p228.
9. *RG*, 20 July 1872, p312; RG, 17 August 1872, p367.
10. *Michigan Railroad Returns*, 1877, p462.
11. Op. cit., p363.
12. MDOT
13. Michael O'Meara, *Oil Springs*, p9.
14. AO, RSP, RG8, Sarnia, Chatham & Erie Railway, letter to T.P. Pardee on 27 March 1875.
15. Elford, op. cit., p159.
16. OSP, Number 26, 1878, p3.
17. *Moody's Transportation Manual*, 1973, p304.

Endnotes to Chapter IV

1. Upper Canada 5 William IV, Chapter 19, cited by Dorman, p204.
2. George Seibel, *Niagara Falls Canada: A History*, p60.
3. C.W. Heard, "The Erie & Ontario Rail Road," *CRHA News Report*, January 1961, p8.
4. Seibel, op. cit., p61; *St. Catharines Journal*, 4 May 1854.
5. J.M. and Edward Trout, *The Railways of Canada*, p35.
6. J.K. Johnson, "One Bold Operator: Samuel Zimmerman, Niagara Entrepreneur, 1843-1857," *Ontario History*, March 1982, pp26-44.
7. Bruce S. Parker, "The Niagara Harbour and Dock Company," *Ontario History*, June 1980, p114.
8. 20 Victoria, Chapter 151, cited in Dorman, p204.
9. George V. Taylor, *Historical Writings of Willoughby Township*, p10; Francis J. Petrie, "The Paddy Miles Road," *Niagara Falls Review*, 5 October 1964.
10. 27 Victoria, Chapter 59, cited by Heard, op. cit., p11.
11. A.W. Currie, *The Grand Trunk Railway of Canada*, p202.
12. R.V.V. Nichols, "The Erie and Ontario Rail Road," *CRHA Bulletin*, Number 11, December 1939, p2.
13. John Jackson and John Burtniak, *Railways in the Niagara Peninsula*, p173, fn 19.
14. Hydro-Electric Power Commission of Ontario, *Official Opening of the Queenston-Chippawa Power Development*, p11.

Endnotes to Chapter V

1. Neutal, op. cit., p130, fn 75.
2. Richard Overton, *Burlington Route*, p114; A.W. Currie, *The Grand Trunk Railway of Canada*, p134.
3. Gustavus Myers, *A History of Canadian Wealth*, p226.
4. Matthew Josephson, *The Robber Barons*, p182.
5. *NYT*, 26 August 1874, p1; Currie, op. cit., p213; *RG*, 29 August 1874, p333.
6. *RG*, 19 December 1874, p498.
7. *RG*, 16 June 1876, p270.
8. *NYT*, 23 September 1877, p12.
9. Thomas Cochran, *Railroad Leaders*, 1845-1890, p30.
10. Ibid., p124.
11. Alvin Harlow, *The Road of the Century*, p240.
12. G.P. deT. Glazebrook, *A History of Transportation in Canada*, Vol. II, p91.
13. CSR, AR 1880, p6.
14. *NYT*, 1 May 1880, p1.
15. Ibid.

Endnotes to Chapter VI

1. James Filby, *Credit Valley Railway*, p85.
2. *SBJ*, 1 December 1883, p3.
3. W.C. Miller, *Vignettes of Early St. Thomas*, p402.
4. *SBJ*, 19 May 1883, p2.
5. *NYT*, 11 November 1883, p9.
6. *Thorold Post*, 23 November 1883, p3.
7. *SBJ*, 15 December 1883, p3.
8. *Engineering News*, January-June 1885, pp171-2.
9. Steinman and Watson, *Bridges and Their Builders*, pp248-9.
10. *Engineering News*, op. cit.
11. Miller, op. cit., p404.
12. Donald E. Loker, "90 Years Ago: Niagara's Cantilever Bridge Opened," *Niagara Gazette*, 16 December 1973, p6-E.
13. Dominion 45 Victoria, Chapter 88, cited by Dorman, p417.
14. *Engineering News and American Contract Journal*. 17 May 1884, p237; *The Globe*, 19 June 1883, p1.
15. *Engineering News*, January-June 1885, p171; Loker, op. cit.
16. *NYT*, 2 September 1883, p2.
17. *Engineering News and American Contract Journal*, 17 May 1884, p239.
18. *SBJ*, 30 June 1883, p3.
19. *SBJ*, 14 July 1883, p3.
20. *NYT*, 11 November 1883, p9.
21. First Minute Book, Leamington & St. Clair Railway Company, 29 November 1877; cited hereinafter as FMB with relevant date.
22. Ontario, 42 Victoria, Chapter 63; cited in Dorman, p326.
23. *Amherstburg Echo*, 15 October 1886, cited in Frances S. Snell, *Leamington's Heritage, 1874-1974*, p78.
24. Ibid.
25. N.F. Morrison, typescript of radio talk on 14 May 1948, Elliott Kimball Tells about Leamington District," p4.
26. CSR, AR 1889, p6.
27. CSR, AR 1896, p11.
28. *Moody's Transportation Manual*, 1973, p304.
29. Neil F. Morrison, *Garden Gateway to Canada*, p159.

Endnotes to Chapter VII

1. E.C. Goodwin, "Canada Southern Railway Company."
2. CSR, AR 1883-84, p8.
3. A.W. Currie, *The Grand Trunk Railway of Canada*, p176.
4. Alvin Harlow, *The Road of the Century*, p240.
5. Thomas C. Cochran, *Railroad Leaders*, 1845-1890, p392.
6. Harold A. Innis, *A History of the Canadian Pacific Railway*, p137.
7. W.C. Miller, *Vignettes of Early St. Thomas*, pp321-22.
8. Ibid., p256.
9. CSR, AR 1889, p6.
10. Ibid., p5.
11. Canada, Department of Agriculture, *Statistical Abstract and Record of Canada*, 1895.
12. Op. cit., 1889, pp356-57; the other railways were the Canada Atlantic and the North Western Coal & Navigation Railway Company.
13. *NYT*, 14 June 1895, p2.
14. Norman Helm, *In the Shadow of Giants*, p52; *R&SW*, March 1899, p79.
15. E.G. Campbell, *The Reorganization of the American Railroad System, 1893-1900*, p263.
16. *Monetary Times*, 12 March 1897, p1211.
17. *Monetary Times*, 9 April 1897, p1885.
18. CSR, AR 1896, p5; CSR, AR 1897, p5.
19. *R&SW, April 1899, p117*; *R&SW*, May 1899, p138.
20. CSR, AR 1903, p10; *R&SW*, July 1903, p227.
21. George Seibel, *Niagara Falls Canada: A History*, p334.

continued

22. *NFG*, 17 January 1940, p10; Andrew A. Merrilees, "International Complications," *Railroad Magazine*, August 1947, p88.
23. Privy Council Order Number 1513, cited in Dorman, p86.
24. *StTTJ*, 9 December 1929, p1.
25. *StTTJ*, 31 January 1930, p9.

Endnotes to Chapter VIII

1. Neil F. Morrison, "Traces of Early Railway Nearly Gone from City," *Windsor Daily Star*, 11 January 1947.
2. Alvin F. Staufer, *New York Central's Early Power*, p312.
3. William J. Wilgus, *The Railway Inter-Relations of the United States and Canada*, p172.
4. Dominion 51 Victoria, Chapter 93, cited in Dorman, p183.
5. Ibid.
6. Jerry A. Pinkepank, "A Tale of Two Tunnels," Part II, *Trains*, October 1964, p41; *R&MW*, March 1906, p3; Wilgus, op. cit., p173.
7. *RG*, 16 February 1906, p149.
8. Paul Leake, "The Michigan Central Tunnel at Detroit," *Moody's Magazine*, December 1906, p42; George F. Kuschell, "The Opening of the New York Central Tunnel between Detroit and Windsor," *The Semaphore*, October 1976, [p7].
9. *R&MW*, November 1906, p639.
10. Leake, op. cit.
11. Pinkepank, op. cit., p45.
12. Archibald Black, *The Story of Tunnels*, p171.
13. Frederick M. Caldwell, "To Sink a Ready Made Tunnel," *Technical World Magazine*, December 1907, p363.
14. Pinkepank, op. cit., p46.
15. *R&MW*, September 1910, p725.
16. *R&MW*, November 1909, p909.
17. Kuschell, op. cit., [p8].
18. Neil F. Morrison, *Garden Gateway to Canada*, p238.
19. *R&MW*, April 1906, p193.
20. Garnet R. Cousins and Paul Maximuke, "The Station That Looks Like a Hotel," *Trains*, August 1978, p45.

Endnotes to Chapter IX

1. *Poor's Manual of Railroads*, 1960, p1454.
2. Christopher Blythe, et al., *Townsend and Waterford: A Double Portrait*, p261.
3. *Canadian Transportation*, September 1930, p561.
4. *Canadian Transportation*, September 1931, p576.
5. Canada, Dominion Bureau of Statistics, *Statistics of Steam Railways of Canada*, 1930, Part II.
6. *The Official Guide*, January 1930, pp187-88.
7. *G&M*, 10 June 1953.
8. Ibid.
9. *WS*, 17 June 1953.
10. *Canadian Transportation*, June 1957, p53.
11. *G&M*, 20 December 1960.

Endnotes to Chapter X

1. Gary S. Daniels, "Canada Division," *Rails Northeast*, March 1976, p18.
2. R&LHS, New York Chapter, *News and Program*, December 1974, p4.
3. See Joseph R. Daughen and Peter Binzen, *The Wreck of the Penn Central*, and Richard Saunders, *The Railroad Mergers and the Coming of Conrail*, Chapter 13.
4. *G&M*, 24 December 1975.
5. *HMS*, 27 March 1976, p37.

Endnotes to Chapter XI

1. *HCH*, 1 February 1979, p4.
2. Letter from National Railroad Passenger Corporation to the author, dated 26 September 1979.
3. *Canadian Rail*, August 1981, p230.
4. CTC Decision 1980, p64.
5. *G&M*, 26 July 1979, p8.
6. CSR, AR 1976, p1.
7. CSR, AR 1981, p1.
8. CTC Decision, 13 August 1981, p52 and CSR Minority Shareholders' Report on the Annual Meeting of 3 June 1981, p2, for Via Rail and GT respectively.
9. *WS*, 19 May 1984, pB1.
10. CSR, AR 1983, p1.
11. CSR Holdings, Introductory Summary, 11 October 1983, p4.
12. CSR, Letter to Shareholders, 18 December 1984.
13. *LFP*, 4 July 1984, p4.
14. CSR, AR 1984, p15.
15. CTC Decision 1984, p46.

Endnotes to Chapter XII

1. Canadian Pacific, Information Statement, p1 and p10.
2. Ibid., p1.
3. CTC Decision 1984, p121.
4. BRAC, 25 November 1982.
5. Ibid.
6. CTC, Notice of Public Hearing, 17 May 1984.
7. *DFP*, 11 July 1984, p9A.
8. *WS*, 26 April 1983; NFR, 1 February 1983.
9. BRAC, 25 November 1982.
10. BRAC, 15 March 1983.
11. *WS*, 3 August 1983.
12. *WS*, 19 May 1984, pB1.
13. *DFP*, 11 July 1984.
14. *G&M*, 25 October 1984, pB6.
15. Trans-Ontario Railway, Summary of Business Plan, p32.
16. *HCH*, 13 July 1984.
17. *LFP*, 9 August 1984.

Endnotes to Epilogue

1. *CN News*, Great Lakes Region, October 1985, p12.
2. UCRS *Newsletter*, July 1985, p12.
3. *Tempo Jr.*, December 1985, p5.
4. *CN News*, op. cit.
5. *Tempo Jr.*, op. cit.
6. *CP Rail News*, January 1987, p12; *HCH*, 13 August 1985.
7. *Tempo Jr.*, September 1985, p2.
8. *CN News*, Great Lakes Region, February 1986, p3.
9. *CN News*, op. cit.
10. *CP Rail News*, February 1987, p3.

Bibliographical Sources

Books, Journals and Articles

Ames, Charles Edgar. *Pioneering the Union Pacific*. New York: Appleton-Century-Crofts, 1969.

Black, Archibald. *The Story of Tunnels*. New York: McGraw-Hill, 1937(?).

Blythe, Christopher, Sarah Brown and David Judd. *Townsend and Waterford: A Double Portrait*. Waterford (Ontario): Waterford and Townsend Historical Society, 1977.

Caldwell, Frederick M. "To Sink a Ready Made Tunnel." *Technical World Magazine*, Number 8, December 1907, pp360-65.

Campbell, E.G. *The Reorganization of the American Railroad System, 1893-1900*. New York: Columbia University Press, 1938. (Columbia University Studies in the Social Sciences, No. 434; New York: AMS Press, 1968.)

Canada. Department of Agriculture. *Statistical Abstract and Record of Canada* (1886 to 1904, later *The Canada Year Book Second Series*, 1905 to 1929).

Canada, Department of Transport. *A Statutory History of the Steam and Electric Railways of Canada, 1836-1937*, with separate Appendix. Ottawa: King's Printer, 1938. (Compiled by Robert Dorman)

Canada. Department of Transport. Canadian Transport Commission, Railway Transport Committee, Decision 13 August 1981 re Consolidated Rail Corporation and The Canada Southern Railway Company.

Canada. Ministry of Transport. Canadian Transport Commission, Railway Transport Committee, Decision 13 December 1984, with separate Appendix, re Objections to the CNCP Acquisition of Consolidated Rail Corporation's Interests in The Canada Southern Railway Company.

Canada Southern Railway Company. Annual Reports, 1873, 1880, 1883-84, 1889, 1896-97, 1903, 1976, 1981, 1983-84.

———. Letter to Shareholders, 18 December 1984.

———. *Prospectus, Reports and Other Documents*. New York, 1872.

Canadian Rail. Canadian Railroad Historical Association. August 1981.

Canadian Transportation, September 1930, September 1931, June 1957.

Chicago and Canada Southern Railway Company. *Prospectus and Other Documents*. New York: Sackett & Bro., 1872.

CN News. Public Affairs, Great Lakes Region, Canadian National Railways. Toronto, October 1985, February 1986.

Cochran, Thomas G. *Railroad Leaders, 1845-1890*. New York: Russell & Russell, 1965.

CP Rail News. Canadian Pacific Limited. Montreal, January 1987, February 1987.

Cousins, Garnet R., and Paul Maximuke. "The Station That Looks Like a Hotel." *Trains*, Vol. 38, No. 10, August 1978, pp40-48.

Currie, A.W. *The Grand Trunk Railway of Canada*, Toronto: University of Toronto Press, 1957. Reprinted 1971/72, Scholarly Reprint Series.

Daniels, Gary S. "Canada Division." *Rails Northeast*, Vol. 4, No. 2, March 1976, pp16-27.

Daughen, Joseph R., and Peter Binzen. *The Wreck of the Penn Central*. Boston: Little, Brown & Company, 1971.

Elford, Jean Turnbull. *Canada West's Last Frontier*. Sarnia: Lambton County Historical Society, 1982.

Engineering News, 1885.

Filby, James. *Credit Valley Railway*. Cheltenham (Ontario): The Boston Mills Press, 1974.

Finlayson, Isabella. "Railroad Built to Courtright to Aid U.S. Line." *London Free Press*, 4 June [1941] (year unclear on photocopy).

Fogel, Robert. *The Union Pacific Railroad*. Baltimore: John Hopkins Press, [1966].

Glazebrook, G.P. deT. *A History of Transportation in Canada*, Volume II. Toronto: McClelland & Stewart, 1964.

Harlow, Alvin F. *The Road of the Century*. New York: Creative Age Press, 1947.

Heard, C.W. Kenneth. "The Erie and Ontario Rail Road." *CRHA News Report*, January 1961, pp8-11.

Helm, Norman. *In the Shadow of Giants*. Cheltenham (Ontario): The Boston Mills Press, 1978.

Hilton, George W. *The Great Lakes Car Ferries*. Berkeley: Howell-North, 1962.

Holt, William J., ed. *Niagara Falls, Canada — A History*. Niagara Falls (Ontario): The Kiwanis Club of Stamford, 1967.

Innis, Harold A. *A History of the Canadian Pacific Railway*. Toronto: University of Toronto Press, 1971. Originally published in 1923.

Jackson, John N., *Welland and the Welland Canal*, Belleville (Ontario): Mika Publishing Co., 1975.

Jackson, John N., and John Burtniak. *Railways in the Niagara Peninsula*. Belleville (Ontario): Mika Publishing Company, 1978.

Johnson, J.K. "One Bold Operator: Samuel Zimmerman, Niagara Entrepreneur, 1843-1857." *Ontario History*, Vol. LXXIV, No. 1, March 1982, pp26-44.

Josephson, Matthew. *The Robber Barons*. New York: Harcourt, Brace & Company, 1934.

Joy, James. "Railroad History of Michigan." *Historical Collections*, Vol XXII, Michigan Pioneer and Historical Society, 1894, pp292-304.

Kuschell, George F. "Canada Southern Bridge Company." *Western Ontario Historical Notes*, Vol. 10, No. 3, September 1952, pp92-97.

——. "The Opening of the New York Central Tunnel between Detroit and Windsor." *The Semaphore*. CRHA Windsor-Essex Division, October 1976, pp7-8.

Leake, Paul. "The Michigan Central Tunnel at Detroit." *Moody's Magazine*, December 1906, pp41-5.

Magill, M.L. "James Morton of Kingston — Brewer." *Historic Kingston*, Number 21, March 1973, pp28-36.

Merrilees, Andrew A. "International Complications." *Railroad Magazine*, Vol. 43, No. 3, August 1947, pp76-88.

Michigan Commissioner of Railroads. Annual Reports, 1872, 1877.

Miller, Warren Cron, ed. *Vignettes of Early St. Thomas*. St. Thomas: City of St. Thomas, 1967. See Chapter 32, "Railway Development in St. Thomas," pp231-43.

Monetary Times, March-April 1897.

Moody's Transportation Manual. New York: Moody's Investors Series, 1973, 1974.

Morrison, Neil F. *Garden Gateway to Canada*. Toronto: Ryerson Press, 1954.

——. "Traces of Early Railway Nearly Gone from City." *Windsor Daily Star*, 11 January 1947.

Myers, Gustavus. *A History of Canadian Wealth*. Toronto: James Lewis & Samuel, 1972. First edition published in Chicago, 1914.

Nelson's Biographical Dictionary and Historical Reference Book of Erie County, Pennsylvannia. Erie: S.B. Nelson, 1896.

Nicholls, R.V.V. "The Erie and Ontario Rail Road." *CRHA Bulletin*, Number 11, December 1939, [five unpaginated pages].

The Official Guide of the Railways. New York: National Railway Publication Company, June 1868, (reprint edition); January 1930.

Ontario. Hydro-Electric Power Commission of Ontario. *Official Opening of the Queenston-Chippawa Power Development*, [Toronto]: Hydro-Electric Power Commission of Ontario, 1921.

Overton, Richard C. *Burlington Route*. New York: Alfred Knopf, 1965.

O'Meara, Michael. *Oil Springs*. Oil Springs (Ontario): Centennial Historical Committee, 1958; 1976 printing.

Parker, Bruce S. "The Niagara Harbour and Dock Company." *Ontario History*, Vol. LXXII, No. 2, June 1980, pp93-121.

Petcher, Charles R. "The Canada Southern Railway Co." *The Michigan Railfan*. Michigan Railroad Club, April 1982, pp8-9.

Petrie, Francis J. "The Paddy Miles Road." *Niagara Falls Review*, 2 October 1964.

Pinkepank, Jerry A. "A Tale of Two Tunnels," Part 2. *Trains*, Vol. 24, No. 12, October 1964., pp40-7.

Poor's Manual of Railroads. New York: H.V. and H.W. Poor, 1960.

Railway & Locomotive Historical Society, New York Chapter, News and Program, December 1974.

Railway and Marine World, various issues.

The Railway and Shipping World, 1898-1904.

Railroad Gazette, 1870-1883, selected issues.

Saunders, Richard. *The Railroad Mergers and the Coming of Conrail*. Westport (Connecticut): Greenwood Press, 1978. (Contributions to Economics and Economic History, Number 19.)

Snell, Frances Selkirk. *Leamington's Heritage, 1874-1974*. Leamington (Ontario): Town of Leamington, 1974.

Staufer, Alvin F. *New York Central's Early Power, 1831-1916*. Medina (Ohio): The Author, 1967.

Steinman, David B., and Sara Ruth Watson. *Bridges and Their Builders*. New York: Dover Publications, 1957.

Stevens, G.R. *Canadian National Railways, Volume I: Sixty Years of Trial and Error*. Toronto: Clarke, Irwin & Company, 1960.

Taylor, George V., ed. *Historical Writings of Willoughby Township*. Niagara Falls (Ontario): Historical Committee, Willoughby Township, 1967.

Tempo Jr. Forest City Historical Society, London, various issues.

Trout, J.M. and Edward. *The Railways of Canada*. Toronto: Monetary Times, 1871; Facsimile Reprint, Toronto: Coles Publishing, 1970.

Upper Canada Railway Society *Newsletter*, July 1985.

Wilgus, William J. *The Railway Interrelations of the United States and Canada*. Toronto: Ryerson, 1937.

Wing, Talcott E., ed. *History of Monroe County Michigan*. New York: Munsell & Company, 1890. See Chapter XIX, "Railroads," by A.B. Bragdon.

Maps

Colton's Township Map of the State of Michigan. New York: Colton & Co., 1874. National Map Collectic #44693, Public Archives of Canada, Ottawa.

Cram's Railroad and County Map of Ontario. Chicago: Western Map Depot, 1882. National Map Collectic #2940, Public Archives of Canada, Ottawa.

Map of Canada Southern Railway Lines. [New York: D. Appleton & Company, 1878?]

Map of the Canada Southern Railway. Canada Southern Railway Company, circa 1880.

Map of Western Ontario Canada. Ottawa: Department of Agriculture, 1897.

Michigan Official Transportation Map. Lansing: Michigan Department of Transportation, 1984.

New York Central Lines. New York: New York Central Railroad Company, circa 1929.

Niagara-on-the-Lake, Plan of the Town of Niagara. Toronto: Ontario Department of Lands, Forests and Mine May 1910. Amended August 1966.

Ontario. [Toronto]: Imperial Oil Limited, 1964.

Newspapers

Chatham Tri-Weekly Planet
Halifax Chronicle-Herald
Halifax Mail-Star
London Free Press
Montreal Gazette
New York Times
Niagara Falls Gazette (Niagara Falls, New York)
Niagara Falls Review
St. Catharines Constitutional
St. Catharines Journal
St. Thomas Weekly Despatch
St. Thomas Times-Journal
Suspension Bridge Journal (Suspension Bridge, now Niagara Falls, N.Y.)
Thorold Post
Toronto Globe
Toronto Globe and Mail
Toronto Star
Windsor Star

Manuscript Sources

Canada Southern Railway Minority Shareholders. "Report on the Annual Meeting of Wednesday, 3 June 1981 of the Canada Southern Railway Company." Privately held, Halifax.

Courtright, Milton, Biographical Sketch. Erie County Library System, Erie, Pennsylvania.

CSR Holdings. Introduction Summary, 11 October 1983.

Erie Express Railway Corporation. Final Filing to Erie Express Submissions, November 1984. Privately held, Halifax.

Goodwin, E.G. "Canada Southern Railway Company." MSS, MG29 A26, Public Archives of Canada.

Leamington & St. Clair Railway Company. First Minute Book [1877-1882]. Private MS Railway Collection, MU2370, Archives of Ontario, Toronto.

Michigan Department of Transportation. Letter to author, 2 April 1979.

Michigan Central Railroad, Canada Division, St. Thomas. "Plan Showing Shop and Part of Yard." Scale 1 inch equals 50 feet. 15 August 1934. Privately held, London.

Morrison, Dr. N.F. "Elliott Kimball Tells about Leamington District." Typescript for radio talk on 12 May 1948 on behalf of Essex County Historical Association.

Neutal, Walter. "From 'Southern' Concept to Canada Southern Railway, 1835-1873." M.A. Thesis, University of Western Ontario, London, 1968.

Ohio Public Utilities Commission. Letter to author on 24 January 1979.

Scott, J.G. to [B.W.] Gossage, C.E., authorizing him to inspect the Canada Southern Railway, 27 May 1873. Railway Sessional Papers, RG8, Archives of Ontario, Toronto.

INDEX